## About This Book

*Conan Doyle And The Mysterious World of Light* traces the Spiritualist career of Sir Arthur Conan Doyle between the years 1887 and 1920.

Starting with his early psychic investigations in Southsea, it tracks his development from a fascinated dilettante to becoming the leader of a world movement. Throughout these years, *Light*, a weekly magazine dedicated to the mystical and occult, traced his journey through his letters and articles, many of which he wrote exclusively for the journal.

Everything Conan Doyle wrote for the magazine during this period is here reproduced, often for the first time, as well as correspondence and articles bearing on his Spiritualist career.

The book sets the story of Conan Doyle's Spiritualism in the context of the discussions, debates and controversies of his time.

It shows how the Great War was a powerful impetus for his public declaration of faith in 1916, and how his powerful imagination coupled with his indefatigable energy made him a highly effective missionary.

To the question "how did the creator of the arch-rationalist Sherlock Holmes also come to believe in ghosts?" this book holds the fascinating answers.

GW00580067

# CONAN DOYLE AND THE MYSTERIOUS WORLD OF *LIGHT*

## 1887-1920

MATT WINGETT

*Life Is Amazing*

**A Life Is Amazing Paperback**

Conan Doyle and the Mysterious World of Light

First published 2016 by Life Is Amazing
ISBN: 978-0-9572413-5-0
First Edition

# Contents

Acknowledgements                                                    6
Foreword                                                            7
Preface                                                             9
Introduction                                                       13
Chapter 1: Psychic Investigations                                  19
Chapter 2: The Soul Flies Free                                     37
Chapter 3: Prelude to the Revelation                               43
Chapter 4: Spiritualism versus Religion                           51
Chapter 5: The New Revelation                                     65
Chapter 6: In Memoriam                                            94
Chapter 7: Turbulent Priests                                     104
Chapter 8: Contact                                               136
Chapter 9: Cynics, Materialists and Pressmen                     148
Chapter 10: Of Spiritualist Science                              173
Chapter 11: The Need For Energy                                  190
Chapter 12: The Great Debate                                     214
Chapter 13: Departures                                           231
Chapter 14: Future Controversies                                 248
Afterword                                                        252
Appendix A: Further Adventures in the World of Light             255
Appendix B: People and Organisations in this Book               289
Appendix C: A Glossary of Spiritualist Terms                    299
Appendix D: Bibliography                                         303
Appendix E: Index of Letters and Articles                       307
Index                                                            311

## Acknowledgements

I would like to thank Michael Gunton at the The Arthur Conan Doyle Collection - Lancelyn Green Bequest, for his help in researching this book; David Saunderson of The Spooky Isles for his encouragement; Leslie Price, archivist at the College of Psychic Studies for his humour and deep insight. Also, thanks must go to the Conan Doyle Encyclopedia online, to Tom Harris for his diligence in proofreading and editing and Portsmouth Library Service for allowing me access to their Conan Doyle Archives and helping me along the way and to Alan Murdie of The Ghost Club. Thank you all.

# Foreword
## by Michael Gunton
(Senior Archivist, Portsmouth Library and Archive Service)

Though Conan Doyle is now known around the world as the creator of Sherlock Holmes, he was a man of many other interests. Throughout his long life he was fascinated by science, exploration, and current affairs.

Thanks to his Sherlock Holmes stories and to his books, pamphlets, talks, and letters to newspapers, he became a public figure. He commented on political issues of his day, such as the campaign for women to have the right to vote, was among the first to publicise and comment on photographs of atrocities in the Belgian Congo (now the Democratic Republic of Congo); and even campaigned to right several miscarriages of justice, such as the cases of George Edalji and Oscar Slater.

While working on *The Lost World*, Conan Doyle spoke to Shackleton and Scott about polar exploration. As a doctor with the British army in the Boer War he not only tended the wounded, but also observed how the British campaign was organised and resourced, writing and lobbying about these things after he returned home. During the First World War Conan Doyle visited the Western Front and wrote about what he witnessed, as well as producing a history of the war.

While Sherlock Holmes is now known worldwide, Conan Doyle himself took much greater pride in the historical and science fiction stories he also wrote: *The White Company*, *Micah Clarke*, *Rodney Stone*, and the Professor Challenger stories.

He was a keen sportsman, who enjoyed watching and playing many different sports: he was among the first to popularise skiing as a sport, he boxed and played cricket, as well as being goalkeeper for Portsmouth Association Football Club.

This, then, is the man who became convinced of the reality of Spiritualism while he was in Portsmouth, and who spent much of his later life trying to spread awareness of what he had discovered.

This book draws largely on the archives left to Portsmouth City Council in 2004 by Richard Lancelyn Green, a collector with a lifelong interest in Conan Doyle and his works. He bequeathed his collection of 40,000 documents, 16,000 books, and 3,000 objects to Portsmouth

Library Service. We are indebted to him for his assiduous collecting and his final act of generosity that means his archive has been saved for future researchers.

It is fascinating to see how much Conan Doyle's towering presence continues to shape popular culture through television, plays, radio and books. And it is fascinating, too, to see how Lancelyn Green's archive inspires and informs so many different research projects which feed into the cultural phenomenon that is Sir Arthur Conan Doyle.

If you would like more information about the collection and how to access it, please visit www.conandoylecollection.co.uk.

MICHAEL GUNTON

# Preface
## by Leslie Price
### (Archivist, College of Psychic Studies, London)

Modern Spiritualism began in the United States about 1848, and spread across the world, reaching a peak of cultural influence around 1875, when the naturalist Alfred Russel Wallace and chemist William Crookes published influential supportive works. It was based on mental mediumship (communication with those who had died who gave information via mediums) and physical mediumship (the movement of objects by spirits, and the production of ectoplasm, a mysterious substance about which Doyle was later to lecture on the radio.)

The London Spiritualist Alliance, the most reputable Spiritualist body, was formed in 1884; it considered Spiritualism as the preamble to religion, rather than a new religion. The LSA leaders were also involved in the weekly newspaper LIGHT, started in 1881, which Doyle evidently began reading, and to which in 1887 he wrote two letters, (reproduced here) identifying himself as a Spiritualist. In the 1890s, Doyle was a major private donor to LIGHT, and it was primarily to LIGHT and the LSA that he turned in 1916 when he gradually came out as a Spiritualist. To what extent he had retained his Spiritualist convictions in the intervening years since 1887 is a moot point. The accounts he gave of how he came to faith (in this book and elsewhere) are at times conflicting.

In 1882, a number of Spiritualists and independent investigators formed a Society for Psychical Research. Doyle was listed as a new member in February 1893, but never became prominent in its affairs. Its scientific concerns were clearly not central to him. It was the implications of mediumship for religion that moved him.

So, we see him in LIGHT from 1916 assembling the building blocks of his missionary faith. He could have preached just survival and communication as scientific facts, but he went further, making a central assault on orthodox Christianity. This endeared him to the rapidly growing Spiritualist churches, but aroused additional hostility. One wonders if his memory of his boyhood membership of the Roman Church caused him to seek its overthrow.

Since the time of its first president, Stainton Moses, (the medium for the classic book *Spirit Teachings*), the LSA had always favoured a

Unitarian[1] interpretation of Christianity, but had not been belligerent, preferring the diplomatic approach of Sir Oliver Lodge, who was a liberal Christian and keen survivalist. Lodge was a good friend of the LSA, though he did not join this or any other Spiritualist body.

There was a palpable hope among radical Spiritualists in that immediate post war era that survival might now be accepted generally, and that orthodox religion could quickly be overthrown. We detect that mood in these pages - the sorrow of the grieving with the hope that a new age was dawning.

National Spiritualism, centred on the churches of the Spiritualists National Union, was also growing in those years. Conan Doyle supported them, especially their leader Ernest Oaten, editor of the weekly newspaper *Two Worlds* published in Manchester. But Doyle wanted the leadership[2] of Jesus Christ to be accepted by the SNU. The Union debated this, but shortly before his death in 1930, voted against this addition to their Seven Spiritual Principles. This significant defeat showed the limitations of Conan Doyle's leadership of the Spiritualist Movement.

From 1916, when Sir Arthur Conan Doyle went public with his convictions, until 1920, he was at the height of his powers in the psychic field. Through Sherlock Holmes, he had earned by proxy a reputation as an astute investigator. He had the energy to lecture persuasively up and down the country. The people in the audiences were in an emotionally heightened state because of the trauma of the Great War. An estimated 7000 attended one event in this work.

Doyle's opponents soon emerged. There were the Rationalists, who usually denied all psychic phenomena. There were the orthodox religious leaders who saw his new revelation as subversive of the old. At least one Christian Spiritualist, Rev. Fielding-Ould became alarmed at the assault by Doyle on the biblical faith. Later in life, Doyle became also critical of the Society for Psychical Research, the non-committed body of which he was a member, but at first it was Lodge, an SPR leader who tried tactfully to restrain Doyle.

Later, Lodge could not dissuade Doyle from his most disastrous case,

---

1    the belief that Christ was human, rather than divine.
2    ie: a recognition of the primacy of Christ as a medium, and the importance of his teachings as recorded in the Gospels.

the Cottingley fairies, which were brought to his attention in 1920 by an LSA friend, Felicia Scatcherd, and which he very publicly endorsed. In the 1920s Doyle was also to be injured by his friendship with the illusionist Houdini, and by another investigator, Harry Price. In his home circle, through his wife's mediumship, Doyle began to be haunted by prophecies of planetary disaster and it is fair to say that his powers declined. But in the years covered by this volume, Arthur Conan Doyle was a commanding figure. LIGHT recognised how he had transformed the prospects of Spiritualism, and supported him in his efforts, while printing the occasional letter of sympathetic dissent. Spiritualists could be forgiven if they could scarcely believe that so famous a name, so energetic a worker, had come to support them.

It is remarkable how Doyle, though lecturing so often, managed to say new things. Many of the questions, such as the problems of mediumship, and how it relates to religion, are with us still. Doyle and those who debated with him in LIGHT and elsewhere, continue to illuminate the issues.

There are many books about Conan Doyle, and a few about the history of Spiritualism. There's even a useful book about the link between the two – Kelvin I. Jones, "Conan Doyle and the Spirits: The Spiritualist Career of Sir Arthur Conan Doyle" (Wellingborough, England: Aquarian Press, 1989.) This new book, however, provides a valuable perspective on the formative years of that link.

In Matt Wingett's book we are able to share in the discussions and controversies in a detailed way that is not possible in ordinary biographies; and it is only thus that we can come to a just assessment of Conan Doyle's thought.

LESLIE PRICE

# Introduction

"How could Arthur Conan Doyle, the man who invented the ultra-rational Sherlock Holmes, believe in séances, mediums - and even fairies?"

That question had been on my mind for some time. Friends I spoke with expressed opinions such as "it's totally schizophrenic" or "he must have lost his marbles when he got older." With that second statement there often came a supplementary question: "Was he still writing Holmes stories when he believed in this stuff?"

They always looked surprised when I told them he was.

That was the starting point for my journey into the world of *Light*, a magazine I found in the Arthur Conan Doyle Collection - Lancelyn Green Bequest held in Portsmouth Central Library.

Subtitled *A Journal of Psychical, Occult, and Mystical Research*, *Light* was one of several magazines dedicated to Spiritualism during the period Conan Doyle was an active Spiritualist; others including *The Two Worlds* (1887) and *The Occult Review* (1905).

Founded in 1881 by Edmund Dawson Rogers and originally subtitled *A Journal Devoted To The Highest Interests Of Humanity Both Here And Hereafter*, it was the first "high-toned and impartial weekly journal" dedicated to Spiritualism. It dealt with a massive subject area, covering all manner of unexplained phenomena; from ghostly sightings to telepathy, from scientific breakthroughs to ancient mysteries, from alchemy to the spiritual meaning of nuclear physics, it had it all. In fact, it still does. The magazine is still published to this day.

Vitally, *Light* was the first magazine to publish a letter by Doyle expressing interest in the subject into which he later directed all his passion. It followed Doyle throughout his long Spiritualist career.

My love of Conan Doyle came alive as a boy when I read *The Lost World*, watched Sherlock Holmes on the tv, and went on to enjoy all the Holmes stories. My interest in Doyle's Spiritualism was originally piqued in *The Unexplained*, a 1980s magazine which investigated strange phenomena. In later years, I discovered Doyle's historical romances and horror tales - the latter of which I devoured greedily. I was deeply impressed by Doyle's zeal, his wide-ranging imagination and his mastery of storytelling.

I read his Spiritualist works; *The New Revelation*, *The Vital Message* and *The Case for Spirit Photography*, among others. They are fascinating as works that stand alone, but they didn't really answer *how* and *why* Conan Doyle came to be the leading Spiritualist of his age.

*Light* provided the key. With original letters and articles by Doyle and references to other magazine and newspaper contributions, it enabled me to track his Spiritualist progress, very often in his own words rather than through others' theories about him. It set him in context, revealing with whom he was talking and sharing ideas. It reflected the mood of the time, uncovering how Conan Doyle came to be the *de facto* leader of a world movement, into which he threw his extraordinary energies with the ardent fervour of the evangelist.

Though *Light* was (and still is) a serious magazine dedicated to discussion of all things psychic, it nevertheless dealt with mysteries, first-hand accounts of unexplained phenomena and tales of half-hidden secrets that were bound to appeal to Conan Doyle's powerful imagination.

An otherworldly ethos also at times pervaded Doyle's Sherlock Holmes stories - though apparently baffling mysteries were always unravelled with materialistic solutions. Even the most Gothic of the Holmes tales, *The Hound of the Baskervilles*, with all its psychic trappings - an ancient curse laid on a family, a massive glowing spectral hound - is in the end explained by an attempt to steal an inheritance by the application of phosphorus to a killer dog.

Nevertheless, the story's genesis was a great example of how the supernatural acted on Doyle's creativity. Part of its impetus came from a story told to Doyle by a friend, Fletcher Robinson, an expert in folktales. The legend of Richard Cabell, tells of the cruel squire of the manor of Brook in seventeenth century Dartmoor, whose wife made a desperate bid for freedom to escape his brutality. He hunted her down on the moors and stabbed her and her dog to death. As punishment for his nefarious crime, his ghost was forever hunted by the monstrous spirit of that faithful hound. A variation on the Dark Huntsman and wisht hounds legends, the story is gloriously eerie, with its vast, empty moors and supernatural retribution.

No doubt, some of the phenomena reported in *Light* had the same hackles-raising effect for many of its readers. It is not difficult to imagine that the Spiritualist explanation of paranormal phenomena fitted Doyle's emotional, scientific, religious and indeed, creative, needs.

There are already in existence several authoritative works which shed light on Doyle's Spiritualism. As Leslie Price has previously mentioned, Kelvin I Jones's *Conan Doyle and the Spirits* traces closely his involvement with the paranormal. Daniel Stashower's *Conan Doyle, Teller of Tales* also deals with Doyle's faith in some chapters – especially (rather tellingly) the one entitled: *Is Conan Doyle Mad?* Andrew Lycett's *Conan Doyle, The Man Who Created Sherlock Holmes* provides impressive detail about his life and his Spiritualist investigations and is an extraordinary work of scholarship. Geoffrey Stavert's *A Study In Southsea* investigates his time in Portsmouth during that crucial early period and postulates that Doyle's book *The Stark Munro Letters* provides a fictionalised description of his real life in the town.

Whilst I recommend them all to anyone seeking more information about Doyle's faith, my book does something different. It is not a conventional biography. It reproduces in whole all Doyle's articles written for *Light* (a magazine with which he became uniquely close), and parts of many more he wrote for other magazines and quoted by *Light*, as well as the responses of those who knew him, argued with him and admired him. It doesn't give the minutiae of his life: those others I name have already done that brilliantly. This book, I hope, answers the enigma of the man in a different way from those other, excellent works. It is focused on the narrative of his Spiritualist development and relates it as it happened, often in his own words.

You will will hear other long-silent voices speak again: the devout and passionate Rev. F. Fielding-Ould; the usually urbane but occasionally petulant editor of *Light*, David Gow; the obdurate and piously narrow-minded Father Bernard Vaughan; the fantastically disdainful but equally witty Joseph McCabe – all these voices combine to paint a vivid picture of the period.

In the later chapters, there is some overlap. I have traced Doyle's attitudes in specific chapters toward the Church, his materialist critics and his devotion to the cause. Events in some chapters run parallel with each other because this is a useful way to consider his different facets, so this is not a chronological account of his letters to *Light*. I have, however, listed all his letters and articles at the back of this book, so they are easy to find.

Occasionally, I comment on Conan Doyle's thinking. I am not in any way making a case for or against Spiritualism, but tracing the development of Doyle's thoughts to reveal how they made perfect sense in the context of his life. In this context, I also at times report that "so-and-so received a message from a spirit." I am neutral in such cases. Repeatedly using "believed he received" or other such formulæ would impede the flow of reading.

I don't often apply theories or offer deep psychological interpretations of Doyle's actions. These appear in some of the books I have already mentioned and stand scrutiny to varying degrees. Instead, I allow Doyle to speak for himself.

To help contextualise Doyle's faith, in Appendix A I have included a selection of *Light* articles by other authors. They deal with all manner of phenomena; from the Angels of Mons to the Mummy of Evil; from articles about hypnosis to true ghost stories. Over it all hangs the spectre of the Great War. The articles reward perusal. Some are genuinely spine-tingling.

In Appendix B I've included "potted biographies" of some of the more prominent names in Spiritualism in the period covered by this book.

In Appendix C, you will find a glossary of Spiritualist terms, Appendix D includes a Bibliography, and E lists the articles and letters in this book by Doyle, and some of the important ones written about him.

On a minor note, the name "Conan" was not a family name, but appears on his certificate of baptism as a given name. For brevity, I often refer to Sir Arthur Conan Doyle simply as "Doyle".

I have learned much from writing this book, and have come to a much clearer – and more sympathetic – view of the men and women who drove the massive movement of Spiritualism in the early years of the 20th Century.

I have done so while keeping in mind the goal of being entertaining.

I hope I've succeeded.

*Matt Wingett, Southsea, March 2015*

"How often have I said to you that when you have eliminated the impossible, whatever remains, however improbable, must be the truth?"

# Chapter 1
## Psychic Investigations

When in 1882 the young Arthur Conan Doyle took up residence above his new practice at No.1 Bush Villas, Elm Grove, Southsea, it is said he was astonished to find piled in his basement stacks of human jaws grinning at him - the jawbones of numerous people who had visited that building in the preceding years.[3]

It is a detail from his life worthy of an episode of his great detective, Sherlock Holmes, whom he was to create during his extraordinarily fruitful stay in Southsea between 1882 and 1890.

From the very beginning, elements of the Gothic filled Conan Doyle's stories, revealing an imagination and a thought process fascinated by the unknown and apparently inexplicable.

Long before he strode on to the world's stage to evangelise Spiritualism his tales already included moments of spiritual contact. In the spine-tingling conclusion to his 1890 short story *The Captain of the Polestar,* the narrator observed near the body of the eponymous Captain an inexplicable vision in the vast Arctic wastes.

> He was lying face downwards upon a frozen bank. Many little crystals of ice and feathers of snow had drifted on to him as he lay, and sparkled upon his dark seaman's jacket. As we came up, some wandering puff of wind caught these tiny flakes in its vortex, and they whirled up into the air, partially descended again, and then, caught once more in the current, sped rapidly away in the direction of the sea. To my eyes it seemed but a snow-drift, but many of my companions averred that it started up in the shape of a woman, stooped over the corpse and kissed it, and then hurried away across the floe. I have learned never to ridicule any man's opinion, however strange it may seem.

It is a moment straight from the Romantic tradition. The Arctic setting echoes the denouement of Mary Shelley's *Frankenstein* – another

---

3   See Geoffrey Stavert, *A Study In Southsea*

writer who skilfully combined elements of science and spirit to ask philosophical questions and create a supernatural thrill.

Other early works also show his love of the unexplained and the occult. His horror novel, *The Mystery of Cloomber* employs reincarnation, karma and astral projection in a tale of vengeance involving a cursed army General who killed a Buddhist in India, for whom it all ends badly in the desolate Scottish countryside.

Conan Doyle's love of the apparently inexplicable also suffused the stories starring his greatest creation, Sherlock Holmes. From the glowing supernatural appearance of *The Hound of the Baskervilles* through the macabre murder near the beginning of *The Sign of Four*, in which a mysterious small-footed creature appears to materialise inside the victim's bedroom, to the sprawling ivy-covered mansion of *Abbey Grange* where a body is discovered with its head battered in using, as Conan Doyle tells us for extra detail "his own poker", there is a gory and otherworldly aspect over which Holmes eventually casts the cold light of reason.

Reading the Holmes stories in isolation, one might not guess the driving force in Doyle's nature – an imagination that revelled in mystery of any kind, be its genesis material or spiritual.

Just so with the short story *Lot No 249*, published in 1892[4], the same year *The Adventures of Sherlock Holmes* began to appear in *The Strand*. It tells the ghoulish tale of Edward Bellingham, an Oxford student with an unhealthy interest in necromancy, who shares a Gothic turret with two other students and an ancient Egyptian mummy which Bellingham bought at auction.

After reanimating the long-dead mummy, Bellingham uses it to remove one of his room-mates as a rival in love. Finally, he is forced at gunpoint by his other room-mate to destroy it. Doyle describes the moment with wonderful ghastly detail:

> In frantic haste he caught up the knife and hacked at the figure of the mummy, ever glancing round to see the eye and the weapon of his terrible visitor bent upon him. The creature crackled and snapped under every stab of the keen blade. A thick yellow dust rose up from it. Spices and dried essences rained

---

4   Also collected in *The Captain of the Polestar*

down upon the floor. Suddenly, with a rending crack, its backbone snapped asunder, and it fell, in a brown heap of sprawling limbs, upon the floor.

Doyle was a master of horror as well as the detective fiction he is renowned for. Both genres reflected two of the main currents in Victorian culture.

On one side, the world was yielding its mysteries to the microscopes and scalpels of doctors and professors. Darwin's startling theories had made enquiring minds think anew. If he were right and humankind really had evolved from lower life forms, then at what point in evolution had God inserted the soul into the human body - if at all? Alternatively, if it were true that we are merely animals and not the wingless angels humankind had for millennia conceived itself to be, then did animals have souls, too? Or did none of us? Conventional religion was on the retreat. People sought new proofs and new solace.

Meanwhile, invisible agency was discovered all around. Wireless transmission, the strange burns left on the skin by radium, X-rays which though invisible to the eye could activate a photographic plate, were all indications of an unseen world that interacted with the seen. Nobel prize-winner Marie Curie investigated the spirit manifestations of medium Eusapia Palladino, as did eminent scientist, Spiritualist and, later, Theosophist, Sir William Crookes. To many intelligent, enquiring minds, anything seemed possible and everything was worth evaluating and considering. Alfred Russel Wallace, the scientist who published his first paper on evolution at the same time as Darwin, was also a convinced Spiritualist.

Spiritualism itself came from a time before X-rays and wireless communication, and was taken up by some scientists as part of their inquiry into the world of unseen forces. Many Spiritualist historians date its emergence in Hydesville, New York, to March 31st, 1848. That night, two sisters, Kate Fox (12) and Leah Fox (15) began to communicate with the entities causing unexplained knockings in their reportedly haunted house. Soon, they attracted members of the local Quaker community, who questioned conventional religious structures that excluded women from spirituality, and who saw these phenomena as evidence that spirit was as much women's realm as men's. From here, and in nearby

Rochester, the girls gained a large early following which grew into a worldwide movement that eventually took them around the globe. Victorian England was as much bitten by the bug as anywhere else.

Materialism also had powerful proponents. Indeed, it was Doyle's chosen stance as a young man. Schooled at Stonyhurst College, Lancashire, by Jesuits, he had experienced a dogmatic brand of Roman Catholicism interlaced with physical punishment. Here, he encountered the *tolley*, a thick slab of rubber used for beating errant schoolboys. He took his punishment without complaining, but noted that he would have been better taught through affectionate kindness than the instilling of fear[5]. Of the thunderings of an Irish priest, Father Murphy, who promised damnation for everyone outside the Church, he later wrote, "to that moment I trace the first rift which has grown into such a chasm between me and those who were my guides."[6] So it was that he came to reject Catholicism outright. Rejecting a specific religion, however, did not necessarily mean that the religious impulse itself was so easily suppressed.

Some writers[7] comment on the psychological effect on the young Doyle from a second influence. His father, Charles Altamont Doyle (1832-1893), was an artist of middling talent, who interestingly, considering the direction his son's later life took, was primarily known as a painter of fairies. From the 1860s onwards, Charles was prone to bouts of depression and alcoholism, and in 1885, after drinking alcohol against doctor's advice, he started hearing voices and hallucinating. He was admitted as a long term patient in Montrose Royal Mental Hospital, known as Sunnyside.

For the young Arthur, his father's condition confirmed the materialist's view of the world: something in his father's physiology made him react adversely with alcohol, his brain had been affected by the physical world. No soul was involved. The materialist hypothesis fitted the facts.

This book picks up Doyle's life after he left Edinburgh University in 1881 on completion of his medical degree, filled with a spirit of rationalistic enquiry. Having studied anatomy, optics and pharmacology

---

5   Andrew Lycett, *Conan Doyle, The Man Who Created Sherlock Holmes*
6   Kelvin I Jones, *Conan Doyle and the Spirits*
7   Andrew Lycett, Kelvin I Jones, Daniel Stashower.

he was steeped in the Enlightenment tradition. He wrote later of his belief at this time in *The New Revelation*, his manifesto and statement of faith:

> When the candle burns out the light disappears... When the body dissolves, there is an end of the matter.

Yet for the ever-seeking Conan Doyle, this conclusion was *not* the end of the matter. The Holmes in him had not completely quashed the Bellingham, the enquirer after occult knowledge, and it is possible that in later years this unresolved question about the relationship between mind and body contributed to him seeking an answer which in some way exonerated his father's illness, leaving his soul unsullied.

Despite his materialist leanings, for the young Doctor living in Southsea, no matter how great the allure of science, it became clear to him that it did not hold all the answers. He later wrote in *The Stark Munro Letters*:

> I ask myself, where is the man, the very very inmost essence of the man? ...It does not lie in the limbs which serve him as tools, nor in the apparatus by which he is to digest, nor in that by which he is to inhale oxygen. All these are mere accessories, the slaves of the lord within. Where, then, is he?

He sought to answer this question in his precious spare time. Away from his doctor's practice he was an active participant in Portsmouth society, gave lectures for the local Philosophical Society, played bowls with the Lord Mayor and was goalkeeper for Portsmouth AFC, under the pseudonym "A C Smith", to hide his identity from those who disapproved of gentlemen engaging in a working class sport.

In Southsea, Doyle befriended the architect Henry Ball (designer of St Agatha's Church, Landport), who shared his fascination with the paranormal.

Doyle was at the time developing a theory that the mind produced an *excretion of thought* that a sensitive person could detect. This, he thought, explained telepathy. The two friends embarked on a series of experiments aimed at proving the theory. They employed what Doyle described as a "scientific method" to see whether thoughts could be transferred between their two minds. His conclusion was clear: "Again and again," Doyle recalled in *Memories And Adventures*, "sitting behind him, I have drawn diagrams, and he in turn has made approximately the same figure. I showed beyond doubt whatever that I could convey my thought without words."

Through his energetic networking in Southsea, in 1883 he also befriended a notable local character with strong Spiritualist beliefs, Major-General Alfred Wilkes Drayson of the Royal Artillery. Drayson had written a book entitled *The Art of Practical Whist*, dozens of articles published in *The Boy's Own Paper* and produced several learned astronomical works, one of which propounded a theory of a "second rotation" to the earth, which Drayson argued, accounted for the Earth being plunged into the Glacial Periods. Conan Doyle considered the older man a true genius. Drayson had been converted to Spiritualism upon receiving a spirit message from his late brother; because of his respect for him, Doyle could not discount his opinions easily.

Drayson introduced Doyle to A P Sinnett, a former associate of the Theosophist Madame Blavatsky in India, and read his book *The Occult World*. For some time Doyle was fascinated by Theosophical ideas – which later manifested in his aforementioned 1888 novel *The Mystery of Cloomber* with its Buddhist monks bent on rather unBuddhist revenge.

Drayson, and later, his new wife, Louise, encouraged Doyle to go deeper in his paranormal investigations by applying his scientific mind.

Another military man, Lieutenant-General Thomas Harward invited Doyle to attend a table turning séance held on 24th January 1887 at Kingston Lodge in the north of Portsmouth. Doyle went along with an open and enquiring mind. The group comprised Doyle, his new wife, Louise, his telepathic-experimenter-friend Henry Ball, Lieutenant-General Harward and Nancy, his 22-year-old daughter. They were guided in setting up the séance by instructions they read in *Light* magazine.

The sitting began with a reading from the *First Book of Ezekiel*, in which a spirit appears before the Prophet.[8] "And I looked, and, behold, a whirlwind came out of the north, a great cloud, and a fire infolding itself, and a brightness was about it, and out of the midst thereof as the colour

---

8   Andrew Lycett, *Conan Doyle, The Man Who Created Sherlock Holmes.*

of amber, out of the midst of fire. Also out of the midst thereof came the likeness of four living creatures. And this was their appearance; they had the likeness of a man."[9]

After much waiting, the message the group finally received was somewhat opaque and no doubt an anti-climax:

"You are going too slowly; how long are you going to take?"[10]

Doyle was not impressed by his early Portsmouth experiments. He recalled in his autobiographical *Memories And Adventures*:

> They sat around a dining-room table which after a time, their hands being upon it, began to sway and finally got sufficient motion to tap with one leg. They then asked questions and received answers, more or less wise and more or less to the point. They were got by the tedious process of reciting the alphabet and writing down the letter which the tap indicated. It seemed to me that we were collectively pushing the table and that our own wills were concerned in bringing down the leg at the right moment.

Nevertheless, further séances followed. Nine days later a message came through for Nancy from her cousin, Henry Hastie, who had died three years earlier, "I have not nor ever shall forget you, darling little Nancy. Please love another for my sake. Henry Hastie."

At the same time, Doyle noted that the temperature in the room plummeted and Nancy Harward "became icy cold and experienced a sensation as of soft hands patting her upon the palm with a strong feeling that someone was standing behind her. At the command of the spirits we discontinued the sitting."[11]

Doyle attended 20 sittings with this group in total, but remained unconvinced.

Then, at the end of June, his spiritual leaning was confirmed by a singular event, when he was introduced to a Mr Horstead, an elderly gentleman reputed to have considerable mediumistic power. He wrote his very first letter to *Light* about the encounter.

---

9   Conan Doyle would repeat this imagery decades later during his own prophetic period.
10  Andrew Lycett, *Conan Doyle, The Man Who Created Sherlock Holmes*
11  *Ibid*

*Light, July 2, 1887*

## A TEST MESSAGE

Sir, — I believe that it has been found a useful practice among revivalists and other excitable religionists of all types, for each member to give the assembled congregation a description of the manner in which they attained the somewhat vague result known as "finding salvation." Now among Spiritualists there is really a good deal to be said for such a practice, for the first steps of the inquirer after truth are along such a lonely and treacherous path that it must always be of interest to him to hear how some other wanderer has stumbled along it, uncertain whether he was following a fixed star or a will-o'-the-wisp, until at last his feet came upon firmer ground and he knew that all was well. To the humble inquirer, distrustful of self and fettered with the prejudices of early education, it is of no avail to speak of psychography, materialisation, or advanced phenomena. He yearns for some proof which shall be more within the range of his own personal experience and which shall be decided enough to convince his reason without being so overwhelming as to stagger and confuse it. This must be my apology, therefore, for dwelling upon the incident which, after many months of inquiry, showed me at last that it was absolutely certain that intelligence could exist apart from the body.

Some months ago I read Judge Edmonds' Memoirs, and I have since read Alfred Russel Wallace's book, Major-General Drayson's tract, and other writings on the subject. After weighing the evidence, I could no more doubt the existence of the phenomena than I could doubt the existence of lions in Africa, though I have been to that continent and have never chanced to see one. I felt that if human evidence — regarding both the quantity and the quality of the witnesses — can prove anything, it has proved this. I then set to work to organise a circle of six, which met nine or ten times at my house. We had phenomena such as messages delivered by tilts, and even some writing under control, but there was never anything which could be said to be absolutely conclusive. That complicated machine, the human body, is capable of playing strange tricks, and what was the possibility of unconscious cerebration, of involuntary muscular action, and of the effect of a dozen heavy hands on one light table, I was never entirely satisfied. I was convinced that others had obtained the phenomena, but not that I had done so myself.

Last week I was invited by two friends to join them in a sitting with an old gentleman who was reputed to have considerable mediumistic power. It was the first time that I had ever had the opportunity of sitting with anyone who was not a novice and inquirer like myself. I may remark here that for some days I had been debating in my mind whether I should get a copy of Leigh Hunt's *Comic Dramatists of the Restoration* — the question being whether the mental pollution arising from Messrs. Congreve, Wycherley, and Co. would be compensated for by the picture of the manners and customs of those days to be gathered from their pages, and which I had particular reasons for wishing to be well up in. I had thought the matter over, but had dismissed it from my mind a day or two before the seance. On sitting, our medium came quickly under control, and delivered a trance address, containing much interesting and elevating matter. He then became clairvoyant, describing one or two scenes which we had no opportunity of testing. So far, the meeting had been very interesting, but not above the possibility of deception. We then proposed writing. The medium took up a pencil, and after a few convulsive movements, he wrote a message to each of us. Mine ran: "This gentleman is a healer. Tell him from me not to read Leigh Hunt's book." Now, sir, I can swear that no one knew I had contemplated reading that book, and, moreover, it was no case of thought-reading, for I had never referred to the matter all day. I can only say that if I had had to devise a test message I could not have hit upon one which was so absolutely inexplicable on any hypothesis except that held by Spiritualists. The message of one of my friends, referring to his own private affairs, was as startlingly correct as mine.

Let me conclude by exhorting any other searcher never to despair of receiving personal testimony, but to persevere through any number of failures until at last conviction comes to him, as come it will. Let him deserve success by his patience and earnestness, and he will gain it. Above all, let every inquirer bear in mind that phenomena are only a means to an end, of no value at all of themselves, and simply useful as giving us assurance of an after existence for which we are to prepare by refining away our grosser animal feelings and cultivating our higher, nobler impulses. Unless a man starts with that idea the séance-room sinks to the level of the theatre or the opera — a mere idle resort for the indulgence of a foolish, purposeless curiosity. Let a man realise that the human soul, as it emerges from its bodily cocoon, shapes its destiny in exact accordance with its condition; that that condition depends upon the sum result of his actions and thoughts in this life; that every evil deed stamps itself upon the spirit and entails its own punishment with the same certainty that a man stepping out of a second floor window falls to the ground; that there is no room for deathbed repentances or other nebulous conditions which might screen the evil doer from the consequence of his own deeds, but that the law is self-acting and inexorable. This, I take it, is the lesson which Spiritualism enforces, and all phenomena are only witnesses to the truth of this central all-important fact.

Pray excuse my encroachment upon your space.

Yours faithfully,

A. CONAN DOYLE, M.D.

Southsea

*

Beautifully stylish, this forthright letter reveals his attempt to square the circle. Doyle sought to synthesise science with séance. Thus, he leapt from the description of an experiment to a proof for morality. For him, the raw data of existence were given meaning by evidence of a spiritual life.

Doyle believed the reason he had received advice about Leigh Hunt's book was because something had entered his memory and probed it. This was something above and beyond simple telepathy. It was active rather than passive, and was proof of spirit communication. Doyle excitedly asserted that all that was posited by Spiritualism was proven. In his notebook at the time he wrote of the event: "This message marks in my spiritual career the change of 'I believe' to 'I know'."[12] This pattern of *thinking in large bounds* would stay with him throughout his life.

In Southsea in the 1880s, Doyle went on to investigate all manner of psychic phenomena. He attended demonstrations of hypnosis, writing in his notebooks about its implications for free will, and went on to become

---

12   Andrew Lycett, *Conan Doyle, The Man Who Created Sherlock Holmes*

a founder member and vice-president of the Hampshire Psychical Society. At séances, when he was disappointed by apparently misleading replies from spirits, Drayson encouraged him to persevere. Drayson's rationale for incorrect messages from beyond The Veil painted a picture of a rather mundane afterlife. Doyle explained later in his book *The New Revelation* that Drayson told him:

> "This world is full of weak or foolish people. So is the next. You need not mix with them, any more than you do in this world. But suppose a man in this world, who had lived in his house alone and never mixed with his fellows, was at last to put his head out of the window to see what sort of place it was, what would happen? Some naughty boy would probably say something rude. Anyhow, he would see nothing of the wisdom or greatness of the world. He would draw his head in thinking it was a very poor place. That is just what you have done. In a mixed séance, with no definite aim, you have thrust your head into the next world and you have met some naughty boys. Go forward and try to reach something better."

In the 1880s, while travelling through France with his family, Doyle was inspired in Paris to write *The Ring of Thoth*. With the Louvre as its backdrop, it was his first story featuring a reanimated Egyptian mummy. The arcane and occult were ever potent fuels for his imagination, and *The Ring of Thoth* is oft-credited with starting the mummy story genre, of which the modern film franchise is the latest expression.

As he crystallised his own beliefs in Southsea, Doyle grew increasingly willing to voice his opinions about religion. In a letter to the Portsmouth *Evening News*[13], he took issue with critics of a Southsea public meeting who had denounced Spiritualism as "an old snake of Satan's in a new dress". Signing himself "Spiritualist", he commented:

> When any new form of knowledge arises about the mental horizon of the human race there are always a certain number of well-meaning but narrow-minded men who are ready to denounce it as being opposed to Scriptural teaching.

---

13  Andrew Lycett, *Conan Doyle, The Man Who Created Sherlock Holmes*, p155.

Dismissive of people who adhered to narrow doctrine, he wrote of his encounter with one Southsea "High Church Curate" (actually Reverend Charles Russell Tompkins), in *The Stark Munro Letters*:

> I have no love for the cloth... Just as cotton, which is in itself the most harmless substance in the world becomes dangerous on being dipped in nitric acid, so the mildest of mortals is to be feared if he is once soaked in sectarian religion.

Yet, if Doyle thought Spiritualism might provide an escape from doctrinal dispute, he was wrong. Factions had already formed, with the London-based Society for Psychical Research holding a reputation among some Spiritualists for focusing too much on the unmasking of frauds. Doyle was prompted to write his second letter to *Light* when the magazine reprinted a warning originally published in the *Sunday Boston Herald*. A Mr Hodgson, "an employé *[sic]* of this society, at a salary of £300 per annum", whose business was "to investigate mediumship, and break down and destroy, as far as possible, all mediums" was about to be sent to America "to investigate, and if possible, to prove our prominent mediums cheats." The article gave a description of Hodgson, and told how he had visited India seeking to discredit the great Theosophist Madame Blavatsky. It finished: "We warn all mediums to look out for him, and on no account to hold séances with him."

Such a warning was fertile ground for critics. The following week a correspondent signing himself "A STUDENT" observed that the article was a "puerile confession of weakness" on behalf of Spiritualists.

Conan Doyle, ever ready to rise to a challenge, and motivated by a sense of fair play, replied in bullish tone.

*Light, August 27, 1887*

## MR. HODGSON.
### To the Editor of "LIGHT"

Sir,— I most cordially agree with the letter of "Student," in your recent issue. The flutter which appears to be caused by Mr. Hodgson's descent upon the American mediums would certainly give an unbiassed observer a poor opinion of their honesty. As a Spiritualist, I for one should like to see every possible facility given to Mr. Hodgson in his investigations. If Spiritualism be true and the phenomena genuine, why should the mediums be warned against Mr. Hodgson, or any other inquirer? The worst that could happen would be that his mental attitude might cause inharmonious conditions, and so bring about a negative result. If, however, the phenomena are not genuine, as in some of the cases investigated by the Seybert Commission[14], then, in Heaven's name, let the rascals be exposed. Are we, in our enthusiasm for our belief, to continue to bolster up men who are more vicious than the burglar, meaner than the area-sneak? The Spiritualist ought surely to be keener than any other man in holding up to odium the villains who degrade and prostitute a religion in order to put a few dishonest dollars in their own pockets. Far from throwing difficulties in Mr. Hodgson's way, a fund might very well be set on foot by Spiritualists to assist him in cleaning out the Augean stables of professional mediumship.

Spiritualism in the abstract has no "weak points" because it is *pro tanto* truth. As actually practised, however, it has one weak point more serious than any which have been commented upon in "LIGHT." That is, that respectable Spiritualists persist in supporting and employing men who have been proved, as far as anything mundane is capable of proof, to be swindlers of the lowest order. It may be, as some apologists assert, that they have real but intermittent psychical powers, and that they eke them out by "naive and child-like trickery." If mediums understood definitely that a single instance of this trickery would turn every Spiritualist and every spiritual organ against them, they would be more chary of employing it. While the present loose and easy regime continues, however, in which a medium may be caught tripping one day and be received into the most select spiritual society the next, we have only ourselves to thank if their standard of morality is not a very high one, and if they have successively lost their characters until few of them have any character to lose. A few Hodgsons, backed up by a unanimity of feeling on the part of prominent Spiritualists, would put an end to these

---

14 The Seybert Commission was an academic group at the University of Pennsylvania, who investigated several Spiritualist mediums between 1884 an 1887, uncovering fraud in many cases.

noxious parasites and remove from Spiritualism what Professor Sidgwick justly described as its greatest bane.—Yours faithfully,

A. CONAN DOYLE, M.D. SOUTHSEA,

AUGUST 20th, 1887.

\*

This letter lays bare the basic assumptions in Doyle's thinking that surfaced so publicly nearly 30 years later. Even at this early stage he identified himself as a Spiritualist, and classed Spiritualism as a religion, whereas for many it was an area of scientific investigation. He argued that mediumistic powers were intermittent, and criticised dishonest mediums for bringing the religion into disrepute – levelling his most withering criticism at paid mediums. Furthermore, he criticised Spiritualists for supporting mediums caught in cheap trickery.

In every point – except the last – these opinions were exactly those which formed the basis of his public confession of faith, decades later.

By the time he left Southsea in 1890 Doyle was strongly minded to believe in a world beyond the physical. He held that the Supreme Being alluded to by other religions was also implied by Spiritualists. He hadn't sharpened his view into a coherent belief, but was actively interested by Spiritualist phenomena in the way many other scientifically-minded people were – yet, it was clear that at times at least he had a feeling that disposed him to think of Spiritualism as his religion, though it had not yet coalesced as such, intellectually and intuitively.

After living for a year in Vienna studying ophthalmology, Doyle moved to London and to South Norwood, Croydon. Here, in 1893, Doyle joined the Society for Psychical Research. At this time, he was still grappling with basic theological questions about humanity's relationship with the universe[15]; with these unresolved, he couldn't fully commit to Spiritualism.

In 1894, at the invitation of the Society for Psychical Research, Doyle figuratively donned his deerstalker and accompanied researchers Frank Podmore and Dr Sydney Scott in their investigation of a haunted house in Charmouth, Dorset, that was suffering poltergeist activity. Strange

---

15  Andrew Lycett, *Conan Doyle, The Man Who Created Sherlock Holmes*

phenomena had made the house unbearable to its owner, Colonel Elmore.

On the second night of their stay, the researchers woke to unexplained noises. A sound like a cudgel being repeatedly struck against a heavy table emanated from the locked kitchen. When they unlocked it, they found nothing and no-one there. None of the threads they had set up to mark the passage of a physical presence were broken. The noise was unaccountable.

Ten years later, Doyle was informed that the remains of an infant had been found in the garden. For Doyle, the presence of these bones accounted for the phenomena.

At least, that is how he remembered events 24 years later, when he used the experience to justify his beliefs during the War years. However, recent study of his contemporary notes that were for many years locked in legal battles tell a startlingly different story.

Biographer Andrew Lycett describes the story thus:

> Arthur later offered different versions of what happened, not all of them featuring an ex-army officer. Luckily he provided James Payn with a contemporaneous account of events which must be as close to the truth as possible. According to this, he stayed in the Coach and Horses Hotel in Charmouth. From there, he and his colleagues had access to the supposedly haunted house, a thatched former smuggler's retreat, which was inhabited not by a Colonel but by a cheerful, though somewhat apprehensive, Irish family, comprising mother, son and daughter. Also living there was a forbidding middle-aged maid, also Irish, whom the investigators suspected of instigating the supposedly ghostly disturbances.
>
> On the first night they sat up with a camera and magnesium wire, hoping to take a spirit photograph, but nothing happened. On the second, Dr Scott left early, and the mother and daughter went to bed, leaving Arthur and Podmore talking to the son, who was in his early twenties. After they declined his offer of a drink, he left the room for ten minutes. When, on his return, they made to leave, he begged them to stay. About five minutes later there was a loud crash in the kitchen, and a noise, so Arthur told Payn,

like a table or door being hit with a stick. After half an hour this commotion happened again, but when the investigators went to look they found nothing. Arthur stayed up till two in the morning, hoping to catch someone or something, but to no avail. He eventually decided that the young man of the house was responsible, with an accomplice, since the maid was too stupid to devise such a ruse.

-Andrew Lycett,
*Conan Doyle, The Man Who Created Sherlock Holmes.*

The conclusions he drew later in his life were far removed from this early account, which Lycett notes, concurred with Podmore's.

Was Doyle delusional later? Did he lie for his own purposes? Had he simply forgotten? Did he tell Payn a different story for a particular reason? Or muddled the story?

Another event also took on psychic significance for Doyle. In 1892, travelling through France, he conceived an idea for a story set in the Gemmi Pass, in which a group of travellers stranded by snow take refuge in an inn, with dire consequences. By chance, he bought a book of Maupassant stories and happened upon a story set in the same place, with the same plotline. "Everything that I imagined was there," Arthur later wrote, "save that Maupassant had brought in a savage hound."[16]

For Doyle, this confirmed the notion of divine intervention, which had saved him the embarrassment of being accused of plagiarism. It is a conclusion many of a pattern-making mind commonly draw from what others less willing to join the dots call coincidence.

Later in the year, Doyle's father died in Sunnyside mental hospital. Rather than travel to Dumfries to oversee the funeral, he chose to stay in South Norwood, and hear Spiritualist scientist F W Myers talk on "Recent Evidences As To Man's Survival After Death."

In 1894 Doyle befriended eminent physicist Sir Oliver Lodge, who had recently investigated American medium Leonora Piper. She had also persuaded hard-headed fraud-buster Richard Hodgson (about whom Doyle's second letter to *Light* was written) of survival after death. The friendship between Lodge and Doyle would grow, but Doyle at this time

---

16  Andrew Lycett, *Conan Doyle, The Man Who Created Sherlock Holmes*

clearly saw himself as a humble inquirer overshadowed by Lodge's expertise.

Although Doyle's Spiritualist leanings were largely private and he later described himself during this period as a dilettante, he was inquisitive and committed enough to reach into his pocket. Starting in 1896, over a period of 17 months, he donated to *Light* magazine the sum of £4,250[17]. Reckoned by the Bank of England's inflation calculator to be equivalent to over half a million pounds in 2015, it leads one to wonder just how undecided was he, really?

The message was certainly out there among occultists that Doyle was a seeker after truth. Writing in *Pearsons Magazine* in 1924, he recalled how in 1897 he was approached by a general practitioner named "Pullen-Bury" (actually Henry B Pullen Burry) who had attracted Doyle's interest because he kept a room in his house that was reserved for "mystic and philosophic purposes".

Pullen Burry invited Doyle to join a Rosicrucian-like secret society of which he was a member. The group was the Hermetic Order of the Golden Dawn – a cult that practised ritual magic, astral projection, divination, astrology and Qabalism. Pullen Burry promised Doyle "great powers" if he joined. But, he explained, the powers could do great harm in the wrong hands, so the initiate would need to be examined by a group based in London.

Some time later, Conan Doyle awoke with a peculiar sensation. "It was not a nightmare or any prank of dream... I can only describe it by saying that I was tingling all over. It was not painful, but it was queer and disagreeable, as a mild electric shock would be."

Within a few days, Pullen Burry informed him he had passed the test. Doyle, however, had reconsidered and declined the invitation.

Around a month later, Doyle was visited again by Pullen Burry, this time in the presence of a mutual acquaintance, a Dr Felkin, who described experiences in astral projection. "It was not spiritualism and it was not theosophy," Doyle later wrote, "but rather the acquisition of powers latent in the human organisation, after the alleged fashion of the old Gnostics." After continued resistance to the group's advances, he did not see Pullen Burry for many years.

---

17  Andrew Lycett, *Conan Doyle, The Man Who Created Sherlock Holmes*

These spiritual incidents to one side, for the 20 or so years after his departure from Southsea, Doyle's life was busy and in many ways happy. He was successful and wealthy, and had two children with wife Louise. Life was marred by her contraction of "galloping consumption", a.k.a. tuberculosis, which he sought to treat by frequent trips to foreign climes. Not long after her death in 1906, he married his second wife, Jean Leckie, whom some describe as his former mistress. Though his interest in the paranormal continued, he had little incentive to contact his departed wife. He was unconvinced by séance phenomena and had a new wife to consider, who perhaps jealously advised against investigations which she described as "uncanny and dangerous".[18]

Thanks to his Sherlock Holmes stories, Doyle was wealthy beyond his imaginings and was always busy. There was not much time for thoughts of spirit during this fertile period, though he did with some ambivalence sit in at séances from time to time.

Yet in his creative life, reason jostled the macabre, as was obvious in his Holmes stories and his other tales. These involved mysteries, murders, hypnosis and thought transference. Conan Doyle was irresistibly fascinated by the mysterious, and that fascination only strengthened over the years. Indeed, asked in 1907 to recommend books from his library, he included among classics such as Gibbons' *Decline and Fall of the Roman Empire* and Charles Reade's *The Cloister and the Hearth*, F W Myers' *Human Personality And Its Survival of Bodily Death*.

The beginning of this chapter made mention of the macabre detail of human jawbones grinning at Doyle from the basement of Bush Villas. They have a rational explanation worthy of Holmes. They were casts of patients' jaws left in a pile by the previous incumbent, a dentist. But in his creative life, so central a part to this fascinating man, there was still enough room in Conan Doyle's imagination for the spirit of the uncanny and the unexplained to take wing, as his horror stories revealed.

More room would be made for that spirit with the unfolding of an unprecedented tragedy.

---

18 Andrew Lycett, *Conan Doyle, The Man Who Created Sherlock Holmes*

## Chapter 2
## The Soul Flies Free

Why, in 1916, after a gap of 29 years, should Doyle decide to write to *Light* again?

In his 1926 *The History of Spiritualism*, he revealed some of his motive. He, like so many others, was responding to the Great War:

> The deaths occurring in almost every family in the land brought a sudden and concentrated interest in the life after death. People not only asked the question, 'If a man dies shall he live again?' but they eagerly sought to know if communication was possible with the dear ones they had lost. They sought for 'the touch of a vanished hand, and the sound of a voice that is still.'

Doyle's interest was not an abstract recognition of others' pain. He, too, lost people. At home in Windlesham Manor, he and his wife Jean arranged séances to contact his deceased brother-in-law Malcolm Leckie. In January 1916, Lily Loder-Symonds, Jean's companion and nanny to their children, died. Doyle later wrote of the profound effect her death had on him; for now, suffice to say that at the start of 1916, Doyle was attempting to draw his psychic experiences into a coherent world view.

In March 1916, the first letter Sir Arthur Conan Doyle wrote to *Light* since 1887 began a trickle of activity that soon became a flood. It is tempting to imagine Doyle dipping his toe in the water to test public reception of his Spiritualism with this first letter (if it is possible to imagine the ever-forthright Doyle doing anything tentatively), or to consider him almost "musing aloud" about his views.

The letter this time shared another of Doyle's psychic experiences, not this time discussing the evidence for spirit communication, but for consciousness to remain active when the body is unconscious.

*Light, March 11, 1916*

## WHERE IS THE SOUL DURING UNCONSCIOUSNESS?
## (FROM SIR ARTHUR CONAN DOYLE)
### *To the Editor of* LIGHT.

Sir,— I have had my attention drawn rather strongly to this point by two instances of recent occurrence, one personal and the other in my family.

The first and slighter of the two occurred to myself. A fortnight ago I had laughing gas at the dentist's. I was taken there inside a cab, my wife and two little boys being with me. The cab drove on whilst I was being operated upon. While under the gas I was intensely conscious that I had returned to the moving cab, and that I could very vividly see the occupants, while well aware that they could not see me. This, of course, might be subjective entirely, but the impression was very clear.

The second incident is more convincing. My son Adrian, aged five, was grievously ill of pneumonia, and was lying half comatose with a temperature of 105°. My wife, who was nursing him, left him for a moment and went to fetch something from the nursery, two rooms away. The elder boy, Denis, was standing on a chair, and on getting down he trod upon some tin soldiers on the ground. My wife, anxious not to leave the invalid too long, hurried into the sick room. The child opened his eyes and said, "Naughty Denis, breaking my soldiers!"

He had never spoken of soldiers during five days of illness, so that the remark was beyond the reach of coincidence. Nor was it thought-transference from my wife's brain, as she is clear that she was thinking only of the invalid. I can only explain it by the supposition, which can be supported by a volume of evidence, that the soul can be, and probably is always, out of the body at such times, and that occasionally under rare conditions which we have not yet been able to define, it can convey to the body the observations which it has made during its independent flight.

Such conditions must have existed in the classic case of Sir Rider Haggard. It will be remembered that he wrote a letter to the "Times" some years ago giving the circumstances in detail. He had lost a favourite dog. In his sleep he saw it lying near a certain point of the railway. Upon searching it was actually found there. There was no particular reason why this point should have suggested itself to him, more than any other in the neighbourhood.

Another classic case is that of the Red Barn murder in the eighteenth century. In this case the mother dreamed three times that she saw the corpse of her daughter hidden in a certain loft. The loft was examined and the corpse was found. There are a great number of such cases on record. They are all readily explained on the supposition that the soul drifts out like a captive balloon, attached always by some filament which draws it back in an instant to its body. There is nothing supernatural in such a supposition. It is only the unfolding of a fresh law in a region which is still but little known. There is apparently a "switch-off" between the body life and the extra-body life. Should the switch for any reason hang fire, then we have memory of one carried into the other.

The matter is of profound religious significance. There is, as it seems to me, something very surprising in the limited interest which the churches take in psychical research. It is a subject which cuts at the very root of their existence. It is the one way of demonstrating the independent action of soul, and therefore, to put it at the lowest, the *possibility* of its existence apart from bodily organs. If the balloon can really drift forth upon a filament and retain its own individuality, then it is no great further step to say that when the filament snaps the balloon is still self-sufficient. A fresh unfolding of knowledge — and each such unfolding is in truth a renewed divine revelation — has given us reassurances. Myers, Gurney and Hodgson[19] are messengers, of truth from the Beyond as surely as Isaiah or Amos, but, British fashion, they speak coldly and clearly with none of the passion and declamation of the East. Their message has fallen on many ears and strengthened many spirits, but it has never, as it seems to me, had the direct religious effect which one might have expected. Personally I know no single argument which is not in favour of the extinction of our individuality at death, save only the facts of psychic research. But these are so strong that they must outweigh all others, as the positive must always outweigh the negative. A hundred who have examined and tested and seen must always be more convincing than a million who disagree without investigation.

---

19 F W Myers, Edmund Gurney and Richard Hodgson, prominent psychic investigators and members of the Society for Psychical Research.

—Yours faithfully,
ARTHUR CONAN DOYLE.
Windlesham, Crowborough, Sussex.
February 28th, 1916.

*

Conan Doyle raised themes that would recur throughout his long association with Spiritualism. His assertion that evidence of out-of-the-body experiences entailed the whole of the rest of Spiritualist religion echoed the conceptual leap he expressed when receiving the recommendation not to read Leigh Hunt's book from Mr Horstead in 1887. Another belief, that the amount of research that had been done in psychic research far outweighed all arguments against it, he would adhere to for the rest of his life. He also never wavered from the idea that psychic research was a natural ally of Christianity, though over the years his stance hardened toward the latter when it became clear many Christians did not reciprocate his view.

His letter prompted several replies by the wider Spiritualist community. On April 15th, 1916, *Light* reported one correspondent's remarks in another Spiritualist magazine, *The Occult Review* that "the fact of the soul perceiving things at a distance does not necessarily imply a passage through the intermediate space." *Light* took up the discussion, pointing out that the facts involved a conception of space and distance, and the idea expressed in the original question was "near enough for practical purposes".

Other Spiritualists proposed their own theories. American author, journalist and Spiritualist Lilian Whiting (1859–1942) argued that there was no "floating forth" as Doyle described[20]. Rather, spirits had vastly superior senses that reached further, in just the way our own senses are superior to those of the deaf and blind. Before finishing the letter she noted with obvious warmth "how interesting it is to see the distinguished name of Sir Arthur Conan Doyle in the columns of LIGHT, as the writer of a letter so suggestive and noteworthy."

In Conan Doyle's reply to the many letters he received, he mentioned the "mischievous guttersnipe" argument – revealing how strong was the

20  *Light*, April 22nd 1916

influence on him of Major-General Drayson, his erstwhile spiritual mentor.

*Light, May 13, 1916*

## WHERE IS THE SOUL DURING UNCONSCIOUSNESS?
### (FROM SIR ARTHUR CONAN DOYLE.)
*To the Editor of* LIGHT.

Sir, — I must write again under the above heading in order to thank the numerous correspondents who have thrown various lights upon the question which I raised. Besides the letters in LIGHT I have received many private instances, and another correspondence has treated the matter in a well-known London weekly paper ("T.P.'s Weekly"). The result is a mass of definite testimony which I may elaborate into a longer article where I might have space to dissect the evidence and draw some general conclusions.

Lilian Whiting and one or two other correspondents dissent from my view that the soul or spirit at such a time is floating from the body like a captive balloon on a psychic rope by which it can be drawn instantaneously back. They prefer the view that we have a natural spirit vision which is all-embracing and is only clogged by the body. Since, however, in all the cases cited the result is definite in time and place, and since it does not include a general view of everything but only of one particular thing, I still hold that the floating forth of a sensitive organism which is limited in its perception is the presumption which comes nearest to an explanation of the facts.

The instances are so numerous, so well attested, and so utterly beyond the reach of coincidence that one marvels that any man calling himself a scientist could dismiss them as unworthy of scientific consideration. Such scientists, having formed an *a priori* conception of the universe, simply ignore the plain facts which stand in the way of their hypothesis. One marvels that minds so acute within their own limitations should be so slovenly and illogical outside of them. One cannot forget the famous dictum of Huxley after hearing or reading some inanities of a séance room. "If they are true," said he, "they interest me no more than the gossip of curates in a cathedral city." This was a man who had made his name by a careful classification of crayfish and sea jellies. Yet he dismissed a whole new order of beings because the particular mental phenomena which he first encountered were not up to his preconceived ideas of what they should be. It would be as reasonable for a recluse coming out into the world to abjure the whole human race because the first gutter-snipe whom he encountered made a bad impression on him. Science (so-called) denied mesmerism for a century. Then it renamed it "hypnotism" and adopted it. Some day, no doubt, it will find a new name for the various psychic phenomena which are now under discussion, and will then find itself in complete agreement. — Yours, &c.,

ARTHUR CONAN DOYLE
Windlesham, Crowborough.
April 30th, 1916

\*

In a letter of May 27th, 1916, correspondent James W Sharpe trotted out his own theory – there was a kind of *Russian doll* of self, comprising numerous types of body: "...the soul, during the unconsciousness of the visible mundane body, is contained within some one or other of the inner bodies, two of which, the astral body and the *boule mentale*, are known to us experimentally," he wrote, giving a long description of how these bodies were constituted and used.

For Doyle, this first public outing into the world of Spiritualism was a success. Overall, the tenor of commentators in *Light* was instructive and supportive, with minor differences over details. Since Doyle was a massive celebrity, at the time probably the second most famous author after Rudyard Kipling, Spiritualists who had not previously known of his leanings were clearly pleased to count him among them.

It would not be long before Doyle wrote in upon a new theme that he would return to at greater length.

That theme was that Spiritualism was nothing less than a New Revelation.

# Chapter 3
## Prelude to the Revelation

As has already been noted, Doyle was personally affected by the losses of the Great War.

His brother-in-law, Malcolm Leckie was killed at Mons in 1914. His nephew Oscar Hornung died at Ypres in 1915. The husband of his sister Lottie, Major Leslie Oldham, died at Festubert in the same year.

Even so, when asked by *The International Psychic Gazette* in 1915 for words of comfort for the bereaved, he said: "I fear I can say nothing worth saying. Time only is the healer."[21]

The final catalyst came from a source surprisingly close to home.

Throughout 1915, Lily Loder-Symonds, the Doyle children's nanny and close companion to Lady Jean Conan Doyle, grew increasingly ill. Soon, she was slipping into trance and performing automatic writing.

Spiritualists believe the psychically sensitive convey spirit messages through automatic writing. A medium may be in a trance, may be only just conscious – or may look on with detached curiosity as their hand takes on a life of its own.

Several messages impressed Doyle. Firstly, Lily pronounced on the sinking of the *Lusitania* in May 1915, correctly predicting that the loss of some 1,200 lives (including Doyle's personal friend Charles Frohman, producer of William Gillette's play *Sherlock Holmes*) would have a profound effect on the war.

Daniel Stashower, in his book *Conan Doyle, Teller of Tales*, points out it wasn't obvious the sinking would help draw the United States into the war. On the other hand, he notes that Lily would have been familiar with the public debate about merchant shipping that Doyle's story *Danger!*[22] had stirred. Nevertheless, for Doyle, Lily's observation displayed strong psychic insight.

More convincing was Lily's prediction of "the arrival of an important telegram upon a certain day." She even "gave the name of the deliverer of it – a most unlikely person," Doyle explained in his 1918 book *The New Revelation*.

---

21 Kelvin I Jones, *Conan Doyle and the Spirits*.
22 First published in *The Strand* in July 1914.

Furthermore, Lily's communication with her three brothers killed in the war provided convincing information about the battlefields – though, Doyle conceded the detail could have come from newspapers.

What finally convinced him was Lily's reference to a private conversation between Doyle and and his deceased brother-in-law, Malcolm Leckie, which, he insisted, no-one else knew about. This was the turning point.

Lily's death in January 1916 profoundly affected him. It sealed his belief, perhaps because the phenomena could not be further questioned, and set him on his Spiritualist course.

Another event reinforced his belief after his former sister-in-law, Nem, died of an overdose of chlorodyne, a mixture of opium, cannabis and chloroform. In a visit to medium Vout Peters a few days later, a message came through. "There is a lady, here. She is leaning on an older woman," said Peters. "She keeps saying 'Morphia'. Three times she said it. Her mind was clouded. She did not mean it. Morphia!"

Piecing all the evidence together, Doyle came to what he considered an inescapable conclusion. Toward the end of 1916, he publicly announced Spiritualism to be nothing less than "a New Revelation" - a phrase that would ring through the years. With that realisation, he had found the grand theme of his life.

*Light. November 4, 1916*

## A NEW REVELATION.
## SPIRITUALISM AND RELIGION.
## BY SIR ARTHUR CONAN DOYLE.

If anyone were to look up the list of subscribers to LIGHT for the year 1887 I think that he would find my name. I am also one of the oldest members of the Psychical Research Society[23]. Therefore if, after thirty years of thought, I venture to respond to the Editor's invitation to say a few words upon spirit intercourse, I cannot be accused of having sprung hastily to my conclusions. Those conclusions can be expressed concisely in one sentence. In spite of occasional fraud and wild imaginings, there remains a solid core in this whole spiritual movement which is infinitely

---

23 Correctly, *The Society for Psychical Research*

nearer to positive proof than any other religious development with which I am acquainted. The days are past when the considered opinions of such men as Crookes, Wallace, Flammarion, Lodge, Barrett, Generals Drayson and Turner, Serjeant Ballantyne, W. T. Stead, Judge Edmonds, Vice-Admiral Usborne Moore, the late Archdeacon Wilberforce, and such a cloud of other witnesses, can be dismissed with the empty-headed "all rot" formula. As Mr. J. Arthur Hill has well said in a recent number of the "National Review," we have reached a point where further proof is superfluous, and where the weight of disproof lies upon those who deny. If, to take one of a thousand examples, the only evidence for unknown intelligent forces lay in the experiments of Dr. Crawford recorded in a true, scientific spirit of caution in your columns, I do not see how it can be shaken. We should now be at the close of the stage of investigation and beginning the period of religious construction.

For what is this movement? Are we to satisfy ourselves by observing phenomena with no attention to what the phenomena mean, as a group of savages might stare at a wireless installation with no appreciation of the messages coming through it, or are we resolutely to set ourselves to define these subtle and elusive utterances from beyond, and to construct from them a religious scheme, which shall be founded upon human reason on this side and upon spirit inspiration on the other? These phenomena have passed through the stage of being a parlour game; they are now emerging from that of a debatable scientific novelty; and they are, or should be, taking shape as the foundations of a definite system of religious thought, in some ways confirmatory of ancient systems, in some ways entirely new.

Where are they confirmatory? They are confirmatory as to all those moral laws which are common to most human systems and, which are so sanctioned by reason that where reason is developed they need no further support. They are confirmatory as to life after death, which has been taught by most religions but has been denied by many earnest and thoughtful men. They are confirmatory as to the unhappy results of sin, though adverse to the idea that those results are permanent. They are confirmatory as to the existence of higher beings whom we may call angels and of an ever-ascending hierarchy above us, culminating in heights which are beyond our sight or apprehension, with which we may associate the idea of all-power or of God. They are confirmatory as to the existence of the "Summer-land" or heaven, but assert that every human being finds his or her ultimate, but not necessarily final, resting place therein. Thus this new revelation, so far as it has been systematised, supports many of the more important contentions of the old ones. If this compass points true then our old compasses did not work so badly after all.

But now for the points of correction or addition. These take the form of more positive teaching as to the nature of death and of the world beyond. By this teaching death makes no abrupt change in the process of development, nor does it make an impassable chasm between those who are on either side of it. No trait of the form and no peculiarity of the mind are changed by death, but all are continued in that spiritual body which is the counterpart of the earthly one at its best, and still contains within it that core of spirit which is the very inner essence of the man. Nature develops slowly, and not by enormous leaps, so that it would seem natural that the soul should not suddenly become devil or angel but should continue upon its slow growth. Such would appear to be a reasonable solution, and such is the spiritual teaching from beyond. Nor apparently are the spirit's surroundings, experiences, feelings, and even foibles very different from those of earth. A similar nature in the being would seem to imply a similar atmosphere around the being to meet the needs of that nature, all etherialised to the same degree. What of the colours which we know to exist beyond the violet of the spectrum? What of the notes which we can detect by the vibration of the diaphragm but which are above the pitch of the human ear? We can see for ourselves how in these instances there is an unseen and unheard physical world close to our own; I do not say that it is this world which the spirits inhabit, but at least it shows how very near to us, even in the space which we ourselves occupy, other worlds may exist as oblivious of us as we of them.

It is in the possibility of communion that the main feature of this new teaching lies. The conditions being similar on either side of the partition of death make the idea of communication more feasible. Spirits claim that they are happier than we, but they have no more force of intellect than they brought over with them and they have the same difficulties in solving the question of communication as their relatives on earth. On both sides of the partition the vast majority would appear to be absolutely indifferent and ignorant upon the subject. But also on both sides there are bands of pioneers who, as we know in this world, comprise some of the best intellects of humanity, and who are, as we are told, reinforced upon the other side by more advanced spirits. These are beating down the partition, and hear the sound of each others' picks. Many ways have been devised, all imperfect, but some of them fitfully and wonderfully successful. Clairvoyance, clairaudience, the direct voice, automatic writing, spirit control — these are the various methods, all depending upon that inexplicable thing called mediumship, a thing so sacred, and sometimes so abused.

Such, in brief, is the spiritual philosophy where faith — a most two-edged virtue — is replaced by actual demonstration. The evidence upon which this system rests is so enormous that it would take a very considerable library to contain it, and the witnesses are not shadowy people living in the dim past and inaccessible to our cross-examination but are our own contemporaries, men of character and intellect whom all must respect. The situation may, as it seems to me, be summed up in a simple alternative. The one supposition is that there has been an outbreak of lunacy extending over two generations of mankind and two great continents — a lunacy which assails men or women who are otherwise eminently sane. The alternative supposition is that in recent years there has come to us from divine sources a new revelation which constitutes by far the greatest religious event since the death of Christ (for the Reformation was a re-arrangement of the old, not a revelation of the new), a revelation which alters the whole aspect of death and the fate of man. Between these two suppositions I can see no solid position. Theories of fraud or of delusion will not meet the evidence. It is absolute lunacy or it is a revolution in religious thought, a revolution which gives us as by-products an utter fearlessness of death, and an immense consolation when those who are dear to us pass behind the veil.

There are many superficial inquirers to whom the ideas of a divine revelation and of such humble phenomena as Rochester rappings or moving tables seem incompatible. The greatest things have always come from the smallest seeds. The twitching leg of a frog suggested the whole development of electric science, and the rattling lid of a kettle was the father of steam, as the falling apple is said to have suggested the law of gravity. It is the simple thing that catches the eye. But the wise investigator does not dwell too much upon the first suggestions, but passes onwards to consider what they have suggested and whither they have led.

There remains the question which troubles many earnest souls as to whether such communion is right. Personally I am not aware of any human power which has been given us without our having the right under any circumstances to use it. On the other hand, I know no human power which may not be abused. It is an abuse of such a power as this that it should be used in a spirit of levity or of mere curiosity. It is either an absurd farce or the most solemn and sacred of functions. But when one knows, as I know, of widows who are assured that they hear the loved voice once again, or of mothers whose hands, groping in the darkness, clasp once again those of the vanished child, and when one considers the loftiness of their intercourse and the serenity of spirit which succeeds it, I feel sure that a fuller knowledge would calm the doubt of the most scrupulous conscience. Men talk of a great religious revival after the war. Perhaps it is in this direction that it will be.

\*

The energy and assuredness of the above article simultaneously displays one of Doyle's great virtues and one of his great weaknesses. Though hugely intelligent, he was not immune to logical fallacy. Thus, having decided that "further proof is superfluous" he set out a false dichotomy. His readers had a choice: people who believe in Spiritualism, a) had alighted on the truth, or b) were insane.

Having employed this rhetorical device, he rushed on with characteristic energy to argue that spiritual data should be interpreted through a moral prism. This neatly loaded spirit manifestation with subjective religious interpretation, thus removing it from the statistical or observational sphere of the scientist. He conflated the subjective and the objective.

At the same time, Doyle also sought an alliance between the old religions and his New Revelation – although his appeal was that the New Revelation improved on the old.

Spiritualists were clearly excited that a writer of Doyle's magnitude had taken up their cause.

His friend, Sir William F Barrett was a respected scientist - a Fellow of the Royal Society, a Fellow of the Royal Society of Edinburgh and a Fellow of the Royal Dublin Society. Barrett had also personally witnessed thought transference during a demonstration of mesmerism in the 1860s. In his spiritual trajectory, Barrett had studied poltergeist activity and was a founder of the Society for Psychical Research. He was a scientist, a Spiritualist and a committed Christian.

His response to Doyle in a letter published on 11th November was largely supportive. "I quite agree with Sir Arthur that the evidence on behalf of spirit communications and spirit-identity has now grown so remarkably that we are driven to one of two alternatives – either that it is a genuine momentous revelation of survival after death, or that large numbers of otherwise sane men and women are the victims of a widespread lunacy." He added, "...it is a significant and impressive fact when such a conclusion has been reached by one who not only has a high medical degree, and is therefore acquainted with diseases of mind as well as of body, but who is eminent as a trained observer, and famous for his knowledge of all the methods of detective skill."

On one point they disagreed. "I do not think that Spiritualism is or ever can be a *religion*; in fact, it may be inimical to true religion." In his view, psychical research "may strengthen the foundations but cannot take the place of religion."

This last point would be repeatedly revisited over the years.

Doyle also drew support from the artistic world. H B Marriott-Watson was an Australian-born British novelist, journalist, playwright, short story writer and author of more than forty books including Gothic horror novels. When his wife died in 1911 he was contacted by her at a séance and converted to Spiritualism. In *Light* of November 18th, 1916, he announced:

"At last he, with his keen intellect and after his long experience has been compelled to pronounce in favour of survival and the possibility of communication from the other side of death... Sir Arthur Conan Doyle's open adherence to this belief... is a tremendous gain. I am not of any religion, and I have only founded my faith on scientific evidence." He had not made up his mind about the relationship of Spiritualism to religion, he added.

Another novelist, Mrs Philip Champion de Crespigny welcomed

Doyle into the Spiritualist fold[24]: "I am glad to be able to add my humble tribute to the admiration all interested in this most vital question must feel for Sir Arthur Conan Doyle's recent statement. He argues with the sane open-mindedness and moderation of claim that brings so much more conviction than exaggerated asseveration." She sided with Barrett on the question of Spiritualism as a religion, before going on, "...neither would I call it inimical to religion. It seems to me rather to modify and clarify the religions that be. The Bible confirms it – not to mention other sacred writings – and *it* confirms the Bible, throwing light on many passages that to the enquiring mind have proved stumbling-blocks."

Others sided with Doyle; for example, Major-General Sir Alfred E Turner, a retired British army officer mentioned in despatches in the 1884-5 Nile Expedition which attempted to relieve General Gordon of Khartoum. Turner was a member of The Ghost Club and a keen Spiritualist.

"A declaration of such a kind from a writer of his great ability, wide experience of the world, and well-known level-headedness, on the subject of scientific evidence for the continuity of life, is of infinite interest and importance, especially at this time when hundreds of thousands have lost those near and dear to them in this atrocious war," he commented. The revelation afforded by Spiritualism, "when received in a reverent attitude, cannot fail to make people better and wiser. It prepares them for death, it takes away the terrors of mortality, and convinces them that 'passing over the border' is but one step on the upward path of evolution which we must all tread, sooner or later, slowly or quickly, according to the life we have led on earth, until we come to higher planes and eventually approach the presence of that omniscient and omnipotent Deity... If this is not religion I am unable to define it."

This put Spiritualism in direct competition with Christianity. Could it really be a rival? And if so, where did it leave those who were both Spiritualists and Christians?

Christians would soon have their say.

---

24 *Light*, November 25th, 1916

# Chapter 4
## Spiritualism Versus Religion

The arrival of Spiritualism in the 19th and 20th Centuries divided Christian opinion between those Christians for whom revelations from spirits provided confirmation of the spirit hierarchy of the Bible and those who saw it as directly contradicting the Christian narrative of the soul's onward journey. This latter group were suspicious that there was no wait for resurrection, no purgatory, no heaven and no hell. Spirits appeared straight after death with news of a surprisingly mundane, "morality-lite" afterlife. For some, this smelt of diabolism.

Doyle's sister Ida and his son Kingsley, both devout Christians, disapproved of Doyle's faith. Kingsley told him so, but at the same time, knowing his father's stubbornness, conceded he "would not pretend to argue with Daddy".[25]

However, the Christian Spiritualist message had powerful appeal. Respected scientist Sir Oliver Lodge (a close friend of Doyle by 1916) had revealed his conclusions on the truth of Spiritualism in his 1909 book "Survival of Man". In 1915, his son, Raymond was killed in the The Great War and Lodge contacted him through a series of séances. In 1916, these postmortem conversations were published in *Raymond, or Life and Death,* revealing that life on the other side was more continuation than stop. Lodge's support for Spiritualism confirmed Doyle's conviction that the faith was in the early stages of becoming a recognised science.

Critics saw things differently. One detail in Lodge's book was cited as an example of the preposterousness of its claims: that on the other side, spirits enjoyed whisky and good cigars fabricated from "essences, and ethers, and gases"[26].

The discussion was slightly more subtle than this, with Raymond explaining to his father that in order to acclimatise the newly dead to the Other Side, if they asked, they were given spiritual equivalents to comforts they had enjoyed whilst alive – cigars, meat and strong drink – even "whisky sodas". But, Raymond explained, this earthly appetite soon fell from them: "when they have had one or two, they don't seem to want

25  Andrew Lycett, *Conan Doyle, The Man Who Created Sherlock Holmes*
26  Sir Oliver Lodge, *Raymond, or Life and Death,*

it so much". What such information might have meant to Conan Doyle, whose father's life was ruined by alcohol, can only be guessed.

In Lodge's book, Raymond assured his father he lived happily in a joyous Summerland, enjoying many of the comforts of home.

When *Raymond, or Life and Death* was published, it was exactly the news people needed to hear.

Since Sir Oliver was also a Christian, his message of hope carried both spiritual *and* scientific credibility. Amidst so much loss and slaughter, his book captured the zeitgeist. *Raymond* became a massive bestseller upon its 1916 release, selling not only to Spiritualists, but also to people who regarded themselves as Christians.

As is often the case with nascent religious movements, many Spiritualists hoped their new message would encourage older religions to unite to create a world no longer troubled by division and war. Yet despite such aspirations, criticism of older religions bubbled away.

Just so with the spirit messages received by Reverend W Stainton Moses (1839-1892), a divine from Oxford and a leading Spiritualist of the previous generation who had published several books on Spiritualism. Moses is sometimes described as the most influential medium in late Victorian England. He was the first president of the London Spiritualist Alliance, a founder member and Vice-President of the Society for Psychical Research, a regular contributor to and an editor of *Light*, and a member of The Ghost Club, the world's oldest psychical research organisation.

As his mediumship developed after the commencement of his psychic investigations in 1872, Moses received messages from numerous spirits, including biblical worthies, Greek philosophers, English historical characters and numerous others. His main guide, the prophet Malachi, bearing the pseudonym "Imperator" claimed that the teachings he imparted were part of a plan inspired by Jesus to further divine revelation. Moses heavily influenced later New Age thinking.

Though by 1916 Moses was long-dead, a communication given in 1873 by Moses's spirit guide, "Imperator" and printed in *Light* in 1916[27] revealed a not uncommon adversarial attitude toward conventional Christianity, which Spiritualism, he asserted, was here to supplant.

"You do not sufficiently grasp the scanty hold that religion has upon

---

27 *Light*, April 22nd, 1916

the mass of mankind, nor the adaptability of what we preach to the wants and cravings of men," Imperator informed the séance room. He warned that those with strong reasoning capabilities would realise that "the Revelation of God contains very plain marks of human origin; that it will not stand the test of sifting such as is applied to works professedly human; and that the priestly fiction that reason is no measure of revelation, and that it must be left on the threshold of inquiry, and give place to faith, is a cunningly planned means of preventing man from discovering the errors and contradictions which throng the pages of the Bible."

On the other hand, Imperator warned that those who do not use their reason, "betake themselves to the refuge of Faith, and become blind devotees, fanatical, irrational, and bigoted: conformed to a groove in which they have been educated and from which they have not broken loose simply because they have not dared to think. It would be hard for man to devise a means [more capable] of cramping the mind and dwarfing the spirit's growth than this persuading a man that he must not think about religion."

Imperator's new message was, "That which may have suited a far off ancestor may be quite unsuited to a struggling soul that lives in other times from those in which such ideas had vitality." Beliefs such as Christianity, Islam and other religions were born of geographic accident. "The days are coming when this geographical sectarianism will give place before the enlightenment caused by the spread of our revelation, for which men are far riper than you think."

The rest of the communication was filled with similar prophecy. "The time draws nigh apace when the sublime truths of Spiritualism, rational and noble as they are when viewed by man's standard, shall wipe away from the face of God's earth the sectarian jealousy and theological bitterness, the anger and ill-will, the folly and stupidity which have disgraced the name of religion and the worship of God, and man shall see in a clearer light the Supreme Creator and the spirit's eternal destiny."

In a phrase that will be familiar to any who have seen millennialists and doomsayers preaching on street corners, he said, "We tell you, friend, that the end draws nigh... the night of ignorance is passing fast; the shackles which priestcraft has strung around the struggling souls shall be knocked off, and in place of fanatical folly and ignorant speculation and superstitious belief, ye shall have a reasonable religion and a knowledge of the reality of the spirit-world and of the ministry of angels with you."

Prophetic stuff indeed, predicting the rise of Spiritualism as the one true religion. Coming from a Divine, this sort of language was bound to antagonise some sections of Christianity.

Although Conan Doyle had asserted Spiritualism as a New Revelation, it was some time before he entered the larger debate with religion.

His brand of Spiritualism reflected his bias, which was as anti-sectarian as it was when he had argued with priests in Southsea in the 1880s. Doyle promised no eternal punishment for a life ill-lived on this plane. Instead, people who had lived badly moved on to lower astral planes than they might otherwise have reached, moving up on learning their moral lesson.

Doyle may have been glad of this big-hearted rationalism, but with no punishment in the afterlife, Spiritualism was potentially dangerous in its preaching of little consequence for evil deeds.

In the article below, his measured tone attempted to show that Spiritualist science was the doorway to religion, and that the revelations from the far side must change the current conception of Christianity.

*Light, December 2, 1916*

## SPIRITUALISM AND RELIGION.
### BY SIR ARTHUR CONAN DOYLE.

I would desire to thank Mr. Marriott-Watson (whose evolution seems to have been very similar to my own) for his letter in LIGHT of November 18th last. I am also much strengthened in my position by the general agreement of Sir William Crookes, Sir Oliver Lodge, and Sir William Barrett, who have gone so much more deeply into the subject than I can pretend to have done.

I should like to restate my views upon the subject of the relation between psychical science and religion, not by way of argument, but to define more clearly my personal outlook. It is obvious that the mere fact of being a psychical student will no more make a man a good man than the study of any other form of science. Therefore to say that psychic science and religion are different things is beyond all contradiction. It is for that reason that in my former article I pleaded for a practical application of the results of psychic science. That is quite another matter, and does most directly impinge upon religious dogma, and, as it seems to me, upon formal religious practice.

If we are taking the communications from beyond seriously, and that is pre-supposed in our argument, then we are checking our religious beliefs from the standpoint of two worlds instead of one. Surely that must greatly strengthen those points which remain firm and modify those upon which a new light is cast from a fresh angle. I am not speaking of the real inner spirit of Christianity, which is the highest moral development of which we know, or of which we can conceive, making for gentleness, mercy, unselfishness, and all that is beautiful. No fresh revelation can injure this. Such new lights as come from beyond not only confirm it, but, as it seems to me, greatly strengthen it by simplifying and modifying some other beliefs which have tended to obscure it and to mix it up with doctrines which offend reason and our sense of justice.

The doctrine of nearly all Christian Churches has been that after death the soul lies dormant until the advent at some far future date of a day of doom. After this it is judged upon its deeds in this earth-life, which by that time must be, in retrospect, like to a few seconds of time blurred by the passage of count-less centuries. It is then either ruined for ever in the most terrible manner, or (with or without a term of probation) it is made happy for ever. That, I think, is a fair statement of the usual Christian dogma, but this is traversed at every point by the facts of Spiritualism. We find ourselves in apparent communication with the dead very shortly after they leave us; they seem to be exactly as they were before we parted, and they assert that judgment is a self-acting thing by which like is brought to like, and that none are so lost that they will not work their way upwards, however much sin may have retarded their journey. Every intelligent and unprejudiced man, when he has contemplated the doctrine of eternal punishment, has said to himself, "Surely God could not be so cruel. Even I, a poor mortal, would not punish so vindictively one who had wronged me." This new revelation shows that this reproach was an injustice to the Divinity, whose ways are as merciful as they are wonderful.

Even if there were nothing but this, then Spiritualism must modify not Christianity, but the wrong old-fashioned ideas of what Christianity meant. But there is much more. We cannot accept the opinions of those beyond upon some points and disregard them upon others. If they are agreed upon any proposition it must at least strongly commend itself to us. One message, which I have found to be constant, is that all religions are absolutely equal there, that formal dogma or practice counts for nothing one way or the other, and that the welfare and advancement of the spirit depend entirely upon the degree of refinement and goodness produced by the discipline of earth. This message is too broad to confine itself to Christianity, but extends itself to all creeds or no creeds, so long as an individual result is attained. Many pet texts with which men have belaboured their fellow men are thereby expunged, but surely the general conception is a higher, and, in its essence, a more Christian one than any narrow exclusive view of orthodoxy. Man has made his own difficulties, and all the religious wars, the persecutions, the feuds and the misery have had no relation whatever to true religion or to spiritual progress. The fierce and narrow sectarian who wished to drive his neighbours into what he held to be the path of virtue was in fact simply preparing his own spirit for those lower spheres out of which he will with time and suffering win his way as a kinder and broader soul.

There are many other points, but these two — the sequence of events after death, and the value of special dogma — are enough, as it seems to me, to justify the claim that although Spiritualism is in no way antagonistic to, but, on the contrary, strongly corroborative of, the central Christian idea, it does, as a matter of fact, modify Christian doctrine upon certain very important but not vital points.

*

Doyle believed compromise possible with Christianity, a view echoed by Anglican priest and Spiritualist, the Reverend G Cooper, Vicar of Lower Beeding. It was not echoed by the Bishop of Chichester, however, who criticised Spiritualism and Lodge's *Raymond* in his 1917 Easter Eve sermon, accusing it of being a modern expression of necromancy.

With typical Anglican politeness, the Reverend Cooper wrote to *Light*[28] that the Bishop's inaccurate criticisms of *Raymond* may have been misreported. Optimistically, he asserted "surely it is a gain just now that the Bishop and Lord Halifax should give their challenge and call for consideration as to where the truth lies with regard to Spiritualism."

Using scriptural quotations to prove Spiritualism was not "all necromancy" he argued, "surely the Bible shows that true Spiritualism is a very real part not only of religion but of true Christianity."

Yes, Cooper conceded, there were warnings against the Witch of Endor in the Old Testament, but the New Testament approved of the "true Spiritualism" of the seer and prophet. His conclusion? Christians should reject only "wrong Spiritualism" and "follow the right."

Another Spiritualist Anglican, the Rev. F Fielding-Ould, a regular and oft-lauded contributor to *Light,* also wished to synthesise Spiritualism with Christianity. He demanded his mother Church give Spiritualism a fair hearing.

In his article *On Uninstructed Criticism*[29], he quoted Proverbs xviii, 13 to make his point: *He that answereth a matter before he heareth it, it is folly and shame unto him.*

"Man is for the most part mentally lazy," he wrote, "and for the rest he considers himself sufficiently preoccupied." He cited the Suffragettes' success, which had required them to have "committed a crime or two that people might be compelled to give their serious attention", and considered the process analogous for Spiritualists with their publicity-seeking through the pages of *Raymond.*

Despite ignorant clergy making "pronouncements pompously dealing with the whole intricate subject", he urged: "The book insists that attention should be given to the subject...like that exasperating advertisement which points an impolite finger in your face and will not be ignored."

*Raymond* was criticised mercilessly in some quarters. Paul Carus, a German-American writer and student of comparative religion had written in *The Monist in* April 1917 that the "story of Raymond's communications rather excels all prior tales of mediumistic lore in the silliness of its revelations. But the saddest part of it consists in the fact

---

28  *Light*, May 26th, 1917
29  *Light*, July 17th, 1917

that a great scientist, no less a one than Sir Oliver Lodge, has published the book and so stands sponsor for it."

Meanwhile, many Spiritualists felt aggrieved at being persecuted for their beliefs. In *Light* on June 16th, 1917, a Mr H Boddington decried the double standards with which the British Establishment dealt with spiritual manifestations in the Witchcraft and Vagrancy Acts, while none other than the Established Church supported the reality of spirits. "...As the whole Christian world teaches that there are 'guardian angels' and 'ministering spirits' it is foolish to deny them a mode of manifestation." He castigated "the intolerant bigots and the unscrupulous Press which teaches that Spiritualism is anti-Christian and diabolical," countering: "It is not anti-Christian in the modern humanitarian sense of the word. It most certainly is anti-Christian if they mean to uphold the Christianity of the dark ages which believed that burning, maiming and torturing was acting in accordance with the will of God."

With all this talk of diabolism, like a pantomime devil right on cue, Father Bernard Vaughan sprang into the debate.

A former student at Stonyhurst College nine years before Doyle, Vaughan was an uncompromising Jesuit of unbending faith. He was just the type Doyle had railed against during his time in Southsea, when he had renounced the narrow dogma of Roman Catholicism.

Vaughan saw Satan's hand in any deviation from orthodox scriptural interpretation. A flavour of his attitude can be tasted in an address he gave at a conference of the Catholic Young Men's Society of Great Britain in 1920, in which Vaughan described Spiritualists as a "menace", going on to accuse Lodge and Conan Doyle of having "lost their mental poise". There were, he suggested, demons behind spirit manifestations[30].

To a sardonic eye it might appear that Vaughan's objection was that the séance spirit was a different flavour to the one he preferred. However, his repugnance was visceral. At the same address, Father Vaughan pronounced of Lodge and Doyle, "I would rather be in prison for the rest of my life, than carry on the work that is being done by these two gentlemen."

Father Vaughan's scorn is also revealed in his contribution to a symposium published in 1920, *Spiritualism: Its Present Day Meaning*[31].

30  *Conan Doyle, Teller of Tales,* Daniel Stashower
31  Edited by Huntly Carter

Spiritualism only too often means loss of health, loss of morals and loss of faith. Consult not Sir Oliver Lodge or Sir Arthur Conan Doyle or Mr Vale Owen, but your family medical advisers, and he will tell you to keep away from the séance-room as you would from an opium den. In fact, the drug habit is not more fatal than the practice of Spiritualism in very many cases... be satisfied that yielding to Spiritualism is qualifying for an asylum. You may not get there but you deserve to be an inmate.

In the June 1917 *Pall Mall Gazette*, Father Vaughan derided Sir Oliver Lodge as "The Seer of Birmingham" and hoped that Spiritualism would be swept out of the country. Conan Doyle did not stand idly by at the attack on his friend.

*Light, June 23, 1917*

### FATHER VAUGHAN AND SPIRITUALISM.

The "Pall Mall Gazette," of the 11th inst., contained the following reply by Sir Arthur Conan Doyle to Father Vaughan's recent attack on Spiritualism through the columns of that journal:—

To the EDITOR of the "PALL MALL GAZETTE."

SIR, — Father Vaughan should learn by the history of his own order, which has often been unjustly attacked, to be more moderate in his censures upon others.

His article in your columns upon Spiritism displays all the intolerance and the persecuting spirit of the Inquisition. "So it is that I declare we must sweep the country clear of these charlatans." In using these words he is evidently not referring to fraudulent mediums, especially as the sentence continues with a thinly veiled allusion to Sir Oliver Lodge. If Father Vaughan confined himself to fraudulent mediums he would have both the existing laws of England and all decent Spiritualists upon his side, for they have always been the curse of the movement.

The whole context shows, however, that what he desires to forcibly attack is everyone who believes what few who have really studied the evidence have failed to believe — first, that the dead survive even as we knew them; secondly, that reverent communication with them is not absolutely impossible; and, thirdly, that many people have been confirmed in or converted to the belief in a future life by such experience, and have thus attained great spiritual good from it. Indeed, it may be said that the only valid answer to materialism lies in the phenomena of Spiritualism.

I can assure Father Vaughan that the people who believe this are as good and earnest as he is himself, and very much more open-minded and charitable. When he talks of persecuting them for their beliefs and springcleaning them out of England he is using language which was sinister in the fifteenth century, but is out of place in the twentieth.

ARTHUR CONAN DOYLE.

Windlesham, Crowborough, Sussex.

*

The price of Spiritualism's increased profile, it seemed, was deeper scrutiny, even enmity.

Doyle's was one in a series of replies to Vaughan. A letter from "V.C.D.", *A Question For Father Vaughan*, published on July 7th 1917, pointed out the hypocrisy of the Catholic Church in condemning communication with spirits on the one hand, while in another instance, advocating payment at a shrine to a Saint to help recover a lost 10 shilling postal order. Was such an intercession on the part of the saint more or less illusory than Spiritualist communication? – Why should one be treated with reverence and the other ignored? Around such trifles as a misplaced postal order revolved the salvation of the human soul, at least for "V.C.D."

For writer and Spiritualist J Arthur Hill, the discussion was also about hypocrisy. In the *International Psychic Gazette*[32], he cited the Catholic story of the ailing Friar James who agreed to visit his friend Friar John after his death, on an appointed date. Arriving a day late, the spirit of Friar James was questioned by Friar John about his tardiness, to which he replied: "Because I had need of some purgation."

Hill went on: "I ask Father Vaughan whether we are to consider this (and there are innumerable similar stories in Catholic literature) as a

---

32  Reported as such in *Light*, August 25th, 1917, but cited as *The Psychic Gazette*

vision in which a Satanic spirit was... bamboozling poor Friar John? And if not, why not? There are many similar cases, not only in Catholic literature but also in the Proceedings of the Society for Psychical Research... and I should like to know, as a matter of interesting information, how Father Vaughan will separate — so to speak — the sheep from the goats."

*Light,* in the editorial *Notes by the Way,* took a more disdainful view of Father Vaughan's intervention, declaring that while some argued that religious discussion was above reason, some minds (including Vaughan's) "are below it."[33]

Despite these spats, hopes remained of building bridges between Spiritualists and priests of a more amenable mindset. Hence, Conan Doyle wrote the introduction to the Reverend Fielding-Ould's pamphlet *Is Spiritualism of the Devil?,* quoted in *Light* on August 4th 1917:

> This new message from the unseen and the eternal contains much which, without destroying our old creeds, must at least modify and clarify them, and no one can do this work better than those who search for the necessary formulae with a reverence for the old as well as with a mind that is open to the new. People, especially earnest and educated people, have long been drifting away from orthodoxy because, as presented to them, it offended their whole sense of justice and morality. It had become a perfect nightmare of unreason. But now there come these voices from the beyond explaining away some of the grosser misunderstandings, and shearing through forms and ceremonies right down to the essential spiritual roots of the matter which have been so covered over that their meaning and even their existence have been forgotten. We understand that these spirits of the beyond can no more define Deity than a man standing one rung up a ladder can explain the sun to a man who stands upon the ground. But one rung up the ladder gives a broader view, and when we have learned all that can be seen from there, it is possible that yet another rung may be attained. We have enough in the new revelation to carry us on for some centuries before we

---

33  *Light,* July 14th, 1917

exhaust it, and it will mark the strongest upward heave since the days of the greatest spirit who has ever descended upon earth...

It is this religious side which attracts me. It is human and practical, and must weave itself deeply into our daily lives. As to the evidential and phenomenal side upon which the validity of the messages rests, it has been so thoroughly proved that it seems to be a mere waste of time to continue this line of work. No amount of negative results, or of fraudulent mediums (surely the meanest and wickedest form of fraud in the world) can ever affect the positive results obtained by such a cloud of witnesses. If the definite testimony of Crookes, Wallace, Lodge, Barrett, Myers, William James, Charles Richet, Lombroso, Gurney, Hodgson, Stead and so many more will not carry conviction, what additional evidence is likely to do so? Are greater names needed, or more of them, or what? Psychical Research has, in my opinion, done its work, and the time has come to garner the harvest which for so many years it has been most patiently sowing. That harvest is essentially a religious one, reconciling reason and religion, which have been divorced so long, and yet are so essential to each other.

In his article *Heaven*, published on August 11th, 1917, Reverend Fielding-Ould discussed how ideas of heaven and hell could be squared with Raymond Lodge's afterlife - cigars, whisky and all. He argued that heaven, as well as being a state of mind and a state of closeness to God was also a spatial environment. For those disappointed by the mundanity of séance reports of the afterlife, he pointed out that "ordinary people do not at once" go to heaven. "There are many 'mansions', dwelling-places or states of being," he explained. "We shall gravitate to the one we are suited for. Death is the gate by which all leave this world, but there are many inner doors which must be passed before we enter heaven."

Carried along by the freedom Spiritualism offered him, Fielding-Ould revealed a Romantic mindset in his article of August 18th 1918, *In Here, The Voice In The Silence*. He flirted with the pagans, even advocating a pantheism *à la* Wordsworth or Walt Whitman:

God is everywhere, and man knows it. There is an instinct and subtle consciousness of the all-seeing eye against which he argues in vain. "Whither shall I go from Thy spirit, or whither shall I flee from Thy presence?" In the sunny glades of the forest depths voices whisper His name; among the solitudes of mountain gorges, on snow fields untrodden by the child of man, the inner sense discovers the footprints of the Creator.

"Earth's crammed with heaven,
And every common bush afire with God."

The ancients knew that feeling, and peopled the countryside with rich imagination. The woodcutter would hear Pan's pipes among the trees or the distant baying of Diana's hounds, and bursting through the undergrowth to drink from the running stream would look this way and that for the nymphs whom he had heard splashing in the pools. And yet how rare is the direct vision. "Verily Thou art a God that hidest Thyself." "O that I knew where I might find Him!" cries Job. ". . . Behold I go forward, but He is not there; and backward, but I cannot perceive Him." And when, man calls and there is no answering voice but the mocking echo of material things, he has in exasperation made an idol which shall represent his illusive God.

Yet God may be found in the heart all the time; it is from within that the whisperings come — "Be still and know that I am God." "The kingdom of God is within you." There is the true sanctuary, the only one in which God really dwells on earth; a Presence is there, overlaid, ignored, forgotten, outraged, provoked every day, but ever applauding the good, grieving over the evil and in faithfulness refusing to be quite expelled.

There is a legend that a soul newly passed over heard God say to him," And how did you like my beautiful world?" "Beautiful!" he replied, astonished; "was it beautiful?" Such a thing had never occurred to him. There is a good deal which never "occurs" to us because we are never "still." I have attended service in a church where the ritual was so "advanced" and everybody was so exceedingly busy getting things "correct" that worship was quite out of the question. The Quakers have possession of a great secret — the secret of silence. If we make such a noise we shall never hear the "still small voice." It is because man has been so deaf and preoccupied that God has found it necessary to shout to the world with the insistent voice of war. There are people who will chatter when someone is playing or singing, and there are many who will not attend even to the harmonies of angels.

"Pour not out words where there is a musician, and show not wisdom out of time." The saints with one voice insist on the necessity of meditation, but though many at the present day talk much to God, there are few who quietly listen to what He has to say. We need not be surprised to read that "there was silence in heaven about the space of half-an-hour."

Fielding-Ould's writing was persuasive and effective partially because it was beautiful. With its art he sought to defuse the tensions between the new religion and the old.

Doyle, meanwhile, drew together his thoughts about Spiritualism into a more complete doctrine which he delivered around the country or included in articles for mainstream magazines faithfully reported in *Light*.

His pronouncements on Christianity were starting to alarm more orthodox preachers, leading to warnings of witchcraft and necromancy, as reported in the November 1917 issue of *Light*, in which Rev. G Gilbert Muir of Eastbrook Hall denounced as unChristian a talk Doyle gave in Bradford.

"Quite naturally Mr. Muir fell back on Old Testament prohibitions, and referred also to the monk Rasputin," *Light* reported, before listing other similar Old Testament prohibitions such as the wearing of mixed materials, the eating of meat more than three days old or the reaping of field corners. "The simple truth is, of course, that a prohibition which may have been wise and right in Syria several thousand years ago is not necessarily wise and right here and now."

The matter of Spiritualism's role in the modern world reached a new pitch thanks to an address Doyle gave at Suffolk Street, London, in October 1917.

For Sir Arthur Conan Doyle, that talk would change everything.

# Chapter 5
## The New Revelation

Conan Doyle burst back on to the pages of *Light* in late 1917 with a pivotal address outlining his unshakeable rationale for spirit communion.

Delivered on October 25th at the Salon of the Royal Society of British Artists in Suffolk Street, the talk returned to the theme of revelation. This time, however, Spiritualism was not *A* New Revelation but *The* New Revelation.

Considering the speech today, it's clear Doyle's aim was to present an almost reluctant conversion to Spiritualism. It was the ineluctable conclusion of a man of science's thirty years of studies. Doyle was simply bowing to empirically-observed data. He was Spiritualism's honest broker.

He did leave out some facts. He glossed over his 1887 assertion that he was convinced of Spiritualist phenomena and that even then he described himself as "a Spiritualist". He didn't mention the vast sum he had already donated to *Light*. Perhaps he knew how the impression of early bias would appear to the public; perhaps he had forgotten some of it. After all, if anything shines through in Doyle's writing, it is his sincerity.

The full report of the address is given below, including the editorial. It would also form the main argument of his book published the following year, also entitled *The New Revelation*.

*Light, November 11, 1917*

REASON AND REVELATION.

That Sir Arthur Conan Doyle's address to the London Spiritualist Alliance was a notable event in the history of Spiritualism goes without saying. It was a fine, frank and courageous utterance, and the significance of it will not be missed, for it has already found echoes all over the globe, especially in the United States, whose journals, always alert followers and occasionally leaders of the world's thought, are givingit very full attention.

We do not propose at the moment to enter upon a consideration of any points in the address itself, but rather to deal with the general question, especially the effect of such a message upon public thought at the present time. In the first place, while it will stir up innumerable minor questions, it will serve to awaken the interest of all intelligent minds in a subject which has for a generation been clouded with elements of doubt and confusion. Many of these minds will be gifted with powers of assimilation, critical judgment and clear perception which will be infinitely valuable in placing the subject on a sane and reasonable basis as part of the orderly life and thought of the new generation. We have never disguised our conviction that in its present aspect Spiritualism is a new growth, needing time to render it shapely and symmetrical. As Oliver Wendell Holmes wrote in "Wind Clouds and Star Drifts":—

> Truth new-born
> Looks a misshapen and untimely growth,
> The terror of the household and its shame,
> A monster coiling in its nurse's lap
> That some would strangle, some would only starve;
> But still it breathes, and passed from hand to hand,
> And suckled at a hundred half-clad breasts,
> Comes slowly to its stature and its form,
> Calms the rough ridges of its dragon-scales,
> Changes to shining locks its snaky hair,
> And moves transfigured into angel guise,
> Welcomed by all that cursed its hour of birth,
> And folded in the same encircling arms
> That cast it like a serpent from their hold.

We could hardly have a finer or more concise description of the genesis of our particular truth in its modern presentation.

We have found it profitable, nay, essential, in our attitude towards the subject to concentrate as far as possible on the central and vital aspects. There are a multitude of minor propositions, some of them, to our thinking, highly unimportant and more than a little doubtful. That they should emerge and in some instances endeavour to absorb an undue amount of attention to themselves is quite natural. That those who are mainly concerned with them should resent what may appear a somewhat cavalier treatment of their pet theories is also intelligible. We are for the fundamentals. When the central part of the construction is fixed firmly into its true position the rest of the pieces will fall naturally into their places—*if they belong to it*. We must never forget that we are dealing with a world of human life which, even if transferred to another sphere of evolution, is still imperfect, still capable of error and misdirection. Moreover, we are in touch with those whose voices we hear but faintly, and the possibility of occasional mistakes is ever present. We have great need not merely to try the spirits,"but to test our instruments of communication, to be continually making adjustments that we may get what we see into proper focus. (The simile of the telescope as recently applied to mediumship is an excellent one.) Some of those who have studied the question closely, while they do not dispute the fact that there are tricky and lying communicators (animated, it may be, either by pure wantonness or by a deliberate desire to discredit the subject), are yet of opinion that not sufficient consideration has been given to the psychology of mediumship. Not once but several times in our own investigations we have been able to trace fabrications and spurious matter to the medium's own mental content. Certain automatic powers of the mind, once stirred into action will do a great deal of elaborate and often very ingenious fabrication on their own account without the necessity of postulating any conscious intelligent agency at the back of the work. The "personal equation" is a very important one. Some minds respond only to the impulse of truth and reality: others are "blown about by every wind of doctrine," and start off as readily on a false clue as a true one. Illustrations abound in the world around us. The question is not restricted to the mental phenomena of mediumship. For us the "New Revelation" is the unfolding of a vision of worlds of light, order and beauty beyond this war-racked earth, and of a new humanity with its old familiar virtues and weaknesses making it still akin to the old and very near to us by consequence. That last discovery comes as a shock (and a very healthy shock) to those who have become merged in artificialities and abstractions regarding all that relates to life after death — as though in a Universe of infinite variety this must needs be of all of one pattern.

Our glass is but dim at present. It distorts some of the images. It may be with some of us as with the lady whose experiences we gave in LIGHT some time ago. She was haunted by a weird and terrifying shape that gave her no rest. At last she went to a well-known medium and found that the fearsome apparition was no goblin, but only a loved brother, killed at the Front, anxious to reveal his identity and give her a message that brought sunshine into her life. Many of us could tell of similar experiences. There are "adversaries" in the Beyond doubtless, but here or there there are no greater enemies than Fear and Ignorance.

*

*Light, November 11, 1917*

## THE NEW REVELATION.
## ADDRESS BY SIR ARTHUR CONAN DOYLE.

Summary of an Address delivered by Sir Arthur Conan Doyle before the London Spiritualist Alliance at the Salon of The Royal Society of British Artists, Suffolk-street, Pall Mall East, S.W., on Thursday, October 25th, 1917, Sir Oliver Lodge, F.R.S., presiding.

The speaker commenced his discourse by remarking that it dealt with a subject upon which he had thought more, and been slower to form an opinion, than upon any other subject whatever.

"I can claim," he continued, "to have spent more years in the serious study of the subject than some of our antagonists have spent hours. If I narrate some of my experiences and difficulties you will not, I hope, think it egotistical upon my part, but you will realise that it is the most graphic way in which I can sketch out the points which are likely to occur to any other inquirer."

When he finished his medical education he found himself a convinced materialist. But he was never an atheist, because it seemed to him that to say the Universe was made by immutable laws only put the question one degree further back as to who made the laws. Naturally he had no belief in an anthropomorphic Deity, but believed then, as he believed now, in an *intelligent* Force behind all Nature—a Power so infinitely vast and complex that a finite brain could do no more than conceive its existence. Right and wrong were clearly great obvious facts which needed no divine revelation. But as to the survival of human life beyond death, it seemed to him that every analogy in Nature contradicted the idea. With the burning out of the candle the light came to an end. With the breaking of the electric cell the current ceased. So when the body dissolved there was an end of the individual life. The idea that any form of personal life survived death seemed to him a delusion, but although convinced that death meant extinction of life he saw no reason why that should affect our duty towards humanity during our transitory existence.

That, briefly, was his attitude of mind when psychic phenomena first came under his notice. At first he regarded the subject as merely nonsensical. He heard of fraudulent mediums and wondered how any sane man could believe in the subject. However, meeting some friends who were interested in the matter, he sat with them, out of curiosity, for table manifestations. But although they obtained some coherent messages he regarded the results with suspicion. It seemed quite impossible that the messages were the result of chance, the inference was that someone amongst the sitters manipulated the table. He was greatly perplexed over it. He could not easily imagine his friends to be cheating —and yet he could not see how the messages could come except by their agency.

About this time (1886) he came across a book called "The Reminiscences of Judge Edmonds[34]." He was a judge of the Supreme Court of New York, and a man of high character and intelligence. The book gave an account of the death of the judge's wife, and how he had been able, for many years afterwards, to communicate with her. He read the book with interest, but absolute unbelief. It seemed to him to show how an otherwise sane man might have a defect in his mind, the result of some reaction against the hard facts of daily life. Where did this spirit exist of which he talked? An injury to the brain would change the whole character of a man, and a high nature might become a low one. With alcohol or opium, or many other drugs, one could apparently quite change a man's identity. The spirit, then, seemed to be abjectly dependent upon matter. These were the arguments which he employed

---

34 No book of this title exists. Doyle may be referring to *Letters and Tracts on Spiritualism; Spiritualism, Volume I* (1853); *Spiritualism, Volume II* (1855); or *Uncertainty of Spiritual Intercourse* (1856) by Edmonds.

in those days, not realising that it was not the spirit that was changed in such cases, but the body through which the spirit worked.

Nevertheless, he remained sufficiently interested to read such books on the subject as came in his way, and was surprised to observe how many men whose names were to the fore in science thoroughly believed that Spirit was independent of Matter and could survive it. When he found that Spiritualism was endorsed by a man like Crookes, whom he knew to be the most rising British chemist; by Alfred Russel Wallace, the coadjutor of Darwin, and by Flammarion, the best known of astronomers, he felt he could not afford to dismiss it lightly. On the other hand, he had to consider the attitude of other great men, such as Darwin himself, Huxley, Tyndall and Herbert Spencer, who derided this new branch of knowledge - but when he realised that their scepticism was so profound that they would not even examine it, that Spencer had declared in so many words that he had decided against it on *a priori* grounds, while Huxley had said that it did not interest him, it seemed to him that, however great they were in science, their attitude in this respect was most unscientific and dogmatic. Clearly those who studied the phenomena and tried to discover the laws at work were following the true path which had given us all human advance and knowledge. But although weakened in this direction, his scepticism was somewhat reinforced by his own experiences as an investigator. He was working without a medium, which was like an astronomer working without a telescope. He had no psychical powers himself, and those who worked with him had little more. Among them they seemed to have just enough psychic power to get table movements, with their suspicious and often ridiculous messages. They were not always absolutely stupid. For example, on one occasion on his asking some test question, such as how many coins he had in his pocket, the table spelt out: "We are here to educate and to elevate, not to guess riddles," and then: "The religious frame of mind, not the critical, is what we wish to inculcate." No one could say that that was a puerile message. On the other hand, he was always haunted by the fear of unconscious agency on the part of the sitters. On one occasion long and detailed messages were received, purporting to come from a spirit who gave his name, stating that he was a commercial traveller who had lost his life in the burning of a theatre at Exeter. All the details were exact, and he implored the sitters to write to his family, who lived, he said, at a place called Slattenmere, in Cumberland. Sir Arthur accordingly wrote, but his letter was returned through the Dead Letter Office. He was so disgusted that his interest in the whole subject evaporated for a time.

He was residing in Southsea at this time and there met that well-known Spiritualist General Drayson, a man of very remarkable character, to whom he related his difficulties. The General made light of his criticisms of the foolish nature of many spirit messages. He said :—

> You have not got the fundamental truth into your head. The fact is that every spirit in the flesh passes over to the next world exactly as it is, with no change whatever. This world is full of fools and knaves. So is the next. You need not mix with them, any more than you do in this world. One chooses one's companions. But suppose a man in this world who had lived in his house alone and never mixed with his fellows, was at last to put his head out of the window to see what sort of place it was, what would happen? Some naughty boy would probably say something rude. Anyhow, he would see nothing of the wisdom or greatness of the world. He would draw his head in, thinking it was a very poor place. That is just what you have done. In a mixed seance, with no definite aim, you have thrust your head into the next world and you have met some naughty boys. Go forward and try to reach something better.

The explanation did not satisfy him. He remained a sceptic, although he had learned enough to know how valueless was the objection that Spiritualism was all fraud, or that a conjurer was needed to show it up. True, his own experiences had been unsatisfactory but his reading, which was continuous, showed him how deeply other men had gone into it, and that the testimony was so strong that no other religious movement in the world could put forward anything to compare with it. That did not prove it to be true, but at least it proved that it must be treated with respect and could not be brushed aside.

He still continued to hold table seances which sometimes gave no results, sometimes trivial ones, and sometimes rather surprising ones. He had the notes of these sittings, at which were received descriptions of life beyond the grave so improbable that they amused rather than edified him at the time.

To-day he found that they agreed very closely with the revelations in "Raymond" and in other later accounts, so that he now viewed them with different eyes.

Proceeding, Sir Arthur said :—

"I am aware that all these accounts of life beyond the grave differ in detail, but in fundamentals there is a very great resemblance. Two communicators sent messages, the first of whom spelt out a name, 'Dorothy Postlethwaite,' unknown to any of us. She said she died at Melbourne five years before, at the age of sixteen, that she was now happy, that she had work to do, and that she had been at the same school as one of the two ladies who made up the circle. On my asking that lady to raise her hands and give a succession of names the table tilted at the correct name of the headmistress of the school. This seemed in the nature of a test. She went on to say that the sphere she inhabited was all round the earth; that she knew about the planets; that Mars was inhabited by a race more advanced than we, and that the canals were artificial; there was no bodily pain in her sphere, but there could be mental anxiety; they were governed; they took nourishment; she had been a Catholic and was still a Catholic, but had not fared better than the Protestants; there were Buddhists and Mohammedans in her sphere, but all fared alike; she had never seen Christ and knew no more about Him than on earth, but believed in His influence; spirits prayed and they died in their new sphere before entering another; they had pleasures — music was among them. It was a place of light and of laughter. She added that they had no rich or poor.

Later there came a more vigorous influence, which dashed the table about violently. The communicator claimed to be one who might be called Dodd (that was not the real name). He was a cricketer of some note — a man whom in his life Sir Arthur had met in Cairo before he went up the Nile, where he met his death in the Dongola Expedition. "Dodd" was not known to either of the ladies present. Sir Arthur put several questions, and the answers came back with great speed and decision. The communicator said that he was happy, that he did not wish to return to earth. He had been a free-thinker, but had not actually suffered in the next life for that reason. Prayer, however, was a good thing, as keeping us in touch with the spiritual world. If he had prayed more he would have been higher in the spirit world. His death had been painless. He had work to do. He remembered their conversation in Cairo. Duration of life in the next sphere was shorter than on earth—(both spirits said that). He had not seen General Gordon nor any famous spirit. Spirits lived in families and in communities. Married people did not necessarily meet again. But those who loved each other did meet again.

This message was a very favourable specimen, both for length and for coherence. It showed that it was untrue to say, as many sceptics did, that nothing but folly came through. On the other hand, what proof was there that these statements were true? He (the speaker) could see no such proof; they simply left him bewildered. Now, with a larger experience, in which he found that the same sort of information had come to very many people independently in many countries, it was clear that the agreement of the witnesses did, as in all cases of evidence, constitute some argument for their truth.

Still, the descriptions of the next world were not convincing, and he continued to read books upon the subject. One of these was a book by Monsieur Jacolliot upon occult phenomena in India. Jacolliot was the Chief Judge of the French Colony of Chandragore, with a very judicial mind and rather biased against Spiritualism. He conducted a series of experiments with native fakirs, who gave him their confidence because he was a sympathetic man and spoke their language. M. Jacolliot found among them every phenomenon known in European mediumship, everything which Home, for example, had ever done. He got levitation of the body, the handling of fire, movement of articles at a distance, rapid growth of plants, raising of tables. The natives' explanation of these phenomena was that they were done by the Pitris or spirits of ancestors. They claimed that these powers were handed down from time immemorial and traced back to the Chaldees.

Some time before this, about 1891, Sir Arthur joined the Psychical Research Society[35] and had the advantage of reading all their reports. The world, he considered, owed a great deal to the unwearied diligence of the Society, and to its sobriety of statement, although he felt that in its desire to avoid sensationalism it discouraged the world from knowing and using the splendid work which it was doing. Its semi-scientific terminology also choked off the ordinary reader. But in spite of these little peculiarities, those who had wanted light in the darkness had

---

35 Actually, *The Society for Psychical Research*

found it by the methodical, never-tiring work of the Society. Its influence became one of the powers which helped him to shape his thoughts. There was another, however, which made a deep impression upon him, and that was Myers' wonderful book, "Human Personality," a great root book from which a whole tree of knowledge would grow. While unable to get any formula which covered all the phenomena called "spiritual," Myers so completely proved that action of mind upon mind which he himself called telepathy, that, save for those who were wilfully blind to the evidence, it took its plans henceforth as a scientific fact. This was an enormous advance. If mind could act upon mind at a distance, then there were some human powers which were quite different from matter as we had always understood it. The ground was cut from under the feet of the materialist, and Sir Arthur found that his old position had been destroyed. He had said that the flame could not exist when the candle was gone. But here was the flame a long way off the candle, acting upon its own. The analogy was clearly a false analogy. If the mind, the spirit, the intelligence of man could operate at a distance from the body, then it was a thing separate from the body. Why, then, should it not continue to exist when the body was destroyed? Not only did impressions come from a distance from those who were just dead, but the evidences showed that actual appearances of the dead person came with them, showing that the impressions were carried by something which was exactly like the body, and yet acted independently and survived the death of the body. The chain of evidence between the simplest cases of thought-reading at one end, and the actual manifestation of the spirit independently of the body at the other, was single and unbroken, each phase leading to the other, and this fact seemed to the speaker to bring the first signs of systematic science and order into what had been a mere collection of bewildering and unrelated facts.

About this time he had an interesting experience, for he was one of three delegates sent by the Psychical Research Society[36] to sit up in a haunted house in Dorsetshire. It was one of those poltergeist cases, where noises and foolish tricks had gone on for some years, very much like the classical case of John Wesley's family at Epworth in 1726, or the case of the Fox family at Hydesville, near Rochester, in 1847, which was

---

36 *The Society for Psychical Research*

the starting-point of Modern Spiritualism. Nothing sensational came of their visit, and yet it was not entirely barren. On the first night nothing occurred. On the second, there were tremendous noises, sounds like someone beating a table with a stick. They had taken every precaution, and could not explain the noises, but at the same time they could not swear that some ingenious practical joke had not been played upon them. There the matter ended for the time. Some years afterwards, however, he learned from a member of the family who occupied the house that after their visit the bones of a child, evidently long buried, had been dug up in the garden. This was certainly remarkable. Haunted houses were rare, and it was to be hoped that human remains buried in their gardens were rare also. That they should have both united in one house was surely some argument for the truth of the phenomena. It was interesting to remember that in the case of the Fox family there was also some allusion to human bones and to evidences of murder being found in the cellar. He had little doubt that if the Wesley family could have got upon speaking terms with their persecutors, they would also have come upon some motive for the persecution. It almost seemed as if a life cut suddenly and violently short had some store of unspent vitality which could still manifest itself in a strange, mischievous fashion.

*

*Light, November 17, 1917.*

THE NEW REVELATION.<br>ADDRESS BY SIR ARTHUR CON AN DOYLE.<br>*(Continued)*

From this period until the time of the war he continued to devote attention to the subject. He had experience of one series of séances with very amazing results, including several materialisations seen in dim light. As, however, the medium was detected in trickery shortly afterwards he wiped these off entirely as evidence. At the same time he thought the presumption was very clear that in the case of some mediums like Eusapia Palladino they might be guilty of trickery when their powers failed them, and yet at other times have very genuine gifts.

Mediumship in its lowest forms was a purely physical gift with no relation to morality. Eusapia was at least twice convicted of very clumsy and foolish fraud, but she several times sustained long examination under every possible condition at the hands of scientific committees which contained some of the best names of France, Italy and England.

However, he personally preferred to cut his experience with a discredited medium out of his record. It was the custom of our critics to assume that if we cut out the mediums who got into trouble we should have to cut out nearly all our evidence. But that was not the case. Up to the time of this incident he had never sat with a professional medium at all, and yet he had certainly accumulated some evidence. The greatest medium of all, Mr. D. D. Home, showed his phenomena in broad daylight, and was ready to submit to every test, and no charge of trickery was ever substantiated against him. So it was with many others. It was only fair to add that when a public medium was a fair mark for notoriety hunters, for amateur detectives and for sensational reporters, and when he was dealing with obscure elusive phenomena and had to defend himself before juries and judges who, as a rule, knew nothing about the conditions which influenced the phenomena, it would be wonderful if he could get through without an occasional scandal. At the same time, the whole system of paying by results — which was practically the present system, since if a medium got no results he would soon get no payments — was a vicious one. It was only when the professional medium could be guaranteed an annuity which would be independent of results that we could eliminate the strong temptation to substitute pretended phenomena when the real ones were wanting.

So far he had traced his process of conversion up to the time of the war. It showed, he hoped, no traces of that credulity with which their opponents charged them. But he was, he felt, culpably slow in throwing what influence he possessed into the scale of truth. But for the advent of the war he might have drifted on for his whole life as a psychical researcher, showing a sympathetic, but more or less dilettante attitude towards the whole subject, as if they were arguing about some impersonal thing such as the existence of Atlantis or the Baconian controversy[37]. The war brought earnestness into all their souls and made them look more closely at their own beliefs and reassess their values. In

----

37  The argument that Sir Francis Bacon wrote the plays of Shakespeare.

the presence of an agonised world, hearing every day of the deaths of the flower of the race in the first promise of their unfulfilled youth, seeing around him wives and mothers who had no clear conception whither their loved ones had gone, he realised that the subject with which he had so long dallied was not merely a study of a force outside the rules of science, but was really something tremendous, a breaking down of the walls between two worlds, a direct undeniable message from beyond, a call of hope and of guidance to the human race at the time of its deepest affliction. The objective side of it ceased to interest him, for having made up his mind that it was true there was an end of the matter. The religious side of it he saw to be of infinitely greater importance. The telephone bell was in itself a very childish affair, but it might be the signal for a very vital message. It seemed to him that all these phenomena, large and small, had been the telephone bells which said to the human race: "Rouse yourselves! Stand by! Be at attention! Here are signs for you. They will lead up to the message which God wishes to send."

It was the message, not the signs, which really counted. A new revelation seemed to him to be in course of delivery to the human race, though how far it was still in what he might call the John-the-Baptist stage and how far some greater fullness and clearness might be expected hereafter, was more than he or any man could say. The real value of the physical phenomena lay in the fact that they supported and gave objective reality to an immense body of knowledge which must deeply modify their previous religious views, and must, when properly understood and digested, make religion a very real thing, a matter no longer of faith, but of actual experience and fact. It was to this side of the question he would now turn, merely adding to his previous remarks about personal experiences that since the war he had had some very exceptional opportunities of confirming all the views which he had already formed as to the truth of the general facts upon which Spiritualism was founded. The movement must also gain great additional solidity from the wonderful literature which had sprung up around it during the last few years. If no other spiritual books were in existence than five which had appeared in the last year — Sir Oliver Lodge's "Raymond," Mr. Arthur Hill's "Psychical Investigations," Professor

Crawford's[38] "Reality of Psychical Phenomena[39]," Sir William Barrett's "Threshold of the Unseen[40]," and Mr. Gerald Balfour's "Ear of Dionysius[41]" — those five alone would, in his opinion, be sufficient to establish the facts for any reasonable inquirer.

Before going into this question of a new religious revelation, how it was reached, and of what it consisted he would say a word upon one other subject. There had always been two lines of attack by their opponents. The one was that their facts were not true. This he had dealt with. The other was that they were upon forbidden ground. As he had started from a position of Materialism, this objection had never had any meaning for him, but to those who were troubled by it he would submit one or two considerations. The chief was that God had given them no power which was under no circumstances to be used. The fact that they possessed it was in itself proof that it was their bounden duty to study and develop it. It was also to be remembered that this cry of illicit knowledge had — backed by more or less appropriate texts — been used against every advance of human knowledge. It was used against the new astronomy, and Galileo had actually to recant. It was used against Galvani and electricity. It was used against Darwin, who would certainly have been burned had he lived a few centuries before. It was even used against Simpson's use of chloroform in childbirth on the ground that the Bible declared "In pain shall ye bring them forth." Surely a plea which had been made so often, and so often abandoned, could not be regarded very seriously.

To those, however, to whom the theological aspect was still a stumbling block, he would recommend the reading of two short books, each of them by clergymen. The one was the Rev. Fielding Ould's "Is Spiritualism of the Devil?" the other the Rev. Arthur Chambers' "Our Self After Death." He might add that when he first began to make public his own views, one of the first letters of sympathy which he received was from the late Archdeacon Wilberforce.

He had spoken of a body of fresh doctrine. Whence did it come? It came in the main through automatic writing where the hand of the

---

38  Crawford was actually a Doctor, not a Professor.
39  Correctly titled *The Reality of Psychic Phenomena*
40  Correctly titled *On The Threshold of the Unseen*
41  Fully, *The Ear of Dionysius*

human medium was controlled, either by an alleged dead human being, as in the case of Miss Julia Ames, or by an alleged angel, as in that of Mr. Stainton Moses. These written communications were supplemented by a vast number of trance utterances, and by the verbal messages of spirits, given through the lips of mediums. Sometimes it had even come by direct voices, as in the numerous cases detailed by Admiral Usborne Moore in his book, "The Voices." Occasionally, it had come through the family circle and table-tilting, as, for example, in the two cases he had previously detailed within his own experience. Sometimes, as in a case recorded by Mrs. de Morgan, it had come through the hand of a child.

Now, of course, they were at once confronted with the obvious objection — how did they know that these messages were really from beyond? How did they know that the medium was not consciously writing, or, if that was improbable, that he or she was unconsciously writing them by his or her own higher self? This was a perfectly just criticism. They must have signs which they could test before they accepted assertions which they could not test. But if, as in the case of Stainton Moses, with his "Spirit Teachings," the doctrines which were said to come from beyond were accompanied with a great number of abnormal gifts — and Stainton Moses was one of the greatest mediums in all ways that England had ever produced — then the matter deserved to be regarded in a serious light. Again, if Miss Julia Ames could tell Mr. Stead things in her own earth life of which he could not have cognisance, and if those things were shown, when tested, to be true, then one was more inclined to think that those things which could not be tested were true also. Or, once again, if Raymond could tell them of a photograph, no copy of which had reached England, and which proved to be exactly as he described it, and if he could give them, through the lips of strangers, all sorts of details of his home life, which his own relatives had to verify before they found them to be true, was it unreasonable to suppose that he was fairly accurate in his description of his own experiences and state of life at the very moment at which he was communicating? Or when Mr. Arthur Hill received messages from folks of whom he had never heard, and afterwards verified their truth in every detail, was it not a fair inference that the same people were speaking the truth when they described their present condition? The cases were manifold, and his point was that the whole of the system, from the lowest physical phenomenon of a table-rap up to the most inspired utterance of a prophet, was one complete whole, each link attached to the next one, and that when the humbler end of that chain was placed in the hand of humanity, it was in order that they might, by diligence and reason, feel their way up it until they reached the revelation which waited in the end.

It had been asserted by men for whose opinion he had a deep regard — notably by Sir William Barrett — that Psychical Research was quite distinct from religion. Certainly it was so, in the sense that a man might be a very good psychical researcher, but a very bad man. But the results of psychical research, the deductions which we might draw and the lessons we might learn, taught us of the continued life of the soul, of the nature of that life, and of how it was influenced by our conduct here. If this was distinct from religion, he confessed that he did not understand the distinction. To him it was religion — the very essence of it. The question which faced them was, *How did this religion bear upon the older organised religions and philosophies?*

The answer was, that to only one of those religions or philosophies was this new revelation absolutely fatal. That was to his own old creed of Materialism. He did not say this in any spirit of hostility to Materialists, who, so far as they were an organised body, were, he thought, as earnest and moral as any other class.

But the fact remained that if the human consciousness could survive the destruction of the material organism, then the whole foundation of Materialism went, and the philosophy erected upon it fell to the ground. It was equally clear that acceptance of the teachings which came from beyond the grave would tremendously modify the modern statement of Christianity. It would correct many ideas which offended the reason of thoughtful observers, but it would confirm the truth of some vital dogmas, especially that of life after death. It would prove the disastrous results of evil doing, but would also show that those results were never irremediable. It would confirm the idea of higher beings, those whom we call angels, and of an ever-ascending hierarchy, in which the Christ spirit finds its place. The New Revelation, then, while destructive of the errors in old beliefs, could be welcomed by the earnest souls of all creeds as a Heaven-sent ally rather than a diabolical enemy.

As to the direct effect of the New Revelation on Christianity, although he shrank from hurting the religious susceptibilities of anyone present, it was necessary to be frank. It seemed to him that Christianity, as presented to-day, must change or perish. The falling away of worshippers from the churches meant that people were alienated because they did not believe in the truth of the statements presented to them. So long as there was any "fall of man" in the sense usually assigned to the phrase, there was at least some sort of coherent scheme; but when it became certain that man had never really fallen, since we could trace an upward course from the cave-man and the drift-man, a large part of the Christian system of salvation disappeared.

Dealing with the communications from the next state on this subject of Christianity, the lecturer pointed out that opinion was not uniform there any more than here, but the messages they received amounted in sum to this. There were many high spirits in the next world. High above all the greatest of the spirits of whom they had cognisance was the Christ. His especial care was the earth. He came down upon it at a time of great depravity, in order to give the people the example and teaching of a perfect life. Then He returned to His own high station, having left an example which was still occasionally followed. That was the story of Christ as spirits had described it. If a great Spirit came once, might he not come again? We could do with such a Spirit in London now. But would his fate be very different to-day? There would be no crucifixion since we lived in a milder age. But could we be certain that some Pontius Pilate in a police-court would not be sorely puzzled as to whether he should not be indicted under the Blasphemy Act as unsettling the old religion or under the Vagrancy Act as a prophet and a medium?

*

*Light, November 24, 1917*

## THE NEW REVELATION.
### ADDRESS BY SIR ARTHUR CONAN DOYLE.
*(Continued)*

If this new view of Christianity were generally accepted, reinforced as it would be by assurance and demonstration from the New Revelation, then we should have a creed which might unite the Churches, which might be reconciled with Science, which might defy all attacks, and carry on the Christian faith for an indefinite time. No sudden or violent revolution would bring about such a change. It would come gradually, just as in our own lifetimes such crude dogmas as an eternal hell of material fire and brimstone had gently faded away.

As to man's experiences after death, the evidence on the point was fairly full and consistent. There was a great uniformity in the messages and a consistency of details not at all in accord with any pre-existing scheme of thought. The departed all agreed that death was usually easy and painless, and followed by a great reaction of peace and happiness. The individual found himself in a spirit body which was the exact counterpart of the old one, except that all disease, weakness, or deformity had passed from it. At the moment of passing, the dead man was nearer to matter than he would ever be again, and hence it was at that moment the greater part of those cases occurred where, the man's thoughts turning to some distant friend, the spirit body went with the thoughts and became momentarily visible to the friend. Out of some two hundred and fifty cases of apparitions carefully examined by Mr. Edmund Gurney, it was found that more than half of the number occurred at or about the moment of death. Those cases, however, were but a small proportion of the total number of deaths, partly, perhaps, because the dead man was too much preoccupied with his own astonishing experiences to have much thought for others. The departed spirit soon found that he was mysteriously out of touch with his old environment. He could no longer communicate with his friends on earth, his ethereal voice and ethereal touch being powerless to affect those organs which would only respond to grosser stimuli. Presently, however, he became aware of those on his own side of life — the presence of some he had loved and lost, who greeted him as one newly arrived amongst them. Then in their company, and possibly under the help and guidance of some radiant being who had waited for the event, he rose from the earth conditions to enter on a new life in a realm for which his previous life and character fitted him.

Usually there was a period of sleep before the arisen spirit entered on the active life of his new career. It varied in length, sometimes being of the utmost brevity, at others extending for weeks or months. Doubtless the length of the sleep was dependent on the amount of trouble or the degree of mental pre-occupation which existed in earth life; to some extent also it was determined by the character and strength of the individual spirit concerned.

Then there was the question of probation or punishment. It did not consist of gross bodily pain—hell as a place of torment did not exist. It was simply a question of dwelling in lower spheres, dark and unsatisfying when the spirit became conscious of its situation and found that its own deeds had placed it there.

These probationary spheres were rather sanatoria for weak and undeveloped souls than penal communities. The spirit communicators were all in agreement as to the fact of sunnier and more harmonious conditions of life for the average men and women of earth. That life was full of interest and occupation and there were none who would desire to return. Here, then, was a message of glad tidings — not a vague faith or hope but an account supported by all the laws of evidence which held that where many independent witnesses told the same story their account had a claim to be considered a true one.

It was probable that all those messengers who came back to us were, broadly speaking, in about the same stage of development. Communications usually came from those who had not long passed over, and tended to grow fainter as time went on, which is what might be expected where the line of evolution was away from the earth.

The next life seemed to be primarily a mental life, just as this life was mainly a bodily one. Preoccupations of food, money, pain, and other evils of the body passed away, although they might remain for a time as temporary reactions on the mind from the physical life. Music, the arts, intellectual and spiritual knowledge remained, and progress was made along these lines.

Sir Arthur at this stage dealt with various phases of the after-life, most of which, as being more or less familiar to readers of LIGHT, may be omitted. Touching on the probable ability of experienced spirits conversant with synthetic chemistry to produce simulacra of things which exist upon the earth, Sir Arthur said that the *modus operandi* might well be a matter of speculation to less experienced spirits, just as some of the wonders of modern science are to non-scientific persons amongst ourselves. Raymond, for instance, had spoken of spirit chemists who could produce even such unspiritual forms of substance as alcohol and tobacco — or at least something analogous thereto — to meet some temporary emergency. That had tickled the critics, who talked and wrote (for their own purposes) as though that were the only statement in a book of 400 closely printed pages. Raymond might be right or wrong in what he told his father, but the incident only proved the unflinching courage and honesty of the man who recorded it. (Applause.)

Dealing with the objection to the materiality of the next life as described by spirits, Sir Arthur asked if it was demanded that life after death was to be merely a matter of wisps of gaseous happiness entirely without self-knowledge and individual expression. That seemed to be the idea — an impossible one if there was to be any perpetuation of personality or continuity of consciousness. There could be no glad reunions of those who had lived and loved on earth if they were taken away from all individuality to a vague region of floating emotions.

Sir Arthur next passed to the question of lying communications. Many persons who had investigated had experience of what seemed very like wilful deception, mixed up with good and true communications. It was doubtless of such messages that St. John wrote when he said, "Beloved, believe not every spirit, but try the spirits whether they are of God." There was nothing more puzzling than the fact that one might get long, coherent descriptions, every detail of which afterwards turned out to be a concoction. Akin to these false influences were the "Miltons" who could not scan, the Shelleys who could not rhyme, the Shakespeares who could not think, and all the other absurd impersonations which made our cause ridiculous. These were, he thought, deliberate frauds, either from this side or the other, although something might be set down to the subconscious activities of the medium's mind.

As to the alleged dangers of Spiritualism, so far as accusations concerning insanity, obsession, &c., went, they were almost entirely imaginary, asylum statistics did not bear out such assertions. Still, the cult of the séance might be overdone. When an inquirer had convinced himself of the truth of the phenomena, there was no real need to pursue the matter. To go from séance to séance was to run the risk of becoming a mere sensation hunter. The real object of the investigation was to give us assurance in the future and spiritual strength in the present, to give us a clear perception of the fleeting nature of matter and reveal the eternal values beyond all the shows of time and sense—the things which were indeed lasting, going on and ever on through the ages in a glorious and majestic progression. (Great applause.)

SIR OLIVER LODGE said: Meeting as we do under these circumstances in a dim light, and being informed that the police would be pleased when the meeting terminates, I think we will not have any discussion, and I will close the meeting with a few remarks of my own. Should any contretemps happen, I hope we shall show ourselves worthy of our faith. Sir Arthur has given us an autobiographical sketch of extraordinary comprehensiveness, covering the ground from one end to the other. I shall not attempt to follow him. I will merely say that revelation means that which we do not get directly through the medium of the senses. Our senses give us certain aspects. Though they do not deceive, they limit us to a very great extent. And no wonder! They are the product of evolution, to enable us to catch our food and to do the same sort of things that the animals do. Now we are using them for exploring the mental and spiritual universe. No wonder, therefore, we make mistakes. No wonder some of us think the material aspect is the only aspect, the only thing that is real and satisfactory. The material universe is so beautiful, so complex, so law-abiding, that I am not surprised at anyone worshipping matter and being a materialist. Although restricted in their view, the materialists are to be listened to. Only when they take the negative side and begin denying everything except that which they happen to know, they are not worth listening to, because they are speaking of that which they do not know. Listen to positive statements, but the "spirit which denies" — do not listen to that! That is Mephistophelian. The revelation of astronomy, the revelation of other worlds, the marvellous revelation of the midnight sky — these happen to come within our senses. I want you to notice that they might not have done so. Were the sky permanently opaque, as it too often is over some British towns, we should not see the stars. The atmosphere of Venus is so continually clouded that its inhabitants, if there are any, can know nothing of any other world. Had that been the case with us, how extraordinarily small and insignificant would have been our conception of the universe. I take that as a parable. We do happen to know about the stars, but do we imagine that we know about everything? We have that revelation, but we must not be blind to the immense amount of reality not the less real because we do not happen to get direct impressions of it.

Then there is the revelation of physics, whereby we learn that the fundamental entity is the ether of space, which does not appeal to our senses in the least, but which is more substantial than matter. The omnipresence of the unseen is what we learn by this study. Then we come to the revelation of psychic study, whereby we learn of the existence of discarnate intelligences — discarnate but not disembodied. The union of soul and body is evidently continued. The life beyond is not a shadowy, vague life, but a full-bodied, substantial thing. Then we have the revelation of religion, the value of sacrifice, of redemption, showing us the meaning of existence in the largest sense.

With regard to what the lecturer said about Christianity, when he publishes his address I would suggest that he make a little alteration. When he spoke of Christianity I think he meant Churchianity — the doctrines men have invented and foisted on the pure Gospel of Christ. It is not Christianity which is to change: it is our doctrines, the statements made about Christianity. Partly right and partly wrong, they can be improved. The death of Christ was the climax of His life. There must have been such a death to round off and complete the most beautiful and majestic life which has been lived amongst the sons of men.

I think we shall not separate without feeling strongly that our doctrines, although they may lead away from many of the Churches, will but lead us back to Christ in a real sense; for surely the ambition, the hope, the longing of humanity is that His Kingdom shall come and His will be done on earth as it is in heaven.

*

Doyle's address was a radical and powerful statement of faith bound to rouse a response.

In *Light* in December 1917, Freemasonry and Middle East specialist Bernard H Springett asked *Is A New Religion Needed?* He pronounced an indignant "No", arguing like Lodge that "Churchianity" not Christianity was the problem. In a long, pious letter he described Christianity as "a perfect realisation of union with God through Christ, to all faithful and true hearts, content to accept its original simple, teachings of love, reverence and belief, unsullied by any of the ancient or modern additions and attempted introductions of matters of ritual, matters of individual

construing of forms of doctrinal belief, which must be as displeasing to
the Almighty Father of all as they have been, in all ages, distressing to the
faithful and humbler followers of inspired teachers who have placed
adoration and worship before ritual and doctrinal disquisitions."

No religion had it all correct, he added, declaring "all other questions,
beyond the existence of a supreme Deity and the immortality of the soul,
as matters of opinion, helpful to salvation, but not absolutely and
dogmatically essential."

This type of loosely-formulated faith would never be enough for those
of Doyle's scientific persuasion – but its purpose was noble. Springett
was concerned that yet another doctrine-driven faith was about to rear
up to the exclusion of all others. There was an element of truth in all
religions, he argued, from the Aztecs, the Ancient Egyptians through
Buddhists and Moslems to Zoroastrians, which drew people closer to
God.

"Spiritualism, if used aright, is not a new religion. No new religion
can be wanted, since Christ came and showed us the way to Eternal Life.
Spiritualist teaching... is the keen handmaid of Christianity, not its
opponent or attempted replacer." He went on: "But Spiritualism, like all
other forms of religion, is closely beset by its false teachers, with their
unnecessary and objectionable ritual, satisfying only the cravings of
ignorant, uninspired, and wrongly-ordained followers." After which he
went on to lay out the path to true knowledge.

This rambling letter displayed the problem with the more liberal end
of religious doctrine – whilst appearing to accept all, in the end it laid
out an exclusive path. Trying to make an all-inclusive doctrine that still
points to a particular spiritual programme is like trying to squeeze water
between one's fingers, or nail a cinema projection to the wall.

Overall, Doyle's confession of faith was received with approval,
though one quibbler wrote into *Light* disagreeing with descriptions of
the various spirits Stainton Moses communicated with as "angels". The
same writer signed off positively "I welcome most heartily Sir Arthur
Conan Doyle's admirable address, and I venture to offer him my
congratulations on his escape from the trammels of Materialism, and on
his acceptance of a body of doctrine which is, I believe, destined to
revolutionise the religious thought of the age."

Thus, Conan Doyle was welcomed into the heart of the belief.

Meanwhile, he continued to give talks around the country, varying the emphases to highlight different aspects of the revelation – such as the importance of physical phenomena, or the duty of the Spiritualist to set out the new message to the recently bereaved – an approach which could easily be interpreted by the Church as *poaching*.

Some attempted to downplay the religious implications of Doyle's message. Sir William Barrett closed another Doyle talk by describing Spiritualism as a "preamble" to religion, stressing it was not one in itself.

On November 3rd 1917, *Light* quoted Doyle in *The Sunday Times* talking about communications from beyond the grave:

> They all present a point of view which is not antagonistic to any existing scheme of religion or philosophy, save only materialism, but which greatly supplements any revelation which yet has been conveyed to the human race.

Later, the same column quoted *Sunday Times* journalist Max Pemberton:

> Let us hear the churches upon a gospel so tremendous. Sir Arthur has no rope about his waist – but his voice cries in the wilderness of war and there are thousands waiting upon such words as he has learned to speak.

Doyle's tidings of a pleasant afterlife resonated through the grief of War. That the message came from a trusted messenger, a medical doctor backlit by the scientific glamour of his ultra-rational creation Sherlock Holmes only gave it greater credence.

In December, *Light* published a small piece associating his great fictional creation Sherlock Holmes with psychic goings-on. It shows how Doyle's fame and his Spiritualist message were intertwined in the public psyche:

*Light, December 17, 1917*

In the Christmas Double Number of the "Strand Magazine" Sir A. Conan Doyle gives some interesting "personalia" about Mr. Sherlock

Holmes, from which we gather that many people have the impression that Sherlock Holmes is an actual person – a conclusion distinctly complimentary to the creator of that character. Accordingly problems have been submitted to him from the real world. One of these was "rather upon the psychic plane." It came from a lady who had been given a curious old ring, snake-shaped and of dull gold. This she took from her finger at night. One night she omitted to do this and "had a fearsome dream in which she seemed to be pushing off some furious creature which fastened its teeth into her arm." She awoke with a pain in the arm, upon which appeared the imprint of a double set of teeth. After that she discarded the ring for some time. When she put it on again the strange nocturnal experience was repeated , and the ring was destroyed by being dropped into the hottest corner of the kitchen range. It is, as Sir Arthur remarks, an interesting little problem. We know the phenomena well enough under the name of pyschometry and the stigmata; but who can explain them? In the same issue of the "Strand" Sir Oliver Lodge is the author of the first of a series of papers by the most eminent scientific men of the day dealing with the question, "What is likely to be the next great discovery or invention?" Sir Oliver suggests a reply by discoursing of the utilisation of Nature's more secret stores of energy – intra-atomic and etherial.

*

So far the wider world had only received a foretaste of Doyle's dedication to Spiritualism. The energy he channelled into it would one day eclipse that put into his fictional creations. Another flash of it came soon after, when he wrote a letter entitled

*Light, January 26, 1918*

### THE MAINTENANCE OF "LIGHT."

SIR, — I beg to subscribe my annual donation of £10 to LIGHT. Should there be a deficit I should always be ready to join with others in defraying it. Riches are no doubt enervating either for an individual or for a cause, but you are in a position, I consider, not to beg for but to demand a sufficiency, in the spirit in which St. Paul demanded the needful money for himself and his propaganda from the early Churches. You represent the most living religious cause now existing upon earth, the only conclusive answer against materialism, and to let your work languish for want of funds is unthinkable.

Yours faithfully,

Arthur Conan Doyle.

*

Soon after, in March 1918, his book *The New Revelation* was published, laying out the development of his beliefs, his current attitudes and what he hoped the new faith would deliver. The book followed the programme laid out in his Suffolk Street talk, though it did more fully acknowledge his early interest in psychic phenomena.

The line he trod regarding religion was a fine one:

> It has been asserted by men for whose opinion I have a deep regard – notably by Sir William Barrett – that psychical research is quite distinct from religion. Certainly it is so, in the sense that a man might be a very good psychical researcher but a very bad man. But the results of psychical research, the deductions which we may draw, and the lessons we may learn, teach us of the continued life of the soul, of the nature of that life, and of how it is influenced by our conduct here. If this is distinct from religion, I must confess that I do not understand the distinction. To me it IS religion – the very essence of it. But that does not mean that it will necessarily crystallise into a new religion. Personally I trust that it will not do so. Surely we are disunited enough already. Rather would I see it the great unifying force, the one provable thing connected with every religion, Christian or non-Christian, forming the common solid basis upon which each raises, if must needs raise, that separate system which appeals to the varied types of mind.
>
> *The New Revelation, page 66-67*

Doyle had devised to his own satisfaction a hybrid religio-science which suited his emotional needs. Through Spiritualism all religions and scientific structures would be unified into one continuity, something no other system could achieve. The scale of his message was massive. It required a new physics and biology, inseparable from a new theology.

Despite his assertions to the contrary, one cannot help but ask, if Spiritualism were to become the basis of all faith, what role was left for other religions merely *based* on it?

Also in *The New Revelation,* some of Doyle's generosity of spirit came through in his insistence on the unfairness of a Christian theology that damned to eternal hellfire those who had not even heard of Christ. There were also assurances that death was not painful. This must have been as much of a relief to Doyle, who had lost so many in the war, as to those to whom he preached. Spiritualism assuaged the concern felt by those left behind for their lost ones. There was no hell. Europe had seen enough of hell on earth for a lifetime.

*The Times*, among others, accused Doyle of naiveté for the views expressed in *The New Revelation*, but Doyle continued to convert where he could, including in the military. One young officer from the 1st Norfolks whom he influenced, converted three of his room-mates to the faith. Doyle said confidently, later, "I would go down and take them by their hundreds, but the padres might object."

There is something disturbing in the next article written to *Light* by Doyle.

*Light, May 11, 1918*

## THE MILITARY VALUE OF SPIRITUALISM.
## BY SIR ARTHUR CONAN DOYLE.

This question of military value is one which has not been sufficiently dwelt upon. When a man is convinced, not as a matter of faith but as a matter of personal knowledge, that death is the door which leads to a very homely and happy life with the same individuality, the same body, save for some improvement, similar surroundings and similar pleasures, save that they are more intense and more refined, it is obvious that his fear of death is lessened and his military value as well as his personal peace of mind increased.

As an illustration, I quote an extract from the letter of a fine young soldier whom I had the opportunity of influencing. He says: "Those few short hours of conversation with you have altogether altered my feelings with regard to death. The description of life over there impressed me and pleased me immensely. It takes all the horror away from being killed, and almost makes one wonder whether it is worth worrying about anything so long as one does one's job to the best of one's ability. I feel now that I can go into the line and stick it ever so much better than I could before. It seems so tangible — so natural."

This letter only came two days ago, and the writer is already in the line, testing the results of his knowledge.

In that interesting and valuable book, "Do Thoughts Perish?" (a book which must have been in the press at the same instant as "Raymond," and which confirms Sir Oliver upon many points) the deceased subaltern writes: "If the chaps on the front could realise — which they can't, I know — but if they *could* see the wonderful and miraculous change which comes in a moment to them, there would be no apprehension of death, but they would leap into this life, possibly before their task was over. That is what makes me hesitate to say more. For to me it seems that if they could see through the dividing line, they wouldn't waver, but would jump for it, which would be wrong; for they have got to do their job first, and do it well all the time, if they want to find themselves in the right place over here."

It seems to me that if some attempt were made to place the results of modern psychical research before our fighting men — handling the various sectarian views which they may hold as tenderly as is consistent with truth — great good might come of it.

*

Unlike the letter above, which in its extreme interpretation could be seen as encouraging young soldiers to actively embrace death, the sentiments expressed in *The New Revelation* more closely reflected public sentiment

*The New Revelation* was reviewed in the June 22nd 1918 issue of *Light*.

After picking up on a few areas where the reviewer demurred from the author, the review described it as "an interesting, thoughtful, and instructive work... a valuable contribution to the literature upon this all-important subject."

Throughout 1918, Doyle continued to travel from meeting hall to meeting hall across the country – driven by a moral conviction that his message would bring solace wherever spoken.

This proved true for none other than Doyle himself. Sir Arthur's son, Arthur Alleyne Kingsley Conan Doyle, still weak from injuries sustained in the Somme in 1916 succumbed to the pan-European influenza epidemic and died of pneumonia on 28th October 1918. His father read the devastating news in a telegram two days before he was due to deliver another talk in Nottingham.

Rocked by what he'd read, Doyle quickly stiffened his resolve. Declaring his duty to his fellow mourners, he gave the lecture.

He later told a friend:

"Had I not been a Spiritualist, I could not have spoken that night. As it was, I was able to go straight on the platform and tell the meeting that I knew my son had survived the grave, and there was no need to worry."[42]

---

42  Daniel Stashower, *Conan Doyle, Teller of Tales*

# Chapter 6
## In Memoriam

The Great War came to an end on the 11th of November, 1918, leaving Europe to count the dead and make sense of its loss in the way humans had done for millennia: through rituals and commemorations which acknowledged and then transfigured grief.

Spiritualism, too, enacted its rituals. Early in 1919, the Spiritualists National Union held a National Memorial Service for the fallen, and Doyle was invited as the most prominent speaker to address the congregation.

There was deep optimism among Spiritualists in those heady days for the future of the faith, and satisfaction at the numbers attending - an estimated 7,000 on an icy spring night, filling the Royal Albert Hall to capacity. The report on the *National Memorial Service For the Fallen in the War* appeared in the *Special Supplement of Light* on May 3rd 1919.

It began with a quote from Doyle:

"It is not a Memorial Service, though we call it so. It is rather a joyous reunion." The service was, he said, "an event unique in the history of the world."

In *The White Insignia,* the *Supplement's* opening article, weather omens were observed. "A blinding snowstorm clothed all London in a mantle of white... Really, our organisers will have to be more careful in future; they made it known far and wide that white was to be the colour for the day. Nature rather overdid it in this respect. Not a man or woman who ventured out of doors could escape wearing our insignia."

Among the throng, *Light* listed the prime movers of the Spiritualist world, including editors of magazines, representatives of local Spiritualist associations, councillors, a viscount and viscountess and many others.

The service took a form similar to a church service. After the singing of a hymn came an invocation rich in religious language, which began, "We would address Thee with heart and voice and song for the glorious revelation that has come to us that they whom we once thought of as dead are not dead, but live in very truth, and rejoice with us in Thy love... we thank Thee and the arisen hosts of our fellow men that the time is rapidly coming to hand when the veil shall be clearer and purer, and that as a consequence the knowledge, instruction, inspiration, and love that shall flow to us from higher realms will be dearer and sweeter and have a more holy and mellow influence on the earth life."

The invocation thanked those who had given their lives in the War, and God for the sympathy and kindness the tragedy had drawn one from another, as well as the certain knowledge that mankind had triumphed over death. It spoke of the solace provided by "this truth that there is no death in God's wide world, that the human spirit continues through the Valley of Death, and can come back and relate experiences of the after life, and bring joy where once there was sadness, bring triumph where once there was grief, and sweetness even to the old enemy, Death."

It continued:

> That angel reaper who plucks from our midst those that are near and dear to us, let us, too, praise thee, O Death, that thou dost remove in God's good time those who shall indeed come back to us, and whom we may and need only miss in their physical form. We praise and thank thee that thou dost release the suffering ones and remove them to happier states and conditions. With those who have gone on let us join as in one voice, turning our eyes upwards, outwards, to the illimitable universe, and praise and thank Him who assists us all, through all, in all.

After this, Ernest Oaten, President of the Spiritualists' National Union spoke of the sacrifice of the dead, and noted that many Spiritualists had fought in the war, "From the Spiritualist Sunday Schools of this country alone many thousands have gone into khaki, and some hundreds at least have gone under." He then asserted: "But I am pleased to say that a larger proportion of them than is usual have come back unscathed."

One of the purposes of the service, he said, was "to direct the attention not only of you, but of the whole world, to the fact that life is a continuous thing, and that its continuity is a provable thing." He defended against critics who described spirit communications as trivial, noting that the messages from the Other Side were messages of love. He asked:

> What is life without the sweets of human companionship, without the joys of affection, without the love of those who are dear to us? These men who went abroad to make a sacrifice — what carried them? Not their Army pay, but love of great ideals — love, maybe, of a flag, maybe of a country, but, to sum it all up, human love of ideals.

Love itself, then, prompted the spirit messages that critics complained were trivial.

He finished his address with the rallying cry: "ours is essentially the note of victory." He then asked the audience "for one minute to remain in silence to concentrate its thoughts upon the dear ones who have crossed over, and by thought and desire to bridge that gulf. I believe it will help those who have gone, and I am sure it will strengthen those who remain."

The audience remained in silent meditation for the space of a minute, pre-empting the first Armistice Day Two Minutes Silence by 6 months.

This speech was followed by Chopin's *Funeral March* performed on the grand organ, then the *Hallelujah Chorus*, during which the congregation remained standing. Next followed a sung solo, *O, Rest in the Lord*.

Dr. Ellis T. Powell reinforced the Spiritualist central message of life after death, then predicted that Spiritualism "is going to be the leading power in the social and political reconstruction of the world." Not only were Spiritualists communicating with the deceased, but those who had passed over would be "co-workers with us in the great task that lies immediately before us" - that of saving the fabric of civilisation and handing it on to future generations.

Next, the congregation sang a hymn, *There is no death - tell out the mighty message*.

Now it was Doyle's turn. He addressed the audience with a rousing speech that struck an oddly bellicose tone with its numerous war metaphors.

*Special Supplement for Light, May 3, 1919.*

Our movement, the greatest movement which has been seen in this world for the last two thousand years, has recently been passing through a crisis of contention and of argument. There are many of the more sensitive souls among us who feel very much that a matter which is so delicate, which concerns those whom we have lost, should be exposed to that unseemly levity which is so often the only weapon with which our opponents can attack us. But none the less we are out to fight. We can only fight, and we can only win by fighting. If you have got a thing which is not true, if you are trying to bolster up a thing you are not certain of, then keep it in the dark, and tell people to keep their hands off. But when you know that a thing is true, and when you know that the whole human race is just yearning for that thing, then I say at all costs to your own feelings you must bring it down into the market-place, you must let people see the length and breadth of it for themselves, and, though they may mock and look at it with ignorance, depend upon it the human race is not really foolish, the human race sooner or later, if you put truth before it, will understand that it is true and will follow it. Therefore, I say, although we have got in front of us now a whole Hindenburg Line of ignorance and prejudice, and plenty of theological barbed wire in front of that, we are going to smash through it, because we have got a cause that cannot be beaten.

Fortunately we are not here today to argue or dispute. I get enough of that elsewhere. We are here to greet our dead heroes, those men who cut short their earthly life in order that our earthly life might be tolerable. Only two days ago 5,000 of our brave Australian fellow-subjects marched through the streets of London, receiving from one end to the other the well-deserved plaudits of the Londoners. Then, having done that, they depart to another land to take up their duties in another sphere. Even so tonight far more than 5,000, many tens of thousands of our dead are, I believe, attracted by that spiritual law of sympathy and love down to us tonight. They come to be congratulated, and having been congratulated, for we who represent London and represent those who love them do congratulate them, they go back to that other world and to their high duties in another sphere.

Although we call it so this is not a memorial meeting, for there is something sad in the very word memorial. It is rather a joyous re-union, because those dark days are gone when we used to be taught that we looked after our dead and saw them gradually vanishing away into the mists of eternity without any assurance of how or where we should meet them again. No, thank Heaven, owing to the new knowledge which has come to every man who will only honestly examine it, owing to that new knowledge we know that now we can extend our arms and with smiling faces look up, knowing that we are looking straight into those unchanged faces which once we knew upon earth.

Such a gathering as this is unique in Europe, but it is not unique in the world. I can remember at the end of the Japanese war reading how Admiral Togo went down to some spot — I picture it as a barren place beside the seashore — and standing there alone he invoked his dead seamen who had fought for him in a great battle, he invoked them to gather round him, and, standing there, he told them what the issue of the war had been. He thanked them and told them how far that issue had been due to their own exertions. He said, "You know these things, but it is only out of respect that I, your Admiral, come to tell you." When we have got to the level of Japan in psychical civilisation, it will not be we civilians who will stand here, but it will be those great chiefs of the Army and the Navy who led their men to battle and led them to their death, it will be they who will stand here in a great meeting of this sort and will welcome them and thank them for their services. We know that the Army is largely impregnated with our ideas. It may not be so long before what I say comes true. I know at least one brave Army Commander, the Commander of an Army Corps second to none in the Army, who is as good a Spiritualist as any man in this room. I well know how he would rejoice to stand and address his vanished men.

You may remember that some time ago they had a meeting here to commemorate those of the First Seven Divisions who had fallen. That meeting was held in the most religious, the most solemn, the most sympathetic spirit, but none the less it was not held with the practical knowledge and the realism which we have. It was an interesting thing that on the day following that meeting, at a séance where they had the most unexceptionable results, one of their friends who had lost his life with the Seventh Division came back, as he had been in the habit of doing. His first communication when he came back was that he regretted that his friends at the time had not got tickets for the meeting, as they had tried to do. They explained that that was impossible. The dialogue, which was sent to me a few days afterwards by the gentleman who presided at the séance, then went like this:—

They said to the Spirit: "Have you anything more to say? "

The Spirit: "There was too much ceremony."

They said: "Anything more?"

The Spirit: "All of us felt out of it."

They said: "We are very interested; is there anything more?"

The Spirit: "They praised the dead. We are not dead. They do not see us."

They said: "Then you were disappointed?"

The Spirit: "Yes, a bit."

They said: "Some people surely felt you were there?"

The Spirit: "Many did, but they were so swamped by the scoffers and the unbelievers."

They said: "We are sorry."

The Spirit: "That is all right, that's nothing."

They said : "Were most of those who passed away in the Seven Divisions there?"

The Spirit: "Yes, they were there."

Since then, tonight, at least, I am sure that no fault of that kind could be found by any of our friends on the further side. We know with all our knowledge, with all our intellect, that they have the power to come, and with all our emotions we know that our love, respect, and admiration is the one force in the universe which can bring them here. I have no doubt that at this moment, had we only those eyes of power which are, I believe, gradually developing in the human race, that sense by which all psychic bodies can be known, if we only had that we would realise that this is a double meeting, and that we perhaps are the smaller half of it. We cannot doubt from all that we know of that power of sympathy that they are here — the men who died on the sea, the men who died on the land, and the men who died under the land, and the men, the heroic boys, who, almost before life had dawned upon them, gave their lives in the air for their country. We believe in the depths of our souls that they are here with us tonight. It matters not whether they died in the mud of

Flanders, whether they died in the chalk of Picardy, whether it was on the sands of Kut or Mesopotamia or Palestine, or whether they left their young lives among the swamps of Equatorial Africa. They have died at the ends of the earth, but we have the power, by our love, which is a real invocation, to draw them all to us tonight. We know it even as we know the span of that great roof above us.

They have done much for us, and we have to ask what we can do for them. They tell us one thing we can do is not to mourn for them. They tell us that their lives are spent in such ineffable happiness as they never could have dreamed of on this planet, and nothing on earth except their love for us causes them ever to think again of a world which is so immeasurably inferior in happiness and comfort to that which they inhabit. Therefore, they tell us not to mourn, because when we mourn it is the one thing which casts a cold cloud upon their perfect happiness. The other thing they tell us is not to look upon them as things forgotten and done with, to rule them out of life, but, go where we will, in our hearts to carry them with us, remembering that they are there and making them one of the family circle. That also they beg us to do.

There is much which they can help us to do. They can help us above all to do our duty, they can help us to fight a hard battle just as they fought a hard battle, and not to mind what the consequences may be. We have got this battle before us, and everyone can fight it out in their own little circle, fighting it with tact. We do not want to proselytise, but the day of sorrow and trouble is the day when we can approach a friend and perhaps set him on the right path. That is what we have to do—to fight this battle even as they fought theirs. They have won great things by their death—they have won, I have no doubt, a hundred years of peace in Europe. They have solved a great number of tangled political questions, they have straightened a number of crooked frontiers, they have allowed civilisation to go where barbarism once was unchecked, and, believe me, the greatest thing that will come through the war, the greatest thing that will come from their death is not political at all but religious. Their death has given us a tremendous driving force. The shock of this horrible catastrophe, steadying every man's mind, making him look hard at his old beliefs, has made him say that he has done with phrases and mere words, and wants to get to the facts, to get something which is solid and certain. It is their death which has caused us to take that line of thought and given us the power by which we may drive that line of thought into the heads of the whole human race and into their hearts. That, I believe, will be the permanent effect of the great movement which has gathered you and me together here tonight.

*

The service, which finished with a rendition of *Vale* (*Farewell*) sung by Miss Winnie Bowden, was a high water mark for the Spiritualist movement.

Even the Press, with its fair proportion of hard-headed cynics, largely held back criticism in the face of the grief of the thousands who attended. *Light* seized on this as evidence of the advancement of the cause rather than newspaper publishers' reluctance to alienate readers.

"One of the most noteworthy and gratifying results of the great Memorial Service was the attitude of the London daily and evening newspapers on the day following the service," *Light* declared in the *Special Supplement.* "A very appreciable amount of space was devoted in the columns of all the papers to the outstanding features of the various addresses; the tone and manner of reporting the views of the speakers were indicative of respect and good feeling towards a body of men and women of whose sincerity and conviction there could be no doubt."

The *Times, Telegraph* and *Morning Post* gave a quarter of a column to the event, the *Daily Mail* and *Evening News* close to half a column each, with Doyle's speech highlighted. The other large dailies, the *Daily News, Chronicle, Express, Mirror, Sketch,* and *The Star* also reported largely without the "sensational and grotesque" editorial comments "that have been so prominent a feature in the Press lately when referring to the Spiritualist movement."

The *Evening Standard* of April 28th, under the headline FALLEN HEROES! REUNION. "THOUSANDS OF SPIRITS" AT ALBERT HALL, described how, as Spiritualists gathered to concentrate their minds to draw down the spirits of the departed "you could have heard a pin drop." The audience, wearing white rosettes to signal their belief in spirit communication, "sat in silence, concentrating their thoughts, some staring straight before them, others shading their eyes as if in prayer."

The *Evening Standard* also noted "The applause which greeted Sir

Arthur Conan Doyle's speech visibly agitated the chairman. The clapping of hands is evidently not welcome at spiritual reunions." Spiritualism, it judged, had spread through every class and rank in society, the vast majority being ordinary people, not the "pallid, long-haired persons whose appearance suggested the occult".

In addition to the gentlemen of the Press, another *Supplement* article gave clairvoyants' impressions of the event. Miss Mary Gordon announced that "Right from floor to dome I saw a great concourse of our heroic soldiers and sailors, the whole vast interior of the Albert Hall seemed to be thronged with them. On the platform, when Sir Arthur Conan Doyle spoke, I noticed particularly the presence of Mr. E. W. Wallis and Mr. J. J. Morse.[43]"

Mr Vout Peters[44] stated that his first impression was "the existence of a tremendous psychic power flooding the hall, a power too strong to be almost borne at one time. Next I was conscious of the presence of a host of spirits of all nationalities. There was an army of soldiers." He added: "When Sir Arthur Conan Doyle spoke there was visible a beautiful wave of purple, indicating the triumph over death and despair."

One leading Spiritualist, Percy R Street, summed up the reason that so many had turned to communing with the dead in the *Special Supplement*. "We have a faith that can answer the soul's deepest questionings, and infuse into the heart of humanity the divine fire." Spiritualism "supplies a deep craving of the soul," had "pushed its outpost line of research beyond death and the grave" and offered "a reasonable philosophy of life and death." He went on, "It consoles those who mourn, brings gladness into the lives of the sorrow-laden, and promotes health and joy. It appeals to humanity because it provides a complete answer to the age-old question, *If a man die, shall he live again?*"

Donations poured in. A businessman, "F.L.", *Light* reported on May 10th 1919, had offered £1,000 toward making up a sum of £10,000. Meanwhile, another £1,000 came from "a gentleman in Wales, who, while desiring to support our cause, also wishes to perpetuate the memory of his son, who was lost in the steamer Carthage, torpedoed at sea on July

---

43 The medium and former editor of *Light* and *The Two Worlds*, E W Wallis had died in 1914; J J Morse on February 19th, 1919.

44 See biographical notes.

10th, 1918." The magazine asked: "Who will be the next to come forward?"

The positive mood of expansion rippling through the movement was summed up directly beneath news of these pledges. "The high spirit of confidence which led to engaging the Royal Albert Hall for the great Memorial Service has been thoroughly justified by results. The meeting was a fitting climax to the Spiritualist activities of our time. It was a land-mark in the history of our movement, and prepared the way for the militant side to organise itself and to come forward armed for the fray."

Meanwhile, alarm grew in the Establishment. The Church was drawn into debate in an area which it traditionally considered its exclusive domain. It did so in a way that only a Church as broad as Anglicanism could do – in a self-contradictory, tumultuous and deeply disorganised way.

# Chapter 7
## Turbulent Priests

Throughout the latter part of 1918 and early 1919, while Doyle busied himself with writing his next Spiritualist book *The Vital Message,* as well as *The History of the Great War* and gave numerous public lectures on Spiritualism, his appearances in *Light* became less frequent. Others, however, pointed to the changes blowing through the country's spiritual beliefs – changes in which Doyle was playing a leading role.

In the March 8th 1919 issue, "VCD" wrote that the Church had "thrown away one opportunity after another for leadership", citing its initial response to Darwin, and urging it not to waste another opportunity by rejecting the new psychic science.

Dr Ellis Powell's article in the April 12th issue, *Re-Interpreting Palm Sunday,* argued that the events of that day only made sense from a Spiritualist perspective. Following a Unitarian line, Powell claimed Christ as the "most powerful Psychic of all time", with the ability to read minds, among other gifts.

By the time of the National Memorial service in April 1919, *The New Revelation* was into its sixth edition and Doyle was completing its companion volume. Serialisation of *The Vital Message* began in *Nash's Magazine* in May, before October publication.

The direction of Doyle's thinking was revealed when asked by the *Daily Chronicle* if he opposed Christianity. He replied: "Oppose it..? I am endeavouring to restore it." Christianity had been "mangled beyond recognition", while Spiritualism "reconciles Christianity with proof and reason from which it is at present divorced."[45]

It was typical of Doyle that he would acknowledge the vast edifice of Christianity on his own terms.

His opinion was far from unique. An article in *Light* on February 15th 1919, by watercolour artist E Wake Cook entitled *The Religious Aspects Of The War: The Churches I,* argued that the Church trailed a "hampering load of old-world barbarisms which must be got rid of ere it can bring itself up to date and fit itself anew for its vital tasks." As Doyle did, Cook questioned the "primitive idea" of punishment for Original

---

45 *Light,* March 1st, 1919

Sin, advising, "the Church should strive strenuously to straighten out these matters and bring consistency into teaching. It should denounce as dishonouring to God, Religion, and itself, the many barbarities of the Old Testament, and the frightfulness of everlasting torments in the New." Echoing Doyle's language , he added that the "new revelations" of Pentecostalism, Psychical Research and Science should be incorporated into a fresh conception of the theo-scientific universe.

In the *Special Supplement* commemorating the Royal Albert Hall memorial service, Miss Lind Af-Hageby wrote in her article *Spiritualism And Modern Thought*:

> The general breakdown of conventional religion is apparent to the most casual observer. Orthodoxy is losing its hold on all but the most superficial thinkers... The war has given a new poignancy to questions about the human soul, about moral responsibility, about life after death. It is the great human prerogative to ask questions. Science, religion, art, civilisation are the answers, tentative and imperfect, yet well worth the travail of the mind.

She added that Spiritualism was "fraught with dynamic power of changing belief and conduct. Hence the hostility of the ecclesiastically fossilised mind." This explained "the silly warnings about Satan as the director of every spiritualistic séance, about lunatic asylums as the ultimate place of reception for those who dally with spooks."

She predicted "ecclesiastical hostility to Spiritualism will some day be accounted one of the most remarkable features in the great history of human stupidity", and summed up the role of Spiritualists:

> Whilst the doors and windows of the Church are tightly closed and volumes of sermons and speculations on immortality are poured out before more or less somnolent congregations, there is a loud knock at the door. Spiritualism wants to enter, calls out: "This belief, this hope of yours can be tested, proved; the so-called dead are ready and willing to speak to you; they are alive with greater knowledge. Prepare yourselves for communion and entry into the light of a fuller understanding." But the priest

> will not listen, will not suffer the people to listen. Muttering something about necromancy or demons or lifting the veil, he rushes forward and bolts and bars the door. And the sermons go on and the light is withheld.

She finished the article with the rallying cry: "The future is in the hands of Spiritualism."

It all seemed possible. With Conan Doyle packing meeting rooms with his talks on *Death and the Hereafter,* and other Spiritualists holding services with congregations in the hundreds or even thousands, a new era seemed to have begun.

Father Vaughan remained uncompromisingly critical. "Never since the world began was there so dangerous a time as the present for indulging in the perils of necromancy," he announced in the *Daily Dispatch,* asking, "Who would venture to tell the number of persons who had been mentally unhinged, morally undone, and physically ruined by attempting to force the locks of the gates of Death, and to pry into the secrets of God?"[46]

The Spiritualist medium and Vicar of Orford, Reverend G Vale Owen, denied Vaughan's dire warnings on "the perils of necromancy" in *Light* of May 10th 1919, saying, "That accusation is a lie, for the uttering of which there is no excuse."

Nevertheless, argument about Spiritualism's alleged role in lunacy rumbled on. *Light* replied to Father Vaughan on May 24th by quoting another Spiritualist preacher, the Rev. Charles Tweedale who had gathered statistics on this matter. "It was found that in the asylums from which the statistics were obtained there were very few persons suffering from madness caused by devotion to psychic things, but that there were many cases of religious mania among the orthodox patients." *Light* asked, why did Father Vaughan not also rail against Christianity?

Another combatant in this war for souls was General Booth[47], leader of the *blood and fire* Salvation Army, who deployed his spiritual ordnance in the *Empire News* – his salvo receiving withering fire from an increasingly impatient Doyle in the same paper.

Doyle cited an American investigation showing that out of 13,500

---

46 *Light*, March 1st, 1919
47 Bramwell Booth, the son of the founder, known for his autocratic style.

lunacy patients, four were Spiritualists and two hundred and fifteen were clergymen. Doyle remarked "it is really time this nonsense ceased... That is my answer to General Booth and the others who follow that line of argument."

Nevertheless Father Vaughan continued lambasting Spiritualists from the pulpit and any other public platform he could find. *Light* reported him in the April 3rd issue of 1920:

> What to some folk read like the gibberings of a lunatic in an asylum, to others, like Oliver Lodge, Conan Doyle and Vale Owen, seemed a sublime revelation from a promised land. Without conclusive evidence to guide them, these gentlemen gulped down van loads of rubbish which ought to be tilted on a dust heap.

Reverend F Fielding-Ould captured the national preoccupations of War and spirit at a Spiritualist address reported in *Light,* on May 10th 1919, including an alleged true account from the Front.

> An officer, while an attack was proceeding, became separated from the rest of his men. He found himself alone in broken country in the midst of firing from every side. He had no idea of his whereabouts and had given himself up for lost, when suddenly he encountered two of his fellow officers who shouted, "Come on this way, old chap, it's your only chance," and scrambling on he discovered himself back amongst his own men. They asked him how he had managed to find them, and he mentioned the two officers who had guided his footsteps. "But they were both killed this morning," his companions replied. Many stories of that kind, said Mr. Fielding-Ould, were being reported from the fighting line, and it looked as if the two worlds were drifting closer together...

Fielding-Ould noted that "thousands of people were leaving the old ordered routine of the Christian religion," and quoted some impressive numbers. In the Spiritualists' National Union there were one hundred and eighty affiliated societies, and three hundred and fifty societies held regular Sunday services. Forty of them already had churches of their own. "From the clerical point of view," he surmised, "the movement was not one to be dismissed with a trifling word about *flying tambourines.*"

Fielding-Ould hoped that before long the Church would appoint a commission to investigate. He had, he announced "written to the Bishop of London on the matter." His warning of the impending break-up of the Church was clear: "the Church was drifting, and any nautical man would tell them what a dangerous course that was, in view of possible breakers ahead." As a Christian Spiritualist, he argued that Spiritualism had much good in it and much in common with Christian belief, and its doctrine should be judged on its merits.

An investigation by The Psychical Research Committee of St. Ethelburga's Church, Bishopsgate was arranged. On 12th July 1919 *Light* published a summary of its findings presented to the Church Council, in *A Church Committee Investigates Spiritualism.*

"The results have been definite in fact, even when unsatisfactory in rationality, or inexplicable in theory," the report noted. The Committee was able to say without hesitation that:—

1. The activity of a mind or minds is revealed in the phenomena witnessed;
2. What purports to be a definite personality is as a rule to be got at through one medium alone; it does not come through another medium;
3. The mind which communicates is as a rule dominated by prejudices or beliefs which might be thought peculiar to this side;
4. Messages sent through tend to be diffuse and vague rather than pointed and clear;
5. When a mind communicates with us at more than one sitting a coherent personality is distinguishable;
6. No danger to the medium has been observed when the method used is that of letters of the alphabet spelled out on a table;
7. The mind which communicates speaks frequently of being allowed a definite time and no more; it also appears to be governed by one controlling mind;

8. The hypotheses of the unconscious and of telepathy complicate but do not solve the problems offered by Spiritualism.

The report gave a flavour of the entities investigators had encountered at séance. These included a friar of the thirteenth century, a priest of the sixteenth, a soldier of the seventeenth, an Egyptian of the Ptolemaic period, one spirit calling himself a *watcher* or an *angel*, as well as relatives of some of the sitters who had passed over in recent years.

Two theories for the phenomena were proposed, one accepting a manifestation of the deceased's soul, the other suggesting the more traditional Church line, possession.

"The latter lies more ready to hand, is more intelligible and seems to leave less to be accounted for," the report noted, though it didn't discount the alternative.

It went on to speculate that if the phenomena were really due to communication from the deceased, the vagueness of communication might be down to the spirit's "imperfect control of the brain of the medium."

If these phenomena were the result of possession, the report noted: "The communicating spirits show for the most part little interest in their own present surroundings, and they frequently seem to have lost what we commonly call the personal touch... The limitation of their knowledge and interests is as striking as is the fact that they express themselves at all. Too often they deal in windy generalities about truth, and as frequently when they give definite names or dates, these on inquiry are found to be incorrect."

The writer posited a third hypothesis that "thought-forms" (essentially the psychological residue of thoughts) were captured and replayed by the medium.

Now, seeing that communicating spirits frequently discourse of far-off events and things of long ago, the guess may be hazarded that what comes to us is not a personality but that a cinema film, depicting actual things or forms created by thought in the past, is unrolled before us. In this case we should be compelled to abstain from affirming anything about the present condition of a departed spirit, for the simple reason that he has not been before us. What we have been looking upon is the ideas which a mind has created and left behind in possibly an ethereal form."

The report explained: "The phenomena of materialisation would witness also to this creative or plastic power of thought."

The report described how the spirit of a Father Stephen from the reign of Edward VI was addressed in Latin (a language unknown to the medium), and gave "apposite and rational answers." The same could not be said of communication from Julius Caesar, of whom the writer noted: "The circle would seem here to have entered the memory of some megalomaniac."

Another psychic manifestation was described:

> ...the most interesting person we have come across is Edward Parr, one of the Queen's halberdiers under Raleigh in Queen Elizabeth's time. He claims one of the sitters as an old and beloved boon companion under the name of "gladsome Roger." He has given details of his own life and that of his friend and of that of their families without any undue hesitation, is full of affection, speaks in the dialect of the seventeenth century, and has shown himself at six sittings consistent, lovable and rational. It is difficult to believe that in his case we have not been in touch with a definite personality, whether that personality be Edward Parr himself or some master-mind who has created him for his own pleasure, and perhaps ours."

The report's final paragraph concluded:

> Your Committee, then, is satisfied that "spirits" of some sort are active in the séance-room; that the probability is that some of these at least have been formerly in the flesh; that the double strain of transcendentalism and of the limits set by whatever organ is being used renders great caution necessary in forming a judgment; and that sufficient ground exists to justify religiously-mind people in pursuing reverently and cautiously a scientific inquiry into the phenomena of Spiritualism, so long as they do

not allow themselves to confuse the domain of religion with that of science.

(Signed on behalf of the Committee),

W. F. Cobb, D. D.

Reverend Fielding-Ould neatly epitomised the disarray of the Church of England in two articles. In *The Problem Of The Empty Tomb*, in *Light* on June 14th, he explained Christ's resurrection in purely Spiritualist terms without apparently considering that this meant Christ was an ordinary man. A month later on July 12th, perhaps to correct perceptions about how far he had *gone over* to Spiritualism, he wrote a letter titled *Jesus Christ And Spiritualism*. A red rag to a bull if ever there was one, it alienated many nominally Christian Spiritualists and enraged those who had left Christianity behind. It began:

> No one has a right to call himself a Christian unless he believes in the Divinity of Jesus Christ. He may be a person of estimable character, and greatly developed spirituality, but he is not a Christian. The Christian believes that Jesus is "the only son of God," *i.e.*, a son of God in a unique sense, of a quality, not merely a degree of attainment which transcends that of the highest among merely created being. He believes that in and through Him the supreme Father is Imaged, manifested and revealed to creation. That in the essence of His own nature He is Divine.

On that foundation rock the whole Church was built. "Take it away and the whole elaborate structure falls into ruins." Whereas previously he had warned that the Church was "drifting" toward danger, now he cautioned, "it is upon this rock that the great vessel of modern Spiritualism is in imminent danger of being wrecked."

He mourned the fact that "in the Spiritualist hymn-book, the name of Jesus is deleted, *e.g.*, 'angels of Jesus' reads 'angels of wisdom.'" He complained that Christ's name was "carefully omitted in the prayers." Christian Spiritualists rejoicing in the revelations of the séance room were "alarmed" by the direction Spiritualism was taking. "That they themselves should be considered as having renounced their faith and hope in Jesus Christ is intolerable." He warned:

> If it can be shown that the communicating spirits are the authors of and responsible for this anti-Christian tendency, then, in the eyes of Christendom, the whole vast movement is not only suspect, but utterly discredited and condemned. There can be no compromise whatever, and I personally shall spend the rest of my life in condemning it and warning people against. But if, as I believe, the error originated on this side of the veil then, in the name of God, let it be corrected without further delay.

The replies in *Light* were predictable. Numerous writers expressed exasperation or quoted scripture proving that either Christ was a talented Spiritualist human being, or that all humankind was divine.

Conan Doyle took a line both combative and conciliatory.

*Light, August 9, 1919*

### JESUS CHRIST AND SPIRITUALISM.
### SIR ARTHUR CONAN DOYLE.

What ruined early Christianity and reduced it to a jumble of creeds all at loggerheads over mystical questions? It was the attempt in the second century or thereabouts to closely define things which the human brain is incapable of understanding, and then to quarrel with those who did not agree with the definition. When we consider the breadth and gentle toleration of Christ's teaching we can, it seems to me, see that all those successive Councils of the Church which got more and more dogmatic in their teaching were essentially unChristian in their spirit. Spiritualism is, in my opinion, an attempt to get back to the simplicity as well as to the phenomena of the early Christian days. We have to cease the twisting of texts and the drawing of iron lines round matters which are admitted to be infinite and therefore beyond our capacity. It would be a thousand pities if any considerable body of Spiritualists began to excommunicate their neighbours upon such grounds. Every Spiritualist whom I know is convinced that Christ is the highest of Spirits. Upon that there is no contention. Why not leave it at that, and let each determine in his own soul and reason how far that highest spirit approached actual divinity? Only in this way can we find unity and mutual tolerance.

*

Committed Spiritualist Miss H A Dallas vainly hoped "that Mr. Fielding-Ould's article will not result in controversial arguments concerning the divinity of Christ. We shall gain nothing by mere arguments", and then went on to lay out her particular view of Christ as "the Highest Spirit known to us." She urged Spiritualists and mediums to keep Christ in their thoughts because He had urged his followers to "abide in me". Christ, she claimed, was a Spiritualist and contact with Him would have great rewards: "we may expect inward light from the Father in Heaven, who alone can reveal truth to our spirits." Seeking compromise, she went on: "No two minds will have exactly the same revelation; that does not matter."

Another writer, James Coates questioned both Christ's divinity and the Bible's reliability. He saw Christ as an inspired "God-intoxicated" man, "full of the Messianic concept of His time and race." He was a telepath and a "highly gifted man," *ie:* a talented Spiritualist. Coates finished by saying "the teachings of Spiritualism were not given to the world as under-pinnings for any Church, sect or party," thereby inverting the notion of the primacy of Christianity – Spiritualism held a more fundamental truth.

As the letters flooded in, Fielding-Ould wrote, in *Light* of August 9th 1919:

> Now we take our choice. On one side Christ's own claims and the consistent and reasoned conclusions of the great Church, of the best, holiest and most learned men for many centuries, and on the other side "Imperator," "Morambo,"[48] and a few other people of whom we know practically nothing. If dwellers in the beyond are kind enough to come back and tell us something of the conditions under which they live we are grateful and

---

48 Imperator was the leader of the band of spirits who controlled Stainton Moses. Morambo was the control for Mrs Minnie Harriet Wallis.

courteous listeners and learners, but shall we renounce and destroy the most exquisite treasure which man possesses, gathered with infinite pains and protected by the life blood of uncounted martyrs, at the word of someone who, except by the accident of death, may be no further advanced than many still in the world?

The matter came to an uneasy rest when *Light* announced they would take no more letters on the subject.

It was far from the sole spat between fledgling Spiritualism and Christianity. On 27th July 1919, the Bishop of London, A. F. Winington-Ingram, conducted a service to honour the "memory of those fallen in the war," arranged by the snappily named *Metropolitan Divisional Council of the National Federation of Discharged and Demobilized Sailors and Soldiers*. According to *The Times*, "in addition to the 50,000 ex-service men who assembled on the Victoria Embankment and marched in procession to the Park, thousands of people were present."

The Bishop directly addressed the nation's grief, *The Times* reported. "He said that those who had lost loved ones in the war might be comforted by the fact that they had died in a noble cause and that they were with them in spirit." Telling of a mother who had experienced a visitation from her son when she received the sad news of his death, he suggested that such visions "were only very seldom vouchsafed and faith did not depend upon them, but they enforced what they were promised, and that was that their son, their husband, friend, or comrade was the same person five minutes after death as he was before."

He then advised his congregation to have "nothing to do with those who attempted communications with the dead." The Bishop believed it was "a sin to seek to know what we could not know," adding, "let Sir Oliver Lodge and Sir Conan Doyle do what they like, but do not let the ordinary mourner spend his hours in trying to get into communication with the dead."

Doyle and his friend Oliver Lodge were among the many who responded. In *Light* on 9th August, appeared an article called *Is Spirit Communion A Sin? Criticisms On The Bishop Of London's Address.*

Oliver Lodge, more restrained than his friend, did not directly criticise the Bishop, putting forward variously the ideas that the initial report was unreliable, that we didn't know exactly what was in the Bishop's mind, that the Bishop had met "foolish and unbalanced inquirers whom he thinks it wise to restrain," and that therefore the precautionary principle was to be advised. "I also think it probable," Lodge added, "that he has been too busy to go into the subject at all closely."

In carefully couched terms, he added: "...the claim that we ought not to try to ascertain the truth on any apparently hidden matter is one that can be used, and historically has been used, against progress in every branch of knowledge, from Roger Bacon downwards. It is the negation of science... It is the business of myself and other scientific inquirers to make these facts better known. And when they are better known, then their practical application can be dealt with by those in ecclesiastical authority."

Conan Doyle's answer was less tactful. *Light* quoted a reply he had given to the *Evening News*:

> "It is a sin to seek to know what we should not know," the Bishop had said.
>
> "I can conceive nothing that is more vital," replied Sir Arthur, "and no better work than to bring solace and hope to grief-stricken people."
>
> Sir Arthur spoke of the ignorance of the clergy on this great subject.
>
> "If," he said, "a surgeon or a physician is conscientious, he reads up all there is on his subject, but these people who are our spiritual doctors know absolutely nothing on the average about this gigantic development of communication with those who have passed. If one of them writes to the papers about it he exhibits his ignorance at once. He has never read the standard works on the subject, such as Crookes's investigations or Crawford's experiments. If he were to read them he would be converted, because the evidence is absolutely unassailable.
>
> "On the whole I don't feel that the Bishop is antagonistic to our view. He admits the possibility of a return, and since the boy in his anecdote did return, he did so presumably with the permission of God and consoled his mother. The Bishop is

against frivolous indulgence in spirit communication. Most Spiritualists are entirely with him in this. We very much object to see a solemn rite being performed out of mere frivolity or curiosity. We agree with him that it should be restricted to cases of stress, where broken-hearted people urgently desire to reconstitute their lives by some form of personal communication with those they have lost.

"What the Bishop does not seem to understand is that we have no power to call down spirits. We cannot evoke them. All we can do is to make the conditions such that they can come if they desire to come. That the choice of coming rests with them entirely is proved by the fact that very often they do not come.

"We ask them, when they do come, if our communications with them retard their development. They are all unanimous in saying that they are enormously consoled and helped by our efforts. Some of them speak with great bitterness of the fact that those who love them are deterred by empty fancies from enjoying the great privilege which God has granted to mankind."

Other commentators in *Light* were more combative. The Reverend W F Cobb, D.D., the same man who had written the Church Committee's report on Spiritualism, wrote:

It is not very easy to follow the reasoning of the Bishop of London by which he is led to denounce any attempt to open up communication with the departed, while he affirms that those on the other side do communicate with us. This sounds as if Columbus ought not to have discovered America, but that a Red Indian might have discovered Europe... No sane and well-founded religion looks askance at science... That the Church has in the past consistently and disastrously set its face against the active pursuit of new aspects of Truth is the best of all reasons why it should not again repeat its blunder...

The Reverend G Vale Owen joined in. "When a leader of the Orthodox party uses such arguments as he used, the poverty of his case is apparent to all," he wrote. Enquirers after truth would not be deterred "by the bogey of diabolism."

Reverend Fielding-Ould pressed for the Church to adopt an official position: "Can it be denied that all Spiritualists sincerely seek the Truth and the highest benefit of mankind? If their methods are unlawful and their conclusions unwarranted, let the fact be adequately pointed out and exposed, let there be a weighty and dignified pronouncement such as is worthy of the unexampled importance of the subject in question..."

In *Light* of August 23rd 1919, Doyle was quoted as observing, "How strange that the Church should attack us for confirming its own doctrine of immortality, a basic creed, in fact."

In its editorial, *Light* wrote of the Church's disarray:

"Someone has said that the Church is 'all at sea.' But that we do not accept. It is so painfully apparent it has somehow missed the tide."[49]

The onslaught continued, with *Light* publishing a provocative extract from Doyle's new work, *The Vital Message*:

*Light, September 27, 1919*

THE NEW TESTAMENT AND THE NEW REVELATION.

"Nash's" for October contains the fifth and last of Sir Arthur Conan Doyle's series of articles entitled "The Vital Message." In this he takes the New Testament record and points out at some length how close is the analogy which exists between the phenomenal events associated with the early days of Christianity and those which have perplexed the world in connection with modern Spiritualism.

Concluding this part of his argument, he writes:—-

"Enough has been said, perhaps, to show the reader that it is possible to put forward a view of Christ's life which would be in strict accord with the most modern psychic knowledge, and which, far from supplanting Christianity would show the surprising accuracy of some of the details handed down to us, and would support the surprising conclusion that those very miracles which have been the stumbling block to so many truthful, earnest minds may finally offer some very cogent arguments for the truth of the whole narrative. Is this, then, a line of thought which merits the wholesale condemnations and anathemas hurled at it, not only from Rome and Canterbury, but even from Little Bethel?"

---

49 *Light*, August 9th, 1919

At the same time Sir Arthur would not have these remarks quoted as sustaining the literal accuracy of the New Testament record. On the contrary, he holds that it would be "a good, though an unattainable, thing that a really honest and open-minded attempt should be made to weed out from that record the obvious forgeries and interpolations which disfigure it." But it is not only revision that is needed: "a change of emphasis is also needed in order to get the grand Christian inception back into the current of reason and progress." It is still, he holds, beyond doubt that Christianity has broken down (not Christ's teaching, for that has seldom been followed) and that this breakdown has been brought home to everyone by the terrible catastrophe which has befallen the world. He sums up : —

"Is it not time, then, for the religious bodies to discourage their own bigots and sectarians and to seriously consider, if only for self-preservation, how they can get into line once more with that general level of human thought which is now far in front of them? I say that they can do more than get level — they can lead. But to do so they must have the firm courage to cut away from their own bodies all that dead tissue which is but a disfigurement and an encumbrance. They must face difficulties of reason, and adapt themselves to the demands of the human intelligence which rejects, and is right in rejecting, much which they offer. Finally, they must gather fresh strength by drawing in all the new truth and all the new power which are afforded by this new wave of inspiration which has been sent into the world by God, and which the human race, deluded and bemused by the would-be clever, has received with such perverse and obstinate incredulity. When they have done all this they will find, not only that they are leading the world with an obvious right to the leadership, but, in addition, that they have come round once more to the very teaching of that Master whom they have so long misrepresented."

\*

Those whom Doyle described as bigots saw themselves as protectors of their flock. The Dean of Manchester, preaching in Manchester Cathedral in August 1919, warned of the physical and psychological health risks Spiritualism presented, as well as dangers in communicating with spirits "that are not wholesome or desirable"[50]. The Catholic Cardinal Bourne at a service in Kent asserted: "...it is not according to the Providence of God and His will that we should enter into any other sort of communication with them [the dead] than intercession."[51]

For Doyle, this controversy had all been seen before, as another extract from *The Vital Message* showed.

*Light, October 4, 1919*

## AS IT WAS IN THE BEGINNING.

It is interesting to observe the effect which these phenomena, or the report of them, produced upon the orthodox Jews of those days [the time of Jesus]. The greater part obviously discredited them, otherwise they could not have failed to become followers, or at the least to have regarded such a wonder-worker with respect and admiration. One can well imagine how they shook their bearded heads, declared that such occurrences were outside their experience, and possibly pointed to the local conjurer, who earned a few not over-clean denarii by imitating the phenomena. There were others, however, who could not possibly deny, because they either saw or met with witnesses who had seen. These declared roundly that the whole thing was of the devil, drawing from Christ one of those pithy common-sense arguments in which He excelled. The same two classes of opponents, the scoffers and the diabolists, face us to-day. Verily, the old world goes round, and so do the events upon the surface.

\*

When it was published in October 1919, *The Vital Message* pulled few punches. Doyle advocated a root-and-branch reappraisal of Christianity. "...There can be no clear thinking until the old dispensation has been placed on the shelf of the scholar, and removed from the desk of the teacher," he wrote, "...it has no connection with modern conceptions of religion."

50  *Light*, August 9th, 1919
51  Ibid

He dispensed with the Old Testament out of hand as "a document which advocates massacre, condones polygamy, accepts slavery, and orders the burning of so-called witches". He didn't have much truck with the New Testament either, arguing it was unreliable and the book's writers had interpolated their own ideas into it, distorting the true message of God.

He then demolished the basis of Christianity when he described Christ's blood ransom on behalf of humankind as an "injustice" and went on to say: "the student is well aware that the whole of this sanguinary metaphor is drawn really from the Pagan rites of Mithra, where the neophyte was actually placed under a bull at the ceremony of the TAUROBOLIUM, and was drenched, through a grating, with the blood of the slaughtered animal. Such reminiscences of the more brutal side of Paganism are not helpful to the thoughtful and sensitive modern mind."

With the blood of Christ drained from the faith, what bones were left for Christians to pick over? Doyle asserted that true Christianity should focus on the personality of Christ himself, underplay the Passion (more blood and barbarity) and also focus to a lesser extent upon the Resurrection.

Nevertheless, Christ certainly had a role in Conan Doyle's religious view. Christ was, after all, a typological forerunner of the Fox sisters who started the Modern Spiritualist movement in 1848 in Hydesville, USA.

> The circumstances were humble, and even rather sordid, upon both sides of the veil, human and spirit, yet it was, as time will more and more clearly show, one of the turning points of the world's history, greater far than the fall of thrones or the rout of armies. Some artist of the future will draw the scene—the sitting-room of the wooden, shack-like house, the circle of half-awed and half-critical neighbours, the child clapping her hands with upturned laughing face, the dark corner shadows where these strange new forces seem to lurk—forces often apparent, and now come to stay and to effect the complete revolution of human thought. We may well ask why should such great results arise from such petty sources? So argued the highbrowed philosophers of Greece and Rome when the outspoken Paul, with the fisherman Peter and his half-educated disciples,

traversed all their learned theories, and with the help of women, slaves, and schismatic Jews, subverted their ancient creeds. One can but answer that Providence has its own way of attaining its results, and that it seldom conforms to our opinion of what is most appropriate.

*- The Vital Message*

*The Vital Message* rationalised the implications of *The New Revelation*. Christ and his disciples were Spiritualists. "...the phenomena associated with the rise of Christianity and those which have appeared during the present spiritual ferment are very analogous...the only additional point is the raising of the dead." Of Christ's groaning before raising Lazarus, "anyone who has heard a medium groaning before any great manifestation of power will read into this passage just that touch of practical knowledge, which will convince him of its truth. The miracle, I may add, is none the less wonderful or beyond our human powers, because it was wrought by an extension of natural law, differing only in degree with that which we can ourselves test and even do."

In the pattern-making reflex of the religiously inspired, Doyle rationalised why Spiritualism had come to humankind now. The "inner reason" of the Great War had been "to shake mankind loose from gossip and pink teas, and sword-worship, and Saturday night drunks, and self-seeking politics and theological quibbles..." in order to reform religion and bring the one true insight to the world while disposing of "make-beliefs".

Doyle's book is a compelling, persuasive read which shows how far he had travelled in rationalising his religion. *The Vital Message* shifts between appeals to heart and head, speaking in one breath of the weight of scientific evidence and in the next of the comfort Spiritualism provides to the bereaved; at times it declares the new faith to be allied with Christianity against Materialism, at others it claims an as-yet undiscovered *ether* which composes the spirit-substance - thus making Spiritualism an arm of Materialism.

It was explosive stuff.

Some clerics counter-attacked by claiming the view that Spiritualism caused insanity was supported by Dr Forbes Winslow, a psychiatrist renowned for his involvement in the Jack The Ripper case. Forbes

Winslow had died in 1913, but in *Light* of October 11th 1919, Ernest W Oaten, editor of *The Two Worlds* quoted a letter sent him by the doctor in 1912, which eschewed his previous criticisms: "Yes, I wrote that, but I have changed my mind since then."

The letter didn't prevent Father Vaughan and others repeating the charge. Once again Conan Doyle stepped into the breach.

*Light, October 11, 1919*

## SIR A. CONAN DOYLE AT LEICESTER
## REPLY TO CHURCH CONGRESS CRITICISMS.

Sir Arthur Conan Doyle, who was accompanied by Lady Doyle, addressed a large meeting in the Palace Theatre, Leicester, on Sunday last. Mr. Ernest W. Oaten, president of the Spiritualists' National Union, presided. Some 2,500 people were present, and hundreds were turned away. Among those on the platform was Alderman Chaplin, the mayor-elect of Leicester, who has for some years been president of the local Spiritualist Society. We take the following report from "The Times.":—

Having explained the general philosophy of the Spiritualistic movement and the evidence upon which it was based, the speaker, proceeded to deal with the recent discussion of the Church Congress. Nowhere among the speakers did he recognise a strong, clear conviction like that of the late Archdeacon Colley, whose name would live as a fearless pioneer of the truth. Archdeacon Wilberforce seemed also to have left no adequate successor. At the same time every Spiritualist would be grateful to the Dean of Manchester for the moderation and sanity with which he discussed the question. The admission that the explanation by fraud is utterly out of date was an honest and clear one. Though they were unfortunately not represented among the speakers, this philosophy claimed many adherents and some leaders among the clergy. The Rev. Mr. Tweedale, Dr. Cobb, the late Mr. Chambers, Mr. Fielding-Ould, and many other Anglican clergymen knew the truth, and were fearless in asserting it. In Mr. Vale Owen, vicar of Orford, were to be found the highest powers of automatic writing possessed by any medium in Britain. The lecturer had read in script a long and detailed account of the next world written by Mr. Vale Owen's hand, through the impulse of a spiritual guide and he could only say that it was one of the most remarkable and inspiring narratives he had ever encountered. He hoped it would soon be available for all the world, and it could not fail to produce a profound sensation.

The Dean of St. Paul's charged Spiritualists with necromancy. As a scholar, Dr. Inge should know that the word "necromancy" means sorcery connected with a corpse. Far from attaching any importance to the dead body, the Spiritualist looked upon it as a mere collection of chemical elements for the use of Nature, with no future function at all. It was entirely superseded by what St. Paul called the spiritual body. There were some bitter opponents in the Church, who were probably more noisy than numerous, but they were the lineal descendants of the men who burned the witches, who scourged the Quakers, who cast the Dissenters into gaol, and who drove the Pilgrim Fathers out of the country. They had not progressed, but the public had progressed, and they were impotent to do harm.

## MEDIUMS AND SANITY.

Commenting upon the remark of Canon McClure, that mediums were neurotic beings, Sir Arthur said that no doubt the man with psychic powers, whether it was John of the Revelation, or Ezekiel, or any other, seemed neurotic to the more earthly souls around them. As far as physical health went, he could testify that the leading mediums of Great Britain, most of whom he knew personally, would compare very favourably, both men and women, with the average citizen. As to sanity, he had never met a more sane set of people than the Spiritualists. The rate of lunacy among Spiritualists was abnormally low, and the late Dr. Forbes Winslow before his death admitted that he had been entirely mistaken in his assertion to the contrary.

Spiritualism had come as an ally to Christianity in confuting materialism and proving the continuity of life and the evil effects of sin. It was evident to anyone that materialism had been steadily winning since the days of Hume and Voltaire, and the reason was clear. When called upon for a sign, the Church had none. It could only make assertions, and it could not prove them. Spiritualism came along, with proofs, and, if it saw the great Christian episode from an angle of its own, the vital point was that its doctrine was absolutely fatal to materialism.

This should merit some better return from the Church than ignorant clamour and accusations of necromancy.

When a man had again and again, beyond all doubt or question, spoken face to face with the so-called dead, as he, the speaker, had done, how would it be possible for him afterwards to yield to the arguments of those who had not had so sacred an experience?

\*

At the annual Church Congress, *The Times* reported that the Rev A V Magee, vicar of St Mark's, London, had closed a debate on Spiritualism with the following warnings:

> He challenged Sir A. Conan Doyle to deny, if he dared, that this thing involved peril to manly moral and spiritual life. Sir Conan Doyle was asking every young woman in the country to try whether she had the attributes of mediumship. He was incurring the gravest responsibility in making such a suggestion as that. It was possible to become possessed of evil spirits which were earth-bound and trying to get back to this earth, and once they took possession of one they did not go as easily as they came. He had seen a woman stark staring mad under the influence of the planchette. He was told only a fortnight ago of a married man and his wife, who had gone staring mad through this thing. A woman had told him her daughter had become possessed of evil spirits, and had become transformed in character and transformed for the worse.[52]

*Light* also reported that the Rev A V Magee, had "thundered against Spiritualism." It drily continued:

> In this connection it is a little amusing to hear from one of our most respected contributors that Mr. Magee has 'had personal experience' of a haunted chamber, in an old house in the West Country. So vivid was his experience that he abruptly cut short his visit and returned to town.

---

52 "Peril of Evil Spirits", *The Times*, October 16th, 1919

Doubtless, his adventure caused his talk of "evil spirits". "Disconcerted by an experience with which he was entirely unfamiliar, he failed to understand that what seemed to him to be of diabolic origin was readily explainable on much more natural grounds. The poor earth-bound ghost has much to answer for."[53]

Once again, it was only a matter of time before Conan Doyle stepped into the fray.

*Light, November 15, 1919*

### SIR ARTHUR CONAN DOYLE AND THE REV. A. V. MAGEE.

As most of our readers are doubtless aware, Sir A. Conan Doyle has accepted the challenge of the Rev. A. V. Magee in his address at St. Mary's, Soho, on "The Dangers of Spiritualism," in the course of which he gave instances of the effects of dabbling in Spiritualism, and quoted Dr. Forbes Winslow, who stated in 1877 that there were ten thousand people in lunatic asylums as a result. Mr. Magee added that Sir Arthur Conan Doyle had said that Dr. Forbes Winslow had recanted that statement, but a friend of his, a priest, had offered fifty pounds for the production of the recantation. Up to the present he had not been called upon to pay the fifty pounds.

In a letter to the "Evening Standard" and other newspapers last week, Sir Arthur quoted the letter of October 17th, 1912, from Dr. Forbes Winslow to the Editor of the "Two Worlds" ... and invited Mr. Magee to apologise and give the name and address of the priest who is alleged to have offered fifty pounds for the production of the document, which can be seen at the office of the "Two Worlds."

\*

This letter to the Evening Standard was not enough, it seemed for Magee, and so in his undeviating manner, Doyle went a step further, as *Light* reported on December 13th.

---

53 *Light*, October 26th, 1919

Sir A. Conan Doyle, in a recent letter to the "Daily Mail," comments in strong terms on the attitude of the Rev. A. V. Magee. The latter challenged Sir Arthur to produce a letter from Dr. Forbes Winslow withdrawing his charges about Spiritualism being a potent cause of insanity. Sir Arthur writes: "I at once produced it. I have had no explanation or apology, and I think that in decency he should be silent for a while." Sir Arthur adds; "Having been proved to be entirely wrong in his assertion about lunacy, he now takes refuge in fables about evil spirits."

It was clear by late 1919 that the Church needed an official stance on the phenomena and teachings of Spiritualism. The *Diarist* in the London *Star* was reported in *Light* of November 8th as writing that there was "every possibility of a special committee, representing Churches of all denominations, being convened to look carefully into the subject of Spiritualism" in order to meet the "psychological demand that the War has produced."

Without guidance, each clergyman was left to follow his conscience. Thus, *Light* reported that the Bishop of London continued "on his ambiguous way unabashed," advising mourning relatives and friends at a memorial service at Southwark Cathedral on November 5th, for the officers and men of the London Rifle Brigade who fell in the war "that necromancy did nothing but harm. It was cruel in that it had wrecked many minds, and nothing had been recorded of it that was of the least use. The so-called revelations could all be explained by telepathy or thought reading."[54]

This line left Christians in No-Man's Land, as the Reverend Charles L Tweedale pointed out. In a letter to the Bishop published in *Light* on November 15th, he asked whether his warning against necromancy also applied to the messages and revelations of the Old and New Testaments. "It is terrible to have one's belief in the spirit world and its reality swept away like this... if man's experiences, or 'so-called' experiences of another world are due to 'telepathy' to-day, then all the similar experiences, or 'so-called' experiences of the prophets and Apostles may have been equally telepathic in days of old. It is all very disheartening."

---

54 *Light*, November 16th, 1919

This encapsulated the Church's dilemma. If it denied Spiritualist phenomena it brought its own teachings into question; if it accepted them there was potential for reinterpretation of its doctrine. Yet some of Spiritualism's major advocates were eminent scientists and the Church feared being left behind by the scientific facts. How should it respond?

Some Christians ignored these more subtle considerations and simply accused Spiritualism of deviating from Christian teaching. Just so with a letter sent to the *Daily Mail* by Coulson Kernahan, which was replied to by both Bishop Welldon and Conan Doyle.

The article in *Light* from November 15th *Is "Spiritism" Anti-Christian? Views Of Bishop Welldon And Sir A. Conan Doyle* reported the Bishop accepting that the common enemy of Christianity and Spiritualism was materialism, and that Spiritualism "cannot now be laughed out of court" but must be evaluated by competent men of science.

In Sir Arthur Conan Doyle's reply, Doyle used one of his common rhetorical techniques, the appeal to authority, in quoting from the work of medium Violet Tweedale:

> I observe that Mr. Coulson Kernahan [who stated in a letter to the "Daily Mail" that in Sir Arthur Conan Doyle's new book the Founder of Christianity is described as a medium][55] is shocked at the idea that Christ and His disciples were psychic in the modern sense. Will you allow me to quote a conversation with Mr. Gladstone, extracted from the interesting book of reminiscences published recently by Mrs. Tweedale?[56]
>
> "Then, quite suddenly, Mr. Gladstone began to prove to us that the old Biblical scribes were convinced Spiritualists. From his intimate knowledge of the Bible he quoted text after text in support of his contention. 'Here He worked no wonders because the people were wanting in faith' he compared to the present-day medium's difficulty in working with sceptics. When Christ asked, 'Who has touched me? Much virtue has passed out of me,' He but spoke as many a modern healer speaks on feeling a loss of

---

55 This parenthesis was inserted by *Light*, and was not Doyle writing in the third person.
56 Violet Tweedale's *Ghosts I Have Seen* is the book in question.

power. 'Try the spirits whether they be of God' is what all Spiritualists of to-day should vigorously practise.

"Conan Doyle in his book, 'The New Revelation,' touches upon those facts . . . and I remembered the impressive talk I had so many years ago with Mr. Gladstone. As Conan Doyle truly says, 'The early Christian Church was saturated with Spiritualism.'"

This should reassure Mr. Kernahan, unless he includes Mr. Gladstone also in his heresy-hunt.

It is perhaps peculiar for the modern reader to consider that Doyle's argument was essentially that because Gladstone was once a Prime Minister and was a pious man, his opinion on Spiritualism was correct. Yet Doyle and his contemporaries' arguments were carrying the day. "In all parts of the country the provincial Press has letters and notices on Spiritualism. Far too many cuttings reach us for separate notices," *Light* noted on February 14th, 1920.

*Light* predicted the Church's attitude to Spiritualism would be a leading topic for months, and in April 1920, quoted a striking metaphor from Doyle when interviewed by the *Evening Standard* about how he saw the Church's position and future relationship to Spiritualism:

> What has happened to the Christian religion is that they have taken the engine off. The engine was Spiritualism, and the result is that the train is gradually coming to a stop. It is as certain as Christianity renovated Rome that Spiritualism is going to renovate Christianity.[57]

This view informed much of Doyle's speech at the anniversary celebrations of modern Spiritualism held at the Queen's Hall on March 31st, 1920. The report summarised his attitude as he mixed military and religious language in a muscular address.

---

57 Quoted in *Light*, April 10th, 1920

*Light, April 10, 1920*

## SIR ARTHUR CONAN DOYLE
(Doyle's address at the anniversary celebrations)
### THE ANNIVERSARY OF MODERN SPIRITUALISM.

Sir A. Conan Doyle said there was a famous battalion in the British army which carried its badge on both sides of its helmet. Spiritualists, he considered, might well carry their badge all round, because they were attacked not only from the front and rear but on every side. People were content to accept as apostolic what happened in the time of Tiberius Caesar, but when they saw exactly the same events occurring at the present day they considered that they came from the devil. They had never tried, however, to convince us as to what the devil thought he was doing by going about endeavouring to prove to us the immortality of the soul! They were there that night to celebrate the seventy-second anniversary of what Spiritualists considered to be the greatest event which had occurred in the world for two thousand years, and what they considered likely to be also the greatest event in the other world.

This movement was really a return to primitive Christianity, but Christianity had become so twisted that if its august Founder came back He would not recognise His own work. Our movement was a return to the simplicity and purity which marked those early days. To anyone familiar with early Christianity the parallel was extraordinarily close. Seneca deplored the decadence of his age. People had lost their faith in the old gods and he wondered how they would carry on without them. All the time if he had gone down into his own kitchen the cook, who would probably have been a Christian (as most of the slaves were Christians), would have told him that there was a spiritual power at work in their midst that would give them the help they needed. Was that not like Dean Inge? He wrote a book about the decadence of religion as shown by the emptiness of the churches. While all the time there was a power among us that would do the work. If he would only go among the Spiritualists he would realise this.

### NO GREAT OUTSTANDING FIGURE.

A singular fact about the Spiritualist movement was that there was in it no great outstanding figure. That could not be said of any other religion. The reason was that our great men were all on the other side. Here we were only the agents. We had got no one, we had got everybody — we had the whole heavenly host behind us! (Applause.) He spoke of two great men who had preceded this movement — Swedenborg and Andrew Jackson Davis. The Churches made much of the points of difference amongst us. We should, on the contrary, insist upon our points of agreement. He would urge that we ought to hold out our hands to Swedenborgians and Theosophists. Let us make one great phalanx fighting for the spiritual cause!

## SWEDENBORG AND DAVIS.

Swedenborg was one of the most wonderful men that ever lived. In every branch of knowledge, from Biblical criticism to engineering, he was an expert. To this man in his sixtieth year came the power of clairvoyance. "I think," said Sir Arthur, "that Swedenborg's knowledge was his weakness. He could not fit in all his new knowledge into what he knew already. That was the reason why he produced something in the nature of a mystical Bible. But putting aside his rather pompous phraseology we must remember that he was the first man who said that after death we pass into a world very like that in which we now live, and that dying does not alter a man's character, but leaves him the same as before with his tastes and feelings unchanged. These points are the centre of our faith to-day, so that I am not far wrong in claiming that Swedenborg was the father of our movement. He communicated with beings whom he describes as angels, but he discovered that all the angels had lived on this earth."

It was impossible, in Sir Arthur's view, to find two men presenting greater points of difference than Swedenborg and Andrew Jackson Davis. The son of a cobbler, Davis, up to the age of nineteen, had only read one book, and that a bad one. At that age he, in an hypnotic trance, dictated that remarkable book, "The Principles of Nature." Later came the magnificent "Harmonial Philosophy," a work little known here but which had been through forty-five editions in the United States. In it is to be found a depth of knowledge and a breadth of conception, such as few books in the world possessed. Davis had never read Swedenborg, yet in what he depicted of the next state we came back to Swedenborg's line of teaching that it was this world raised to a more etherial plane, that its occupations were similar, and that what we called death would seem, in looking back on it, but a very trifling incident in the soul's long upward journey.

Since the time of these two remarkable men there had been in England two great seers — Stainton Moses and George Vale Owen. He regarded the latter especially with reverence, knowing his simple, honourable character. He thought him one of the greatest seers of all time. Sir Arthur then gave an outline of what occurred with the Fox sisters in 1848 at Hydesville. No man could say what limits might be set to the revelations which were then begun. The gates were down, the barrier was passed, nothing intervened between them and death and that long stretch which was going to carry them through another stage on that eternal journey which lay before them. (Applause.)

*

Celebrations to one side, a more serious matter weighing on Spiritualists' minds was the upcoming Lambeth Conference. When it became clear that Spiritualism would be one of the subjects under discussion, Doyle put in a plea in *Light* to four Bishops who had critiqued Spiritualism to give the faith a fair hearing.

*Light, May 15, 1920.*

As the Bishops will soon be called upon to consider this all-important question, I would earnestly and respectfully beg them to read at least one book which is sympathetic with the subject and written with knowledge. To read books written by its enemies and traducers, such as Canon Barnes or the Rev. A. V. Magee, is as fair as it would be for an inquirer to gain his knowledge of the Church from the writings of Bradlaugh or Ingersoll. The particular book which I should recommend as covering every aspect of the matter is 'Man's Survival After Death,' by the Rev. C. L. Tweedale, published by Grant Richards.

*

It wasn't only Anglicans who were having to deal with this surge in Spiritualism. On March 13th 1920 *Light* reported that "The Pious

Denomination" had appeared in the German town of Falkenberg, near Halle. It was "making converts so rapidly that the remainder of the population has called on the Government to take steps to restrain it." It went on, "Not only do the devotees claim that they are in special and permanent relations with the Holy Ghost, but they also allege that the spirits of their departed kinsfolk regularly appear to them. Particularly are the many war widows of Falkenberg said to be in close contact with their dead husbands."

*The Daily Telegraph* commented on the Great War's effects.

"The war lasted too long," it said, and the Churches "proved as little satisfying to the needs of humanity as any political or social institution." This resulted in "blighting criticism" and the people "turned their faces despairingly elsewhere". The article went on: "...today a restless, weary, uncertain, puzzled, and — in spite of its feverish pleasures — saddened world feels itself untouched by the message of the Churches."

On July 6th, 1920, at the first day of the ten-yearly Lambeth Conference, the Church acceded to requests from Fielding-Ould, Conan Doyle and others to adopt an "official line" on Spiritualism. Although the disparate elements of the Anglican Communion are autonomous, the Lambeth Conference's resolutions would be influential in setting guidance for future thinking throughout the Anglican sphere.

Thirty-seven bishops were specially appointed to investigate and report, while resolutions were passed by the whole assembly. *Light* noted: "The committee find evidence that, especially under the stress of the horrors and anxieties of the war, and particularly in crowded areas, Spiritualism has affected in some instances even regular churchgoers, withdrawing them from the Church. It notes that belief in the reality of the nearness of the other world has been deepened by the war."[58]

The Church's official line appeared as follows in *Light* on August 21st, 1920, in *The Lambeth Conference, On Spiritualism, Christian Science And Theosophy*:

> It is possible that we may be on the threshold of a new science, which will by another method of approach confirm us in the assurance of a world behind and beyond the world we see, and of something within us by which we are in contact with it.

---

58 *Light*, August 21st, 1920

We could never presume to set a limit to means which God may use to bring man to the realisation of spiritual life. But there is nothing in the cult erected on this science which enhances, there is, indeed, much which obscures, the meaning of that other world and our relation to it as unfolded in the Gospel of Christ and the teaching of the Church, and which depreciates the means given to us of attaining and abiding in fellowship with that world.

The united Conference recognised the Church's common ground with Spiritualism, Christian Science and Theosophy in protesting against materialism, but warned that they ignored or explained away Christ's importance. The article went on:

They recognise that new phenomena of consciousness have been presented, which claim, and at the hands of competent psychologists, have received, careful investigation, and, as far as possible, the application of, scientific method. But such scientific researches have confessedly not reached an advanced stage, and they claim to be supported by the best psychologists in warning their people against accepting as final theories which further knowledge may disprove, and still more against the indiscriminate and undisciplined exercise of psychic powers, and the habit of recourse to séances, "seers," and mediums.

Regarding Spiritualism specifically, the Conference awaited more research, and advised that Church teaching must emphasise communion with Christ to counter the movement. It added,

While recognising that the results of investigation have encouraged many people to find a spiritual meaning and purpose in human life and led them to believe in survival after death, grave dangers are seen in the tendency to make a religion of Spiritualism. The practice of Spiritualism as a cult involves the subordination of the intelligence and the will to unknown forces or personalities and, to that extent, an abdication of self-control.

Responses in *Light* were mixed. Convinced medium Reverend Charles L Tweedale complained that:

> ...the dictum of the Conference is that psychologists are to decide on the genuineness of modern psychic phenomena, and that neither Church nor people may receive them until this decision is given. From this it logically follows that the Conference and the Church it represents must forthwith reject and treat as suspect all the Old Testament records of similar visions, voices and other 'supernatural' experiences therein recorded, and all the New Testament ones on which Christianity is based, until psychologists have sat in judgment on them and pronounced them genuine. Will they do this? When did the Church ever submit the Bible psychic phenomena to the judgment of psychologists, or accept the genuineness of these phenomena at their hands?[59]

On the same page, a more conciliatory "Geeson" took a more optimistic tone:

> The position taken by the Bishops at the Lambeth Conference shows a gradual broadening of view and a more dispassionate and much fairer attitude to the subject than of yore. The Conference sees dangers in connection with it, and no intelligent Spiritualist has ever denied their existence, but the active agency, behind the phenomena, of an almost all-powerful spirit of evil is nowhere suggested. The Devil has disappeared from the scene!

By the late summer of 1920, an uneasy armistice broke out between Spiritualism and Anglicanism.

On August 21st, 1920 *Light* commented that the dominating note of Somerset Maugham's play *The Unknown* was the question: "Has the war killed religious faith?"

Perhaps the bishops had begun to wonder this, too.

After the Lambeth Conference many bishops appeared to

---

59 *Light*, August 28th, 1920

acknowledge that at least Spiritualism provided some form of proof that the world of spirit was real.

Even some of Spiritualism's harshest detractors softened. The Reverend A V Magee was noted in *Light* on September 4th as restating his objections in a "much more temperate tone."

Magee wrote, "Let us admit, once for all... that we can get in touch with the dead, because no one who has ever studied the question really doubts this."

Yet he still sounded warnings: "Hitherto, Spiritualists have failed to convince us that the séance and planchette are either safe or certain methods of approaching the dead." This, he contrasted with the Church's approach: "In prayer and communion the Church gets into 'touch with the dead' every day, and she has had visions and voices from the Unseen which cannot be denied." Then, seemingly unable to stop himself from falling back into stronger criticism, he noted the "grave peril both to reason and health" of Spiritualism.

Nevertheless, by the end of 1920, after the Lambeth Conference, the Church's view was that in contrast to materialism, Spiritualism at least advocated spirit.

It is tempting to portray the Church's position as "My enemy's enemy is my friend" - or even - "Better the devil you know than no devil at all."

Those Christians who suspected Spiritualism of diabolism could draw strength from knowing it confirmed the eternal struggle that had marked their religion for millennia.

It was business as usual.

As for the common enemy, the materialists, it was these upon whom Conan Doyle concentrated much of his attention, and who in turn would concentrate their attentions upon him as he grew increasingly vociferous. More so, as the claims he made for his religion and the spirit contacts he experienced became more noteworthy.

One such contact came late in 1919.

# Chapter 8
## Contact

When *The Vital Message* was published in October 1919, its evangelistic tone made clear how far Doyle's publicly-stated beliefs had developed, as did the gruelling tour of talks he threw himself into around the country. There had been so much death in Doyle's life already, and another came in February 1919, when his brother Innes also succumbed to Spanish flu. Was it possible to remain objective in the midst of such death and grief?

While arguments ebbed and flowed between proponents of the crucifix and the planchette, the state of the battle for minds was revealed by the multitudes flocking to hear Doyle's reasoned arguments that resounded with emotional honesty.

On June 28th 1919, *Light* reported that at one address, Doyle criticised "those investigators who talk to the spirit world in the way a sergeant-major might use in addressing the youngest recruit." He spoke from personal experience. He had attended numerous séances. He hit home because he bore witness to events he'd seen with his own eyes.

His bearing witness took on a far more personal tone after his son's death in 1918 and the subsequent communications he received from him. Kingsley first contacted him through Mrs Annie Brittain, the medium to whom Doyle had personally directed numerous sitters, referred to by him as "Mrs B" to protect her privacy

Mrs B. also communicated with Lily Loder-Symonds, war casualties Malcolm Leckie[60], Oscar Hornung[61] and Alec Forbes (Jean's nephew), and also with Innes. Doyle verified Lily's identity through a phrase known only to close members of the family; Malcolm Leckie by the gold coin he carried, which Doyle gave him to celebrate his first medical case; Kingsley by the use of his name (used only in the Doyle family) and a message reminding him of their disagreement about Spiritualism. "When I was alive I did not believe in spiritualism. Now I believe in it. I was a chuckle-headed ass not to believe in it," Kingsley told him.

---

60  Jean Conan Doyle's brother.
61  Doyle's nephew and the creator of fictional thief, *Raffles*.

On October 11th, 1919 an article in *Light* gave an inkling of anextraordinary encounter.

> Sir Arthur Conan Doyle, at his lecture at Wimbledon, on Sunday night, described how he recently heard the voice of his son who has been dead a year. "I was in a darkened room," he said, "with five men, my wife, and an amateur medium. I bound the medium in six places with string. My wife later gave a little cry, and I heard the voice of my son. My son said : 'Father.' I replied : 'Yes, my boy.' He said : Forgive. me.' I knew to what he referred. We had only one difference in all his lifetime — his non-belief in Spiritualism. I reassured him, and he replied: 'I am so happy.' Then his voice faded away. I state definitely that I spoke to my son, and that I heard his voice. I would be a most blasphemous liar if what I told you were not true." Approached by a newspaper representative with a request for further information, Sir Arthur Conan Doyle resolutely declined to be interviewed. "It is too sacred and delicate a subject to be discussed in cold blood," he said.

More detail soon appeared.

*Light, October 18, 1919*

### SIR A. CONAN DOYLE EXPLAINS.

In reply to a correspondent who asked Sir Arthur Conan Doyle, regarding the séance described in our last issue, how it was that the spirit of his son said "Father" when it was a cry from his mother that called him up, and why the room was darkened, Sir Arthur writes in the "Daily Express," in which paper the query appeared: —

"I do not propose to enter upon any discussion over the case which I quoted at Wimbledon, because there is an element of levity introduced too often into these debates which would be offensive to me. In answer to your correspondent's questions, however, I may say: —

"1. That my son called 'Father!' because it was to me that he wished to speak. His mother is with him.

"2. That long experience of psychic science has shown that all physical phenomena are quicker and more powerful in the dark. The probable reason is that the ether which conveys light by its vibration is the physical basis used for the phenomena. A red light has been found, as in photography, to be the least deterrent.

"3. The voice was my son's voice, as also was the manner. Both my wife and I are agreed on that. The gentleman who acted as medium was some yards away. The voice was within a foot or so of my face. The other sitters — four gentlemen, two ladies — had their own convincing experiences.

*

The following month, *Light* published Conan Doyle's full account of this extraordinary séance held in Southsea, the town where his interest in Spiritualism first stirred.

*Light, December 27, 1919*

## A WONDERFUL SEANCE.
## SIR A. CONAN DOYLE'S ACCOUNT.

Sir A. Conan Doyle, it will be remembered, in his recent address at Wimbledon, referred (as already reported by us) to a sitting he had had with Mr. Powell, the Welsh medium, at which he had spoken with his son who had passed over. We are now able to give from the "Two Worlds" Sir Arthur's story of this event in detail:-

Upon the occasion of my lecture at Portsmouth, Mr. Powell returned with me to our rooms, and most kindly gave us a sitting. There were present my wife, sitting on my left, Mr. Frank Blake, President of the Southern Counties Spiritualist Union, upon my right; next to him Mr. and Mrs. MacFarlane, leaders of the Portsmouth branch; and on their right Mr. Harry Engholm, once well known upon the London press, and now one of the leading cinema producers, in the world. This gentleman was intellectually convinced of the truth of Spiritualism, but had never before been to a séance. Mr. Powell insisted upon being searched, and was then bound by me to a wooden armchair. Remembering the possibility of getting out of bonds of rope—especially such cable-like rope as is used by Mr. Maskelyne in his absurd bogus performances—I cut six lengths of stout twine, and tied the medium in six places to the arms and legs of the chair. So thoroughly was this done, that at the end of the sitting it was quite impossible to loosen him, and we were compelled to cut him free. A small megaphone belonging to the late Admiral Moore was placed beside him. This was circled with luminous paint so as to be visible in the dark. The lights were then turned out, and the room in total darkness, we sitting in a semi-circle round the medium, but none of us touching him, though we joined hands with each other, so as to intervene between him and the room.

Within a couple of minutes the breathing of the medium became loud and stertorous. A voice then addressed us, which issued from his own lips, but which was quite unlike his normal voice, and remained absolutely consistent throughout. It was deep, strong and virile, while that of Mr. Powell was essentially Welsh, gentle, musical and rather clipped. The voice greeted the company, and announced the presence of Black Hawk, the control. The deep voice spoke with an air of good-humoured raillery, addressing us by name. I was christened "Great Chief" and Mr. Engholm "Little Chief," with all good wishes to our respective wigwams. There was an interval of silence while the steady snoring of the medium sounded in the darkness. Then we saw the luminous band of the megaphone rise in the air, and it circled round our heads, sometimes slow, sometimes swift, as smoothly as if it were swung at the end of a string. Then it remained motionless, poised in the air above us. Presently it vanished, and returned with flowers taken from the mantelpiece inserted into its narrow end. These flowers, I may say, were at our backs and quite out of reach of the medium. They were carried round to our noses in the dark with an accuracy which showed that whoever held them could see very plainly where we were. We were then touched by various objects which proved to be taken from the mantelpiece and elsewhere, but lay within the circle when the light was eventually turned on.

Black Hawk had spoken from time to time, and the breathing of the medium continued steadily from the same position. The Indian control now said, "Leely is here, Leely wishes to speak with the lady of the Wigwam." A dear friend of ours named Lily died some years ago, and as she had shared our spiritual experiences we had always believed she might be the first to find her way back. We can trace no way by which her name or existence could have been known to the medium. An instant later a quick, excited voice said, "Jean, Jean, I am here." In the darkness I could hear incoherent words of love as the two friends gasped out little messages of affection. My wife assures me that the voice was that of the dead lady, but I could not hear enough to be able to corroborate. Then came silence again, with a brisk current of cold air which played upon our faces. Shortly afterwards we turned up the light, and found to our surprise that a great wooden pedestal, weighing, I should think, from forty to fifty pounds, had been brought from the corner and placed in the centre of our semi-circle. Some people may reasonably ask what is the use of heavy phenomena of that sort in the presence of the finer ones, but at least in its solid materialism it gave a sufficient answer to those who might be rash enough to suppose that our imaginations had produced the other results.

Next evening we sat at the same hour, under the same conditions, save that the medium was weary, having delivered an exhausting address. Physical phenomena and movements of the luminous trumpet were as before, and the huge pedestal was once more lifted into the circle, and was placed upon my head. An examination had shown us that the heavy crown of this pedestal was balanced upon a single loose screw in a wide socket, so that any careless handling would have sent it down with terrific effect upon our skulls. In spite of the darkness it was held so steadily that there was no accident, but the strength which placed it so gently on my head, and afterwards rubbed the side of it down my cheek, must have been enormous.

Then came what to me was the supreme moment of my spiritual experience. It is almost too sacred for full description, and yet I feel that God sends such gifts that we may share them with others. There came a voice in the darkness, a whispered voice, saying. "Jean, it is I." My wife felt a hand upon her head, and cried, "It is Kingsley." I heard the word "Father." I said, "Dear boy, is that you?" I had the sense of a face very near my own, and of breathing. Then the clear voice came again with an intensity and note very distinctive of my son, "Forgive me!" His life was so admirable that I could only think that he referred to our perfectly good-humoured difference about Spiritualism, concerning which, in the bustle of his medical and military life, he really had no chance of forming an opinion, I told him eagerly that I had no grievance of any kind. A large, strong hand then rested upon my head, it was gently bent forward, and I felt and heard a kiss just above my brow. "Tell me, dear, are you happy?" I cried. There was silence, and I feared he was gone. Then on a sighing note came the words, "Yes, I am so happy." Whilst this was going on I was dimly conscious that another conversation, to which reference is made below, was going on between Mr. Engholm and some voice at the other end of the semi-circle.

A moment afterwards another gentle voice, claiming to be that of my wife's mother, recently deceased, was heard in front of us. We could not have recognised the voice as we could the other. A few loving words were said, and then a small, warm hand patted both our cheeks, with a little gesture which was full of affection.

Such were my own experiences. In a letter which lies before me, Mr. Engholm says: "The seance was conducted under unusually strict test conditions, and I for one was very much awake, indeed. All my senses were alert, and whilst Sir Arthur and his boy were carrying on a conversation of a very private and sacred nature, I was suddenly addressed by a very dear old friend, a. well-known newspaper correspondent, in terms and on a subject that left no doubt in my mind as to who the unseen personality was. There were as a result two distinctively different voices speaking at the same time, each of which could be recognised by voice characteristic alone. My ears did not deceive me."

*

Doyle had studied psychic phenomena with scientific detachment for 30 years. He had personally experienced psychic phenomena and communication with loved ones. But he had never before touched his own dead child at a séance.

Spiritualism by now had taken hold of him, intellectually, emotionally and creatively, as evidenced by his book of Spiritualist-inspired poems, *The Guards Came Through,* published in 1919.

A review in *Light* on January 3rd, 1920, described "the stirring vigour of the verse as, with alternating tension and relief, we watched on Flanders fields the tide of battle roll forward and back and again forward, or, standing on the Surrey hills, listened to the distant booming of the guns." In the poem *The Wreck on Loch McGarry* Doyle dealt with "isolated phenomena which have been proved", and in another "poured out his vials of scorn on *The Bigot*."

The final poem (extract below) was dedicated to "one of the most sacred experiences of the author's life -"

> It was granted me to stand
>    By my dead,
> I have felt the vanished hand
>    On my head,
> On my brow the vanished lips.
> And I know that Death's eclipse
> Is a floating veil that slips
>    Or is shed.

The reviewer went on:

> "Sir Arthur is a born fighter, and he cannot feel that such an experience is meant to be received with a gratitude that is silent and actionless. It is rather a call to strike harder against the foes of human progress and enlightenment, and he ends, with a prayer that the great Guide of his life will -"

> Trace my pathway among men,
> Show me how to strike, and when,
> Take me to the fight—and then
>    Oh, be nigh!

Doyle was indeed a "born fighter". He soon became embroiled in arguments with Canon Wilson in an exchange of letters in the *Worcester Advertiser*[62]. Talking with other departed family members was yet more evidence for his case.

> When I have to discuss Spiritualism I always feel as a New Yorker might who heard an argument as to whether there was

---

62  Quoted in *Light*, January 10th, 1920

such a place as America. The thing to him is certain, and yet he can only keep on repeating that he has been there. I have seen and felt these psychic things. I have talked face to face again and again, beyond all question or doubt, with my dead, and yet I can only assert the fact, and mention those others who were present. I want no scientific expert to tell me the truth of it, and yet I have no means of conveying that truth to another.

The last occasion was in Wales this month (December). My brother came to me and announced himself by giving his family pet name, which I will venture to say no one in Wales could know. He then spoke to me about the health of his wife in Copenhagen as clearly as he could have done if he were in the flesh, and finally gave me a Danish name in reply to my question whether psychic treatment might be good in her case. I noted the name, which was pronounced three times, and I wrote to a Danish friend who informed me that there was such a person in Denmark, and that he was interested in psychic matters. I then communicated with my sister-in-law. Now I ask any reasonable person whence came that name? The medium, an amateur, was bound and breathing heavily some distance away. If he had not been, but had been awake and at liberty, how could he know of this person living in the particular town about which I wanted information? It was not telepathy, since I had certainly never heard of the man. It seems to me pure perversity to ascribe such cases to any cause save the one which they claim for themselves —namely, spirit communion.

In the same report, Doyle also commented regarding certain "unfair tactics" of opponents.

It is worth while to draw attention to one disability from which Spiritualists suffer in argument, even at the hands of those who, like Canon Wilson, desire to be fair. Spiritualist writers set out to tell the whole truth and they, do not, as a rule, disguise that mediums are sometimes fraudulent, that communications are sometimes false, and that evil influences may appear. These concessions are instantly extracted and quoted against them, while their, opponents suppress all that is said on the other side, the assured knowledge the deep consolation, the moral help, the certainty in an age of doubt. Thus an entirely false impression is created. To take an obvious example, anyone reading Canon Wilson's paper would really imagine, save for one line, that Sir Oliver Lodge, instead of being the brave protagonist of Spiritualism, was himself in doubt upon the subject. I continually find my own books quoted in the same way against myself. Still I am of opinion that to be truthful and fair is always in the end the better policy, whatever momentary advantage may be taken by our opponents of our admissions, that every good thing may be abused.

Doyle's devotion to Spiritualism also encompassed his family on this side of The Veil, as described at one of the many talks he gave around the country.

*Light, July 17, 1920*

### SIR A CONAN DOYLE AT HOVE

Sir A. Conan Doyle, in a vivid and stirring address, said : "The revelation of Spiritualism during the past few years marks an epoch in the world's history as great as the Reformation, or the discovery of America. We have thrown bridges over the river of death. We have established our posts on the far side. We have made reconnaissances deeply into that formerly unknown country. We have brought back the tidings. The pioneers know all that has been done. The news has not yet penetrated to the whole Army, still less to the rear guard. But once you are across that river, the tendency always is to consolidate, to increase your boundary, until at last that river will be taken entirely inside your own intellectual boundary. From that time onward there will in truth be no death."

Sir Arthur went on: "Think of the fear taken from the human heart. Think of the tears wiped from human eyes. Think also of the enormous consolation given to us when we can realise that, in spite of so much which seems to our blind eyes to prove the contrary, none the less God is really All Good, All Kind. From that vantage point we get a new perspective that enables us to understand the difficult things of life."

Spiritualism was described by Sir Arthur as a kind of three-storeyed house. He said, "the first storey is that of physical phenomena. Rough, puerile as these phenomena often are, they serve as starting points to stir us out of our complacency, and set us studying. Eventually we come to the things that mean the difference between faith and knowledge." As an instance, Sir Arthur quoted a remarkable personal experience, that happened a few days ago.

AN EXPERIENCE IN THE NURSERY.

He, his wife, and two friends were holding a service in the children's nursery. They were singing "Onward, Christian soldiers" (it was a sheer fallacy to say that the Spiritualists did not revere the name of Jesus), when suddenly a fifth voice joined in the singing, beautiful, clear, dominating the other four voices. There could be no possible mistake or doubt about it. There was only one explanation. It was a case of spiritual intervention.

"The second storey of Spiritualism," he continued, "is the effect on the individual, in that it robs him of all the fear of death. (Loud applause.) To the Spiritualist, death is promotion; his friends are waiting for him. The third storey is the application of Spiritualism to the universe. It gives us a philosophy of religion, and an explanation of man's fate in the beyond."

*

Doyle was quoted by *Light* on September 18th 1920 in a letter to *The Banner*, describing how he and his wife, Jean, raised their children in the bosom of the faith. "I bring up my three little children, eleven, nine and seven, as Spiritualists. The result is that they have no fear at all of death, and have no doubts at all about the goodness of God. 'Won't it be jolly when we all come together again?'—they say quite naturally. May your work be blessed."

On September 11th 1920, *Light* quoted a *Strand* article in which Doyle expanded on his beliefs and its meanings.

The question has often been asked, 'What was the purpose of so strange a movement at this particular time, granting that it is all that it claims to be?' Governor Tallmadge, a United States Senator of repute, was one of the early converts to the new cult, and he has left it upon record that he asked this question upon two separate occasions in two different years from different mediums. The answer in each case was almost identical.

"The first said, 'It is to draw mankind together in harmony, and to convince sceptics of the immortality of the soul.' The second said, 'To unite mankind and to convince sceptics of the immortality of the soul.'"

Sir Arthur comments: "Surely this is no ignoble ambition and does not justify those narrow and bitter attacks from ministers and the less progressive of their flocks from which Spiritualists have up to the present day had to suffer."

Sir Arthur adds: "The first half of the definition is, I think, particularly important, for I believe that one of the ultimate results of this movement will be to unite Christianity upon a common basis so strong and, indeed, self-sufficient that the quibbles which separate the Churches of to-day will be seen in their true proportion and will be swept away or disregarded."

So, what did Spiritualism give Doyle that Christianity thus far hadn't? There are many answers. It is possible Doyle found personal solace in the idea that Spiritualism suggested that the soul remained intact despite physical failings. He wrote about his initial materialist position as a young man in his book, *Memories And Adventures:*

From my point of view the mind (and so far as I could see the soul, which was the total effect of all the hereditary or personal functionings of the mind) was an emanation from the brain and entirely physical in its nature. I saw, as a medical man, how a spicule of bone or a tumour pressing on the brain would cause what seemed an alteration in the soul. I saw also how drugs or alcohol would turn on fleeting phases of virtue or vice. The physical argument seemed an overpowering one. It had never struck me that the current of events might really flow in the opposite direction, and that the higher faculties could only manifest themselves imperfectly through an imperfect instrument. The broken fiddle is silent and yet the musician is the same as ever.

This conclusion would have given him consolation in the face of his father's mental illness; only the physical body that received communication from the soul was faulty - his soul remained whole.

Spiritualism also gave him a coherent philosophy and faith which enabled him to shoulder his grief, while satisfying his intellectual, creative, religious and emotional needs. It led to an entire way of life – a religion that encompassed all other religions and showed them the errors of their ways, uniting them into a coherent whole. It even bridged the gap between science and religion.

This last assertion would be examined and tested further when he encountered very different detractors from the Church.

The materialists, too, would have their say.

## Chapter 9
## Cynics, Materialists and Pressmen

While the Church of England hedged its bets about Spiritualism for fear of denying spirit and losing a potential ally, the materialists had no such strategic considerations. There were three main weapons at their disposal: criticism of psychic experiments, arguments from reason - and good old-fashioned mockery. They used all in good measure.

Doyle was unmoved by appeals to reason or to science. After 30 years of investigation, his experience vastly outstripped his critics'. As far as he was concerned, arguments that his conclusions were the result of 30 years of repeated error simply would not stand.

In 1912 Doyle had debated by letter the possibility of human survival with Hubert Stansbury, materialist author of *In Quest of Truth*. In 1913 he had heard that his friend, Sir Oliver Lodge, had told the British Association for the Advancement of Science to use science to study psychic phenomena, he wrote to Lodge, alluding to the exchange between him and Stansbury and affirming his view that spiritual truths "do not depend on that two-edged business, Faith, but upon direct reason."[63]

This line hardened further over the years, as this extract from *Light* of March 1st, 1919, shows:

> Sir Arthur Conan Doyle, speaking at the Theatre Royal, Merthyr, on February 16th on "Death—and the Hereafter," said that Spiritualists knew, from experiments and research, what happened after death. Anyone who studied the evidence had absolute proof of what the truth was. Messages from those who had passed over to the "other side" were in agreement that death, far from being painful, was a pleasant process, and that, experiencing a happiness such as they never imagined in this world, none of them wished to return.

With arguments from science and reason ineffective against Doyle's faith,mockery remained . Serving a purpose different from honest

---

63  Andrew Lycett, *Conan Doyle, The Man Who Created Sherlock Holmes*

debate, mockery can entrench the views of its target, but is effective in the battle for public opinion. No surprise, then, that it was a common tactic of the Press. To mockery, Doyle remained largely silent, with occasional flashes of exasperation.

It is easy to imagine Doyle as a lone eccentric ploughing a deluded, grief-filled furrow in the face of science and reason. Such a picture is wrong. Doyle was only the most famous of an illustrious band of Spiritualist scientists, which included:

- Sir William Crookes, who identified the first isolated sample of helium, and whose work the *Oxford Dictionary of National Biography* notes "made possible the discovery of X-rays as well as of the electron". His experiments were "the foundation of nuclear physics and of the electronic theory that altered the whole conception of chemistry and physics at the beginning of the twentieth century." After experiments in the 1870s and 1880s he became convinced of the reality of psychic force. He joined the Theosophical Society in 1883 and, after his wife's death, accepted the idea of human survival.

- Sir Oliver Lodge, the author of *Raymond*, who developed key patents in wireless telegraphy.

- Alfred Russel Wallace, who independently of Charles Darwin developed his own theory of evolution. His paper on variation, published alongside Darwin's in 1858 prompted Darwin to write *On The Origin of Species*. Wallace later suggested Darwin use the phrase "survival of the fittest" as an alternative to "natural selection" to describe an organism's adaptation to the environment. His influence on modern thought is profound.

Alongside these stood many others, including renowned French astronomer Camille Flammarion. In 1905, Flammarion's compatriots, Nobel laureates Pierre and Marie Curie and Charles Richet had joined other eminent scientists to investigate the medium Eusapia Palladino in the hope of discovering a new source of energy. Pierre Curie reported:

...the phenomena that we saw appeared inexplicable as trickery — tables raised from all four legs, movement of objects from a distance, hands that pinch or caress you, luminous apparitions. All in a [setting] prepared by us with a small number of spectators all known to us and without a possible accomplice. The only trick possible is that which could result from an extraordinary facility of the medium as a magician. But how do you explain the phenomena when one is holding her hands and feet and when the light is sufficient so that one can see everything that happens?

*- Susan Quinn.*
*Marie Curie: A Life. Simon and Schuster.*
*pp. 208-226 (1995).*

Doyle, then, was no maverick mystic from the scientific community.

Ranged against him were materialists and rationalists, including many scientists, a vast corpus of newspapermen who were cynical by training and prone to take nothing at face value, and writers such as free-thinkers Joseph McCabe, Edward Clodd and H G Wells. All had an instinct something was wrong at the heart of Spiritualism which they considered to be either self-delusion or a refined development of the confidence trick found in the fairground fortune-teller's booth.

One of Spiritualism's most trenchant critics was the aforementioned Edward Clodd, a writer, banker and friend of novelist H G Wells. In his 1917 book *The Question: "If a man die, shall he live again?"* Clodd had attacked the mediums used by Sir Oliver Lodge, stating that they "may, with a large charity, be credited with believing themselves to be the vehicles of 'control' revelations, or, with less charity and more truth, be classed with the tricksters who 'work the oracle' by muscle-reading, sham trances, skilful guessing aided by hints from the sitters and by tapping common or special sources of information. They are either dreamy neurotics or humbugs."

Clodd's impatience with Spiritualism was also evident in his book *A Brief History and Examination of Modern Spiritualism,* in which he characterised Lodge's *Raymond* as "nauseating drivel" that "sullies the fair name of science." Clodd went on, "Every aspect of the Spiritualist movement is pernicious, and one which, at all costs, in support of sanity of public outlook, we should seek to stamp out with every weapon at our command."

*Light* reported Doyle defending his friend, Lodge, against Clodd in *The Strand* magazine[64]. Doyle emphasised the scientific rigour he'd applied in studies of psychic phenomena in an article titled "Is Sir Oliver Lodge Right?"

"If human testimony is capable of establishing anything, then it has absolutely proved the fact of survival. If anyone thinks that I exaggerate, let him before expressing his thought read the following books in the order given: Lodge's 'Survival of Man,' Hill's 'Psychical Investigations,' Stead's 'After Death,' Lodge's 'Raymond'..."

Doyle then described his own progress regarding psychic evidences:

> It took me many years to get as far as telepathy. Many more had passed before I could feel sure about survival and communication. I could have reached conviction much earlier had I used the recognised methods. An astronomer who discards a telescope may expect to be handicapped. I pushed caution to an excess. Since then, however, I have had personal experiences which I will not enter into at present which leave no doubt, in my mind.

Even the most hardened believer had to concede, though, that Spiritualism had reputational problems, some of which were to do with the fairground humbugs Clodd painted all Spiritualists to be. It was also open to easy mockery. *The Sybil And The Witch Finder,* in *Light* on October 13th 1917, quoted Mr Harold Ashton, a journalist writing in *Tit-Bits,* who had set out on a crusade among the fortune-tellers of London to expose their exploitation of the War for their own ends. He claimed to have had his fortune told fifty-six times in his researches, with uniformly poor results, but finally announced he had discovered a genuine fortune-teller.

His article was so filled with romantic clichés straight from a Victorian Penny Dreadful, it is difficult to judge whether it was lampooning Spiritualism, or making its case.

---

64  "Is Sir Oliver Lodge Right?" was reported in *Light* of July 7th, 1917.

> At the top of three flights of desperate stairs I found Sarah, the Sibyl of Notting Dale," wrote Ashton. "Gustave Doré , or George Cruikshank, would have delighted in illustrating this direful dame and the miserable surroundings which enfolded her. Her nutcracker face, yellow-toothed and parchment-skinned, was the face of a picture-book witch — her hands were claws. Sarah was the very apotheosis of dismality and dinginess."

So the lurid description continued, painting a picture of Sarah in a "bottle-green dress", sitting in her dingy room swaying to and fro on her bed and even creaking as she did so. He went on:

> The sibyl addressed me as "dearie," and, grabbing my hand in her own clammy claws, bent over it (still swaying), and in a high-pitched voice, and very rapidly, gibbered the main story of my life, from the days of my innocent childhood down to the present time. Changes of career and fortune and health and happiness she told me, without faltering and without a pause. She told me that the mystic figure 7 was stamped deep upon my palm. "Seven generations of the same name are yours," she cried — and that is true enough, as my family Bible testifies. From father to son, seven Williams have been born in a direct line in my family, and I am the seventh. I was christened William, though I never use the name except on legal documents. How came Sarah to know this? and many more strange things, and true, she told me! I had never seen her before — and I hope never to see her again.

Ashton wrote that the fortune teller claimed to once have been a successful clairvoyant to whom the fashionable set had beaten a path, but that her honesty had in the end frightened them off, and she had fallen into drinking gin, and poverty. The next part could have been straight from Dickens.

> "And now," says she, folding her skinny hands and fixing her hobgoblin eyes for the first time upon my face, "I'll tell you your fortune, if you like, for nix! Lie — lie, flatter, and cajole the fools in the world, and you're booked for a soft thing. Honesty's the

worst policy — live honest and you'll die poor! And drunk — if you're lucky!"

For twenty years and more I have sought among the spooks for an honest practitioner; here in the heart of Notting Dale's infamous Black Spot, and in the personality of this miserable old woman, I had found one at last. And this is what she had come to!

In a disdainful afterword, *Light* sought to distance itself from the article's sensationalist style, comparing Ashton to Matthew Hopkins, the great witch-finder general. This was not the scientific Spiritualism *Light* sought to promote.

In contrast to the Gothic squalor of Ashton's crone, an article on the same page entitled *Electrons to Infinity* used the latest theories about particle physics to argue for reincarnation. The two articles present an awkward juxtaposition, and in many ways symbolise the position of Spiritualists attempting to slough off old clichés and project their work as a scientific discipline.

As Spiritualism's influence grew, many in the Press became increasingly critical of its aspirations, and of Conan Doyle's increasing prominence within the movement. With the Great War now behind them, newspapers could afford to spend more time on the Spiritualist mania sweeping the country.

One focus of attention was a séance held in Cardiff in February 1919 by two brothers, mediums Will and Tom Thomas. It was attended by Conan Doyle and a long list of local worthies, including a J.P., the Chief Constable of Cardiff and several other police officers. Tom was strapped by a police officer to a chair beside a cabinet containing various objects including a doll and a tambourine. In the darkened room, amidst the hymn singing of the 20 or so Spiritualists present, the tambourine and doll were hurled across the room, a jacket was inexplicably dropped into Lady Conan Doyle's lap and objects including a guitar and a child's trumpet were observed floating in the air. When the lights came on, Tom was still strapped to the chair, stripped of his jacket, and the cabinet was empty. Conan Doyle, sitting quietly observing these extraordinary phenomena was convinced that this was indeed a genuine case of spirit agency.

Others were less impressed by such phenomena. An article in *The Times* highlighted the business opportunity Spiritualism raised for the sceptical stage magician and impresario Nevil Maskelyne:

*The Times, March 11, 1919*

### "SPIRITUALISM" BY TRICKERY
### MR MASKELYNE'S IMITATION

There has been a good deal of excitement of late in those circles which dabble in spiritualism concerning the Cardiff *séance*, at which, Sir Arthur Conan Doyle declares, there were strange happenings. While the medium was securely bound to his chair, tambourines were played, bells were rung, and the medium's coat was torn from his back.

The inevitable counter-attack, led, of course, by Mr Nevil Maskelyne has come, and at the St. George's Hall, the *séance* is being reproduced, but in this case trickery is admitted. There is not, of course, the same dark room or the same atmosphere of solemnity, but all the manifestations seem to be duly forthcoming. In this case the "medium" is Mr Goff Godfrey... Securely trussed, he is placed behind a screen, and within a minute tambourines and bells are hurtling through the air and his coat is off his back... The medium goes a step farther... he is secured in a sack, and next in a straitjacket. When done in the daylight at St. George's Hall the whole looks so simple – nothing like so difficult as other things one sees there – the disappearance into thin air, for instance, of a full-sized gramophone.

\*

Maskelyne took his show demonstrating what he labelled fraudulent séance phenomena around the country, often appearing in the same venues where Spiritualists had given public séances.

David Gow, editor of *Light,* was not amused by the hue and cry about the Cardiff séance, commenting in the March 1st 1919 issue that "People who had but the vaguest notion of the whole matter and its true meaning burst into the newspapers snorting and bellowing their wrath and indignation..." He went on, "It would be waste of time to go over the questions and comments offered by the opposition. Some of them are so absurd as to suggest that many of the critics did not even stop to think what they were writing about, for a few minutes' reflection would have enabled them to answer many of their own questions and objections. In the 'Daily Mail' of the 19th ult. Sir Arthur Conan Doyle points out that the phenomena he witnessed are 'very elementary and only useful as forming a final argument against materialism by showing that there are unquestionably powers, and intelligent powers, outside our ordinary senses.' That puts the matter in a nutshell, and answers reams of questions and criticisms from the unintelligent powers who live entirely in the radius of their very ordinary senses."

Doyle's thoughts were expanded on the next page.

*Light, March 1, 1919*

### INTERVIEWS WITH SIR ARTHUR CONAN DOYLE.

As mentioned in Notes by the Way, Sir Arthur Conan Doyle has been interviewed by a representative of the "Evening News" on the subject of his account in the Cardiff "Western Mail" of a recent séance for physical phenomena in that town. We give the following quotations: —

"The demonstrations [said Sir Arthur] are simple first lessons. They are the elementary step. Thousands of people come to my meetings already holding the faith that after life the spirit survives: and I tell them as plainly as I can that our religious beliefs are justified by what I state to be incontrovertible evidence of survival. There is more than the body: and without qualification I state now that we have proof of communication after death.

"I have been going about the country addressing meetings at which there was not an inch of room to spare. The audiences have been extraordinarily large. It would be a mistake to talk of the people as enthusiastic. That is not the word. They, if I may say so have been reverent. Wherever you go you find them serious and anxious— wanting light and comfort. . ."

This brought me (writes the interviewer) to the point I had wished to place before Sir Arthur.

He is one of the most famous of war historians and these historians want first-hand evidence and documents for everything that they put on paper. They approach their task pretty much as a judge does his. Then Sir Arthur's detective stories have placed him in the estimation of the public as one of the keenest of analytic minds of our time. I suggested that the ordinary man was the more astonished when he found Sir Arthur Conan Doyle accepting such incidents as that at Cardiff. I added that I had told such people that he never clouded the question in verbiage or vague and stately words, but came down firm, in the same curt English in which he writes, so that every man and woman could understand his bold meaning.

"That is the truth exactly," he replied. "I say that there is survival after death. I say that I have had proofs of it. I stand secure upon that belief. I am as sure of it as I am of the carpet under my feet."

*

In response to the Cardiff séance, the *Daily Express* laid down a challenge for any medium to produce under test conditions the spirit of a person who had died in living memory. If successful the medium would receive a reward of £500. Tom Thomas, initially reluctant to take part, was eventually persuaded to hold a séance in a darkened room before gathered members of the Press and Spiritualists, including *Light* editor, David Gow and Sir Arthur Conan Doyle.

The test proved inconclusive. There were phenomena of sorts. A shirt suspender and a pair of braces appeared, and some present claimed to see an efflorescent outline of a spirit. But since no one had checked to see whether Thomas was wearing braces or shirt sleeve suspenders beforehand, nothing could be made of their appearance. As for the spirit, not everyone saw it. The Spiritualists complained that hostile intentions interfered with the mediumistic process, while the Press essentially refused to believe anything if it came from the mouth of a Spiritualist. Which took the debate back to square one.

In a long article called *Psychic Science, The Press And The Public* in *Light* on March 22nd 1919, the exasperated David Gow bemoaned the *Express's* "obstinate persistence in entirely wrong methods, which lead nowhere except to confusion and distraction."

It was a point reinforced by the esteemed scientist W F Barrett the following week, who commented, "the methods of journalism are not the methods of science. The only useful fact in the 'Daily Express' enterprise is the testimony it affords to the widespread and growing interest in psychical research in general, and Spiritualism in particular."

Barrett's friend, Conan Doyle, set down a challenge to the Press.

*Light, March 22, 1919*

The "Evening Standard," which has given considerable attention to the subject of psychic phenomena, has published a proposal by Sir Arthur Conan Doyle (made to Mr. Ulyss Rogers, a representative of the journal, in an interview), that six newspapers—the "Evening Standard," the "Daily Sketch," "Daily Express," "Daily Mail," "Evening News" and "Daily Chronicle" shall send representatives for the purpose of considering a sheaf of correspondence in his possession. This correspondence consists of some thirty letters from various people who have visited Mrs. B., a well-known medium, and received what is regarded as conclusive evidence that they were actually in communication with departed friends.

\*

If Doyle expected to strike a knockout blow with letters from correspondents, he was to be disappointed. A brief note in the following issue of *Light* noted that the challenge "resulted in the visit to him of several representatives of daily papers, who published accounts of the evidence he submitted... Our readers will doubtless have read the accounts of some of them, so a fuller description here is unnecessary."

The letters had made little impression. If journalists didn't accept phenomena occurring in the room around them, why would they accept letters written by people they had never met?

It was clear Doyle considered the Press's criticisms of the letters dishonest and misguided.

*Light, July 5, 1919*

## NOTES BY THE WAY

In the course of his address at the Queen's Hall last Sunday Sir Arthur Conan Doyle effectively answered some of his critics in the Press. Incidentally he noticed the method of that one of them who, in analysing the letters, in which visitors to the medium, Mrs. B., had recorded their experiences, referred to the failures and the "successes," the latter word being put in inverted commas, to convey a slur by innuendo. We remember how the trick of the inverted commas was used some time ago by Mr. Edward Clodd in the case of Dr. Crawford's degree: "D.Sc." It was designed to suggest a bogus degree. This was very rash, because it was a real degree conferred by a Scottish University, and Mr. Clodd had to apologise. These petty methods, which are worthy of our opponents, suggest a poverty of mental resource and produce on the impartial observer an effect the reverse of that designed. Then there was the argument that the descriptions given by the medium were attributable to "thought reading." Sir Arthur made mincemeat of this objection when he pointed out that thought reading involves an experiment in the possibility of transferring from one mind to another some special idea or image. It could not apply to such cases as the visit of a stranger to the medium, who must, on this theory, be able to select from innumerable ideas, memories and experiences in the visitor's mind the identical ones which would alone fit the occasion. That would be wonderful enough, but in some instances visitors to this particular medium received communications on matters quite unknown to them, but afterwards verified. All this, of course, is elementary knowledge to the experienced Spiritualist, who is getting very weary of the asinine stupidity of some of his critics.

*

The prevailing tone of scepticism in some quarters was neatly summed up by the writer Arthur Machen, whose story *The Bowmen* was believed to be the genesis of the Angels of Mons[65] stories. His ironic tone

---

65  See Appendix A for a contemporary discussion of the Angels of Mons

was not appreciated by Gow whose counter-argument did little for his case.

"I was was once at a meeting of the Spiritualist Alliance," writes Mr. Arthur Machen in the "Evening News," "and one of the speakers observed, quite seriously, how odd it was that 'spirit photographs' were rarely obtained under strict test conditions, but were frequently produced when no special precautions against fraud had been taken. This circumstance did not strike me as odd." That reminds us that a number of credulous (or incredulous?) people do not believe that Mr. Machen's now famous story, "The Bowmen," was his own invention. They could argue that it was not produced "under strict test conditions." If we say that having seen nothing but the story itself, we are, nevertheless, firmly convinced of the true authorship, will Mr. Machen accuse us of credulity? Some day he may go to a psychic photographer—a complete stranger—and obtain a portrait of some departed friend, clearly recognisable, and not a copy of any photograph taken in life. Many people have done so. There are other criteria of the genuineness of a thing than observation of the conditions of its production.[66]

The exasperation of Spiritualists such as Gow and Doyle was palpable. Spiritualists felt they were on the edge of the greatest discovery known to humankind, and blamed critics for being irrationally obstinate.

Now appeared a new figure who came to prove the veracity of psychic phenomena and claim the £500 being offered by the *Express*. "Miss Smith" was a mysterious figure who wore a veil during her séances, thus earning her the sensationalist sobriquet "The Masked Medium". Conan Doyle attended a séance on the 27th March 1919 in a flat in West Central London, alongside other luminaries in the Spiritualist movement, a Superintendent from the CID, another police officer and the editor of *Light*.

Gow wrote:

---

66 *Light*, March 29th, 1919

Light, April 5, 1919

## THE MASKED MEDIUM "PRODUCES A SPIRIT"

The "masked medium," a lady of personable presence, but whose identity is still kept secret, commenced her demonstrations by giving psychometrical delineations of a kind new to us. That is to say, the articles were placed in a closed box and then described by her with striking accuracy; after which, without the objects being taken out and handled, she added some statements concerning the people with whom they were associated. In this respect her delineations were singularly like those given by the average psychometrist. This appeared to make a considerable impression on the uninitiated, and there was much discussion afterwards concerning clairvoyance, thought reading, the powers of the subconscious mind, and so forth. As a cautious observer we could only say afterwards that there seemed to be evidence of some supernormal power, whatever it might be called.

Then followed the sitting for materialisation, the room being in darkness except for the presence at one side of two screened lights of a kind that served little more than to make darkness visible. The music was furnished by a pianiste, and we were not asked to sing (for this relief, much thanks!). The medium appeared to be in some distress—a familiar note of the regular séance for materialisation. She groaned, sighed, and there was also the sound we know so well, stridulous breathing—the breath exhaling with a fluty noise accompanied by a kind of whispering. In short, the symptoms were precisely those of regular mediums in like circumstances. Shortly afterwards we noticed a luminous appearance on the hand of the lady who sat next to us, and examined it with some attention, ultimately finding that it proceeded from the gems in her ring which apparently reflected the light at the back. (Perhaps this is why some suspicious person afterwards detected the presence of a flash-light.)

Then at last came the ghost. A small luminous cloud "like a man's hand," or at least about the same size, appeared near or at the back of the medium; it moved about, enlarged and at last took some resemblance to a human form. It was irresistibly suggestive of the vaporous ghost or wraith of popular legend. It floated, hovering to and fro, and then, like a flying mist-wreath, took a horizontal position, swam back and forth, and finally vanished; after which the masked medium called for the lights to be turned up, and the cords and bandages which secured her to her chair were "inspected and found correct." At least, no one made any complaint.

During the proceedings the medium was stated to be levitated, but of this we saw nothing.

If it were a genuine manifestation, it was certainly a remarkable one, betokening the possession by the unknown lady of mediumship of a rare type, since it could yield such results in such circumstances. There seemed to be at least the preliminaries of materialisation. Assuming the reality of the mediumship and the demonstrations, we concluded that it represented at least a good *prima facie* case for further careful examination under suitable conditions. We are sorry to have to be so cautious and non-committal, especially when there is a lady in the case, but the peculiar circumstances must be our excuse.

*

Conan Doyle was equally circumspect, confirming to the *Sunday Express* that the Masked Medium had identified a ring that belonged to him which had been placed in a sealed box with other personal items of other attendees. She had even read the worn letters on the ring. Of the manifestation of the spirit, he was guarded – perhaps rightly so, before the British Press. "I should have to see it again before passing a definite opinion on it." He then added, "I have my doubts about the whole thing."

Despite his ambivalence in this case, his confidence in Spiritualism and his natural ebullience were much in evidence in an interview he gave during one of his many tour dates around Britain.

*Light April 12, 1919*

The "Daily Record and Mail" (Glasgow) contains an interview with Sir Arthur Conan Doyle, in the course of which he recorded his opinion that the church of the future would be in the home. Asked how the movement would "appeal to the more learned minds of the country," he said, "This thing is being run not from this side, but from the other. I think the question should be addressed there." As to the learned minds he remarked that as a rule the "highbrow" was a hopeless person; he was too clever. Sir Arthur proceeded:—

"We do not read that in the time of ancient Rome the great philosophers recognised the power and beauty of the teachings of Christ. Instead of accepting what is obvious, learned critics go searching round, and inventing the most extraordinary explanations of Spiritualistic phenomena. Credulity is very silly, but incredulity may be infinitely sillier."

Of the general attitude of the public whom he addressed he said: -

"Not once in all my meetings have I been interrupted, and everywhere people listen eagerly. They are tired of words which bring them no comfort and long for solid facts, and it is the solid facts of human survival and spirit communication of which I tell them. They are critical, but receptive."

*

Other sections of the Press were less receptive. In *John O' London's Weekly*, Arthur Machen compared Spiritualism to "methylated spirit" taken as a substitute for the "good drink" represented by mystical religion.

More Press mockery was noted by *Light* in two clearly irritated editorials:

*Light, April 26, 1919*

The "Star" of the 15th inst. has a comic article on the effigies of Mr. and Mrs. Huett, two Millbrook worthies, who died during the first half of the seventeenth century. The presence of the effigies seemed to have something to do with unearthly wails and groans and "nocturnal plaints" frightening many people. The story is too long to give in full; but it is all very funny, almost as funny as the insane attempts to navigate the air with heavier-than-air machines — before the aeroplane became a common object of the atmosphere. "Great Chance for Spook Hunters" is the heading which the evening paper puts to the story.

***

The atmosphere of hilarity deepens. Now we have a mock-serious book by Dr. Charles A. Mercier in which spirit communication is lampooned in a way that will excite annoyance amongst those who have not preserved the sense of fun. There is the episode of Mrs. Lambnard, the medium, and her control "dear little Googoo," who talks baby talk for twenty years and never gets any older. And so forth. The enemy is doubtless doing good work, purging out and testing the doubtful and really absurd elements in Spiritualism, and at the same time illuminating his own position as by a shower of Verey lights. Whether he discharges curses or guffaws, the result is the same. The feeble and the foolish are driven out or frightened away, and the forces of the wise, loyal and brave are consolidated. Sweet are the uses of opposition.

\*

At his public talks, Conan Doyle continued in his indefatigable manner to answer criticisms and mockery in the Press, commenting in *The Sunday Express* that the method of the critic is "to ridicule the observations of the most famous men of science, whose whole reputation is founded upon their power of exact experiment, while taking as absolute truth any wild assertion by an American newspaper man in search of a stunt."[67]

Meanwhile, despite knowing the effect of *The Bowmen* on the public imagination, Arthur Machen couldn't resist fictionalising another of the War's unexplained phenomena – the baffling reports of hearing the beating of Drake's Drum at the surrender of the German Fleet in 1918. Much as he had done with *The Bowmen*, Machen wrote a first person account based on allegedly true reports of mysterious drums sounding in the fog at the moment of surrender. For someone who had decried the Angels of Mons mania, it was an interesting choice for a story.

David Gow, stung by critics who claimed the actions of spirits with their rappings and tambourine shaking to be oddly futile, wrote, "It is a stirring story of the sea. Yet withal there is a touch of comedy about it. It is such a beautiful satire on the argument that the great dead would not come back to earth to play — drums!"[68]

---

67 Quoted in *Light*, May 17, 1919
68 *Light*, May 17, 1919

Another popular author, Jerome K Jerome also took a materialist position in an article called *Idle Thoughts Concerning Spooks*, which drew a parallel between ancient and modern times. "The miracles of Christ fade year by year. They were more or less imagined by loving, over-wrought men in an age when miracles were the common plan of propaganda."[69]

Another respected writer drawn into the debate was freethinker and socialist H G Wells, a close friend of Edward Clodd. Uncharacteristically, Wells wrote a theological work in 1917, *God The Invisible King*, in which he put forward the idea that God was expressed in human ideals such as love and selflessness. The book even led to him being invited to lunch by the Archbishop of Canterbury.

These themes were explored further in his 1919 novel *The Undying Fire*. A modern-day version of the biblical *Book of Job*, it had plenty to say about Spiritualism, with one character ridiculing Arthur Conan Doyle and Sir Oliver Lodge.

Wells's book was reviewed at great length by John H Dixon in *Light*, on July 26th 1919, in an article called *Mr. H. G. Wells And Spiritualism*. Wells had produced "ninety-nine pages of morbidity and tragedy — all the loathsome things that have ever existed on this planet, from the primeval sludge to the horrors of the world-war — to give us the fitful gleam of a candle-flame on the last page." He complained, "He attacks Spiritualism in violent language, rejecting the survival of personality as an idle dream."

Wells's message was straightforward, he went on:

> ...Spiritualists and all those who believe in the survival of the individual are suffering from hallucination. Mediums are egotistical persons, preying upon the credulity of others, delighting in an audience of two or three; they are mediums because they could not get anyone to listen to them in any other way; Mr. Wells has said so!
>
> ...Mr. Wells delivers a smashing attack against mediums, and in that attack, specifically mentions the names of Sir Arthur Conan Doyle and Sir Oliver Lodge. I quote the following: "All this cheap medium stuff has been shot upon the world by Sir

---

69 *Light*, July 12th, 1919

Oliver J. Lodge, handed out by him to people distraught with grief, in a great fat, impressive-looking volume. . . . No end of them have tried their utmost to take it seriously. . . . It's been a pitiful business...

A further attack by Wells was paired with a similar one by the brilliant writer George Bernard Shaw in *The Strand* magazine, both interviewed by American journalist, Joseph Gollomb.

*Light* responded in *Fallacies and Sadducees* on April 10th, 1920. To Shaw's complaint that the ouija board "gives off rank nonsense" *Light's* ill-tempered reply was: "So it does sometimes, and it is rather a pity that the giving off of rank nonsense is not confined to ouija boards." Shaw was quoted as saying that Spiritualism "adds a new terror to death" in confronting passed-over spirits with an eternity of "tipping little tables and ringing bells."

H G Wells, meanwhile, described eminent Spiritualist scientists as "extremely gullible," adding: "The scientist, the professor, the student deep in his speciality, have always been the easy prey of cheats." He then went on to deride the Spiritualist afterlife with its restoration of hair and teeth to the spirit body, before adding that "the whole idea of a personal immortality is absurd."

*Light's* editor, Gow, gave as good as he got in a by now familiar argument, decrying the ignorance of those willing to pronounce on something of which they had limited experience.

The following week on 17th April, 1919, this short announcement appeared:

## MR H. G. WELLS AND THE "STRAND" MAGAZINE

Referring to the leading article in *LIGHT*, "Fallacies and Sadducees" (p.116), Mr. H. G. Wells writes us disavowing responsibility for the statements alleged to have been made by him in the "interview" published in the "Strand Magazine," alluded to in our article. Having no knowledge of the facts of the case, we can only publish Mr. Wells' disclaimer.

Two weeks later, on 1st May 1920, George Bernard Shaw muddied the waters further by completely disowning the Gollomb interview and stating "if the interview in the 'Strand Magazine,' which you criticise, were by me or authorised by me, or had been submitted to me before publication, I should deserve pretty nearly all you say of me. As a matter of fact, I am quite innocent of it, and I daresay Mr. Wells is in the same predicament."

Shaw explained that Mr. Gollomb had called on him "in the character of an American gentleman guilelessly desirous of making my acquaintance." They had chatted for some time on various subjects of the day, amongst them Spiritualism, Socialism and the war. "If I had had the faintest suspicion that I was being professionally interviewed on Spiritualism, I should have refused to receive Mr. Gollomb. I have my opinion on the subject; but I do not intend to give it to the world in the form of an interview, nor in the words of another man who does not know the difference between a ouija board and a planchette and who, when I tell him of the famous hoax perpetrated by Samuel Butler on Alfred Russel Wallace for his amusement, is so hopelessly at sea that he quotes it, and spoils it in the quoting, as an experience of my own. I never used a ouija board in my life. I agree with you that the interview is a string of flippant rubbish which has neither the virtue of being amusing nor the decency of being considerate to my mother or to my friend Sir Oliver Lodge."

It was a regular storm in a fortune-teller's tealeaves, and represented a mystery of its own when Joseph Gollomb wrote in injured tones to *Light* to "offer evidence that Mr. Shaw knew perfectly well he was being interviewed professionally for publication," that "he himself had corrected and approved a long interview I wrote for the *Observer;*" and that "he gave a photograph for publication."

Gollomb offered character witnesses and signed off ambiguously, "Finally, I want you to know that my study and investigation of Spiritualism have impressed me so profoundly that there is nothing in this life I would more gladly have than a strong conviction of the truth of Spiritualism."

In many ways this exchange encapsulated many journalists' approaches to Spiritualism. What did it really matter what Wells and Shaw (neither of whom were experts) knew of Spiritualism? Their fame was their qualification to pronounce. Such interviews meant more controversy and more sales. Was Gollomb telling the truth? With each side contradicting the other, no verdict was possible. Gollomb had been slapped down not necessarily because he had reported falsely, but because he had generated a sensation that the interviewees perhaps later regretted. Interestingly, decades later, Wells described his religious beliefs during this period as a product of regression due to the pressure of the war.

Meanwhile, more mischief was afoot. New information was unearthed in the Press about the veracity of The Masked Medium, over which *Light* had vacillated by conjecturing that though some of the phenomena were fake, some might be real.

*Express* writer Sydney Moseley had been at the earlier private sitting with Conan Doyle and had himself been deeply impressed by the Masked Medium. He later visited Mr P T Selbit, the medium's agent, and coaxed a full confession as to how the tricks were done. The ghostly figure seen at the medium's West End flat had been an accomplice, while the items supposedly identified by psychometry had at some point in the séance been whisked away and looked through.

In the wake of revelations that she had faked the séances, *Light* belatedly issued a report by Dr Abraham Wallace made in May of that year, reviewing her stage performance and criticising it on several levels. Finally published in *Light* of August 23rd, 1919, Wallace's accusations of fakery included:

1. The unusual way psychometry was performed, only describing personal items of individuals placed in a box, rather than giving their histories, as was usual.

2. The medium's representative was Mr. Selbit, a skilled conjurer and illusionist whose presence gave investigators good reason for "extreme caution".

3. There was plenty of opportunity for the psychometry items to be examined and described by the medium's accomplice at the side of the stage

4. The mask worn by the medium meant it was not possible to see whether it was her voice giving descriptions of the items.

5. Direct Voice and materialisation phenomena were performed in a cabinet in which there was room to conceal an accomplice

6. Overall, the night was a trick performance from beginning to end

"without any of the characteristic features of genuine phenomena".

*Light* announced: "It is to be observed that the performances of the 'Masked Medium' were never endorsed as genuine by LIGHT, although they included a few results not easily to be explained. We were frequently asked whether the lady was a genuine medium. It is quite possible that she was. Mediumship is a difficult matter to pronounce upon offhand. But it was clear enough that most of her demonstrations could be explained by the resources of conjuring."

Gow claimed to have held Wallace's report back to see whether a test séance could be arranged before publishing it. Only when it was certain that it couldn't had he gone ahead with publication. Doyle and Gow had both conceded that some of the phenomena might have been genuine, but their instincts for extreme caution proved right. The whole Masked Medium affair had been calculated charlatanry from beginning to end.

Nevertheless, *Daily Mail* writer A Wade commented in November 1919 "Everywhere there is a great and fast-spreading growth of belief in the occult." Spiritualism had unexpected allies, as noted in this story in *Light* from December 20th 1919:

"Only dolts would deny that sometimes there is ever such a tiny jerk of the curtain which covers the window looking into the Beyond," is a statement we are surprised to find in the "Daily Express" (December 15th). It is the prelude to a story which is described as "a pleasantly baffling little study in the occult."

The story is of a girl sitting in a Kensington drawing-room after dinner—a young English girl, cynical of the occult and emotional, who adores Mr. Robert Loraine. Suddenly, without the slightest warning, she is present at a rehearsal of "Arms and the Man." She has never seen the play nor read it, nor has she seen the "Chocolate Soldier" travesty. But she sees the whole first act and part of the second played, with all the halts and the traffic on the stage and repetitions which attend rehearsals. She describes the setting accurately—-Raina's bedroom lit by two candlesticks and the window looking on the Balkan peaks. She repeats the dialogue.

The next night she goes to the theatre and sees the play

exactly as she saw it in the drawing room. The writer states that he can personally vouch for the accuracy of the facts.

In the following week's issue, *Light* reported:

> Sir A. Conan Doyle has written to the "Daily Express" on the subject of the girl (mentioned in our columns last week) who "saw" a play rehearsed while she sat in her 'drawing-room. Sir Arthur dismisses it as a "very simple case of travelling clairvoyance."

It is worth considering how many psychic cases Doyle must have looked into in order to be so off-hand about something *Daily Express* readers found genuinely enigmatic.

Not all Press reports were so supportive. One correspondent to the *Daily Express* asked for the end of Dickens's unfinished novel *The Mystery of Edwin Drood*. *Light* commented drily: "He is evidently one of those simple folk who hold the belief that any of those who have passed over can be 'called up'."

Realistically, there were as many Press opinions as there were individuals, including converted sceptics. One correspondent in the *Daily Mail* who had previously had no faith in "mediums, seances, or table-turning," wrote:

> I refused to believe in automatic writing until I was convinced, against my ordinary reasoning powers, by receiving written messages which, by their characteristics and inner knowledge, proved to me beyond a doubt that they were written by my son in the life Beyond. My pen moves and writes automatically, in a most miraculous manner, remarkable descriptions of his experience in the spirit world. At first I was almost afraid of the pen and felt I must throw it away, I was so astounded at its action, but the wonderful, cheering, and kindly messages it wrote soon convinced me it was my dear son, and not some power of evil, who was influencing the pen.

*The Times* was not converted. In October 1919 it ran a leader decrying the possibility that the Church might take the claims of Spiritualism seriously. In its discussion it ran between the two sides of the debate, starting with the religious and moving over to the scientific. It asserted that Sir Oliver Lodge and Sir Arthur Conan Doyle made the same claims that had been made throughout history, in that they "proclaim the existence of people with two powers, the power of raising spirits and the power of foretelling the future."

It went on: "The spirits raised by contemporary methods are no more impressive, give no more illuminating glimpses of the supernatural world or more certain predictions of the future, than those raised by primitive or medieval rites."

Of the theories behind Spiritualism, *The Times* wrote: "We are disposed to think the spiritualistic theory logically inferior to that of inspiration by the devil, especially in the matter of telling fortunes or predicting the future. If evidence be ever available that a medium can, with fair regularity, beat a good racing tipster or advise us beforehand of one or two important and apparently improbable events, we shall be ready to consider a grave metaphysical opinion on the probable source of the information." In the meantime, the paper referred not to spiritual authorities on the matter of evidence, but "should prefer that of conjurers with regard to fraud, of pathologists with regard to the 'subconscious self,' and that of average men with regard to telepathy."

*Light* magazine of 10th January 1920 reported that Sir Oliver Lodge had replied to *The Times* in the previous month's *Hibbert Journal*, clarifying that he and Sir Arthur Conan Doyle did not have the powers to raise spirits or of fortune telling. *The Times's* long and eloquent response spun Lodge's words into an admission that the claims of Spiritualists had not been examined and supported by high scientific authority – not Lodge's intention. The article went on to critique Lodge's denial of knowledge of necromancy and incantation:

> No doubt medieval necromancers employed magic circles, fat from the bodies of suicides, and prayers said backwards, whilst contemporary "mediums" use darkened rooms, banjos, and hymns. No doubt also the medieval performers attached great importance to the production of visible manifestations, and these have recently been rather "blown upon." But the essential

part of the claim, the claim to get into communication with the dead, is identical in the two cases.

Then after disparagingly listing Lodge's claims in favour of Spiritualism, *The Times* continued:

> We desire neither to interfere with his beliefs nor to place obstacles in the way of his investigations. But we have a right to demand transparent candour from a man who claims to be an exponent of the scientific method and to have applied that method to phenomena which, to say the least that may be said, have sometimes been associated with fraud.

*Light* also printed Sir Arthur Conan Doyle's answer, which appeared in *The Times* on 3rd January.

*Light, January 10, 1920*

### SIR A. CONAN DOYLE'S ANSWER.

As you were good enough to couple my name with that of Sir Oliver Lodge in your original remarks upon Spiritualism, you will perhaps allow me to associate myself with his disclaimer of the views attributed to us. Those views were that mediums had the power "of raising spirits and of foretelling the future." To "raise a spirit" would seem to imply that we had some control over those who have passed into the beyond. Such is not the case. The most that we can do is to make the physical conditions such that if they should of their own desire wish to manifest themselves to our senses, they may be able to do so. As to "foretelling the future," I have expressly stated in my "New Revelation" (p. 123):—"On the whole I preserve an open mind upon the powers and limitations of prophecy." I have known some very remarkable cases of fulfilment, and I have known grievous lapses. From their higher ground the spirit people see the relations between cause and effect more clearly than we do, but I for one would never admit that they have any certain power of foretelling the future. Thus on both counts you have unwittingly misrepresented my views. You add that mediums use "darkened rooms, banjos, and hymns."

The darkened room is common, but by no means universal, the banjo is, so far as I know, unknown, but hymns and prayer do certainly accompany this, the most solemn of all religious functions.

Sir Oliver has published his one war-widow letter as a sample, no doubt, of a large correspondence. I have myself received hundreds. Of these, 60 complete successes out of 72 attempts have been obtained from a single medium. These documents are entirely at the disposal of yourself or of any other competent authority who would care to examine them. My testimony, however, is more direct than this, since I can solemnly declare that, using an unpaid medium, I have beyond all question or doubt spoken face to face with, my son, my brother, my nephew by marriage, and several other friends since their death, there were six or more witnesses.

*

This, then, was the world in which Conan Doyle moved. On one side, famous scientists spoke of extraordinary breakthroughs; on another journalists and writers attacked and mocked; on another side again thousands flocked to hear him speak and themselves testified to real psychic phenomena; on yet another, charlatans and conmen dragged what Doyle saw as a noble faith deep into the mire.

Writing in the *Sunday Chronicle* in 1920 Doyle expressed some of his frustration. "Every Spiritualist is aware that he is only on the edge of an enormous subject which has been ridiculed by the ignorant, defiled by impostors, used for base purposes by worldlings, but sanctified by the devotion and courage of great numbers of men and women who have testified to the truth."

The question, then, remained.

What was the truth?

# Chapter 10
## Of Spiritualist Science

Some of the early appeal of Spiritualism for Doyle was that through experiment he could produce definite results, as he did in Southsea in 1887. Whether the scientific experiment was in thought-transference, table-turning, spirit photography or automatic writing, the data were based on empirical evidence and quickly available for appraisal.

Like many Spiritualists, Doyle didn't believe he had discovered a *supernatural* world, rather, he had exited from an incomplete view of the natural world. At last, in Spiritualism the *true and ultimate nature* of the world was revealed, unlimited by the mechanical limitations of the senses, by preconception or bias. Spiritualists were groping their ways toward substances and natural laws always present, but never classified.

One of the early pioneers of Spiritualist experimentation was renowned scientist Sir William Crookes. The extraordinary experiments he performed caused a sensation in Victorian Britain. He published the results of experiments with medium D D Home in his own journals; those he performed with medium Florence Cook he wrote about to Spiritualist papers. In his 1926 *History of Spiritualism*, Conan Doyle noted his contribution.

> The research into the phenomena of Spiritualism by Sir William Crookes - or Professor Crookes, as he then was - during the years from 1870 to 1874 is one of the outstanding incidents in the history of the movement. It is notable on account of the high scientific standing of the inquirer, the stern and yet just spirit in which the inquiry was conducted, the extraordinary results, and the uncompromising declaration of faith which followed them. It has been a favourite device of the opponents of the movement to attribute some physical weakness or growing senility to each fresh witness to psychic truth, but none can deny that these researches were carried out by a man at the very zenith of his mental development, and that the famous career which followed was a sufficient proof of his intellectual stability. It is to be remarked that the result was to prove the integrity not only of

the medium Florence Cook with whom the more sensational results were obtained, but also that of D. D. Home and of Miss Kate Fox, who were also severely tested.

The Florence Cook mentioned was a medium born in Hackney, East London in 1856. Cook had started by giving séances at home, and early on had materialised spirit faces. By the time Crookes came to hear of her, she was materialising a fully formed person, a spirit known as Katie King. Doyle wrote in *The History of Spiritualism:*

> Professor Crookes published a full account of his methods in the QUARTERLY JOURNAL OF SCIENCE, of which he was then editor. In his house at Mornington Road a small study opened into the chemical laboratory, a door with a curtain separating the two rooms. Miss Cook lay entranced upon a couch in the inner room. In the outer in subdued light sat Crookes, with such other observers as he invited. At the end of a period which varied from twenty minutes to an hour the materialized figure was built up from the ectoplasm of the medium. The existence of this substance and its method of production were unknown at that date, but subsequent research has thrown much light upon it, an account of which has been embodied in the chapter on ectoplasm. The actual effect was that the curtain was opened, and there emerged into the laboratory a female who was usually as different from the medium as two people could be. This apparition, which could move, talk, and act in all ways as an independent entity, is known by the name which she herself claimed as her own, "Katie King."

Such experiments caused controversy in Victorian society, especially because Crookes started off as a sceptic, minded to expose trickery.

At news of Crookes's death in 1919, Abraham Wallace, MD, noted in the *Special Supplement of Light* on May 3rd that the obituaries only meagrely touched on his Spiritualism. He asked why "so-called orthodox scientists and rationalists have not yet realised the great work that he did during the years 1870-73, when he, with rare courage and much pertinacity in face of considerable opposition, laid the true foundation for the scientific investigation of so-called spiritualistic phenomena." Wallace labelled critics who had no first-hand information of Spiritualism as "pseudo-scientists" and listed Crookes's achievements, by no means the least of which was the inspiration he had given to the next generation of psychic scientists.

One such scientist was French psychical researcher Dr Gustav Geley, an account of whose research appeared in *Light* on 29th March, 1919. His studies of two mediums of uncommon ability in France had repeatedly shown them manifesting extraordinary phenomena under what he described as strict test conditions. One of them, a young woman called Eva C, had been stripped and carefully searched before Geley's experiments, to prove no conventional explanation for the bizarre phenomena she manifested, not this time in darkness, but in good light.

Among phenomena Geley observed was the manifestation of ectoplasmic fluid from the extremities of the body, the mouth, nipples, finger ends, top of the head and vagina[70]. The ectoplasm once manifested would take different forms, at times paste-like, at others like threads, or again, membranous. It was at times soft, at others hard to the touch.

The ectoplasm created various structures, sometimes representing faces, hands, fingers and nails. When Dr Geley squeezed these manifested forms, they caused Eva pain.[71]

This, as far as Spiritualists were concerned was real, hard science. *Light* quoted Dr Geley hypothesising that Eva C presented a "supra-normal physiology" that could be explained by analogy with the body of the insect dematerialising in the chrysalis and then reforming into a new and distinct form.

He also noted that ectoplasm was controllable, and posited a whole new area of study, "ideoplastie", in which ideas "model matter, giving to matter its form and attributes." In this case, he wrote "*materialist physiology is totally upset.*"

Many men of science were interested, and Doyle himself requested to witness Eva C's manifestations, though it turned out he was unable to attend. What actually happened in Dr Geley's experiments remains unknown, although later investigations by SPR member Rudolf Lambert

---

70  Kelvin I. Jones's *Conan Doyle and the Spirits.*
71  *Ibid.*

shed doubt on Geley's claims and showed that evidence that would have cast doubt on the phenomena was suppressed by the *Institut Métapsychique*.[72]

Another Spiritualist scientist with much data on ectoplasm was Dr W J Crawford, a Belfast doctor whom Doyle visited in between his gruelling speaking tours of the UK, toward the end of 1919. Since 1914 Crawford had performed countless experiments with members of a talented family of mediums, the Golighers. The most powerful of these was Kathleen Goligher, a girl of 15 when his observations began, who was able to produce various phenomena including raps, the movement of objects at a distance and the levitation of tables. She also emanated spiritual "plasma" and ectoplasm from her body.

In his *History of Spiritualism*, Doyle later wrote of Crawford's research that it gave new understanding to this fascinating substance:

> ...he demonstrated that levitations of the table, raps on the floor of the room, and movements of objects in the séance room were due to the action of "psychic rods," or, as he came to call them in his last book, "psychic structures," emanating from the medium's body. When the table is levitated these "rods" are operated in two ways. If the table is a light one, the rod or structure does not touch the floor, but is "a cantilever firmly fixed to the medium's body at one end, and gripping the under surface or legs of the table with the free or working end." In the case of a heavy table the reaction, instead of being thrown on the medium, is applied to the floor of the room, forming a kind of strut between the under surface of the levitated table. The medium was placed in a weighing scale, and when the table was levitated an increase in her weight was observed.
>
> - *Sir Arthur Conan Doyle, The History of Spiritualism*

Crawford eventually managed to trace back the source of these rods. It appeared that whenever the medium manifested a solid ectoplasmic rod, a glutinous substance which he named *plasma* was also expelled. At first, he thought this issued from Goligher's feet, but through carefully

---

72  Sofie Lachapelle. *Investigating the Supernatural: From Spiritism and Occultism to Psychical Research and Metapsychics in France, 1853-1931*.

analysis of residual stains left on her feet, legs and thighs, and close repeated examination of her as she stood in her knickers for examination, he finally found the source – her vagina.[73]

By laying his hands on her haunches and feeling her body swelling during its reabsorption, Crawford noted how the expelled ectoplasmic material refilled the body as it returned to her. Doyle was suitably impressed, commenting later in *The History of Spiritualism* that Crawford's books on the matter had "probably done as much to place psychic science on an assured footing as any other works on the subject."

Spiritualists continued to press their case that their faith and their psychic experiments be acknowledged by mainstream scientists. On July 5th 1919 in *Light*, Susan, Countess of Malmesbury offered her support for these scientific pioneers. "Every great discovery has been wrested from its secret storehouse by the hard toil, self-sacrifice and, not least, the moral courage of scientists," she wrote, and affirmed how she was sure of the "establishment, beyond doubt, in the sight of all, of the fact that the spirit of man survives the death of the body and can communicate with us who have not yet stripped off the mask of life."

Not every Spiritualist was involved in such experimentation, but many frequently employed the language of science and science-based theory. Scientific metaphor distanced Spiritualists from charges of witchcraft and quackery, and implied that hitherto unknown forces were at last being understood.

Just so in the April 26th, 1919, issue of *Light*, in which Dr Ellis Powell encouraged a re-interpretation of Palm Sunday from a Spiritualist perspective, showing, as Doyle also asserted, that Christ was himself the ultimate Spiritualist. Picking on the detail of how Christ secured the acquiescence of the owners of the colt on which he rode into Jerusalem, Powell offered a striking metaphor synthesising Religion, Spiritualism and Technology.

> They responded to the wireless messages which were continually circling away from Christ, in a manner singularly analogous to that in which a ship answers a Marconi enquiry flashed through the ether of space. They are found, as we should

---

73  Kelvin I. Jones, *Conan Doyle and the Spirits*

say, well-disposed and ready to be utilised up to the limit of their humble ability and resources.

The theme of "Spirit Communication by Wireless" was also the subject of an article by Lilian Whiting on November 15th 1919, while in the same issue Einstein's *Theory of General and Special Relativity* inspired the claim that "the questions of light and gravitation in their scientific aspects have long been under the close attention of investigators into supernatural phenomena, and more than a hint has been given of the discovery now announced." The article intriguingly added, "We are not entirely absorbed in the observation of tambourines and automatic writing, as every serious student of our subject is well aware."

No explanation for this cryptic pronouncement was forthcoming.

Discussion in the scientific journals showed how divided the scientific community was in the face of Spiritualism. *Light*[74] reported three gentlemen in *The Medical Press*, with three different opinions. One believed that the experiments by psychic investigator Dr Crawford had "only fallen into the error, common throughout all ages, of ascribing what cannot be explained in the light of current knowledge to the agency of departed spirits." Meanwhile, another announced that "The time is rapidly approaching when the existence of the phenomena of Spiritualism (so-called) can no longer be doubted by a thinking man," although he would not fully admit the idea of spirit agency. The third observed: "Sir Conan Doyle and others seem to be trying to lay the foundations of a new religion. It is to be based on science, not faith or revelation. Its foundations ought to be indestructible; they are, to say the least, far from solid."

Doyle's scientific explanations of phenomena also came under the scrutiny of the Magic Circle, the association of professional and amateur conjurers, who requested him to submit certain Spiritualistic phenomena to their committee for examination. He told the *Daily Chronicle*:

> There is nothing at present to investigate in me. I am not a medium, and I do not produce any sort of phenomena myself. All

---

74 *Light*, October 11th, 1919.

that I have done in my books is to record a large number of cases, and if the committee choose to investigate those cases they can do so." He added: "I am only presenting the knowledge that I have gained from many different sources. If they take the same amount of trouble as I have taken the same sources are open to them."[75]

Theory upon theory piled up to explain Spiritualistic phenomena. In one sermon, Dr Cobb (who had been instrumental in initiating the Church's investigations into Spiritualism) argued that through physiology science dealt with the finite material body, and through psychology it encountered the soul. Cobb wrote: "...Science will have to take a part in the building of the temple of humanity. For Religion without Science would be like a vertebrate animal without a backbone."

His article would no doubt have been of interest to another scientist also mentioned in *Light,* Swiss psychologist, Carl Jung. He read a paper on *The Psychological Foundations of the Belief in Spirits*, before the members of the Society for Psychical Research on July 4th, 1919.

His theories of the Archetypes, the Collective Unconscious, synchronicity and much more would be oft-cited by later students of the paranormal, but on this occasion, *Light* simply reported: "Dr. Jung said, although belief in spirits dwelling in the neighbourhood of men, invisible yet powerful, was equally to be found amongst primitives as amongst the most highly civilised, among the educated of to-day it had been almost completely suppressed. The primitive spoke of ghosts, and civilised people of phantasies, and the latter attributed less importance to them than the former." Jung made a lifelong study of the subjective mind and created a vast science around it. Perhaps he was the very psychologist whom Cobb in his writings had predicted – a man who regarded himself as a scientist whom many saw as a mystic.

For Doyle, Spirit communication came in many forms. A more novel one appeared in *Light* of February 28th 1920, when it reported "a notable experience with the crystal". Doyle was quoted in the *Sunday Express*:

"I was at Harrogate recently, and among the people I met there was a lady - I say 'lady' in view of her status and education -

---

75 *Light*, August 9, 1919.

who showed me a crystal. She placed the crystal in a dark handkerchief, and gazed at it for a few minutes. Suddenly she said, 'Look! A message for you!' I myself then looked at the crystal and saw, clearly enough, a message from Raymond to his father, Sir Oliver Lodge. I have forwarded the message."

Doyle was not only interested in communication with the dead – his ever-roaming mind was always inquiring into strange phenomena. On August 14th, he was reported as experimenting with a "sideric pendulum" - the movement of a ring suspended on a thread that could supposedly determine the sex of newly born animals, or indeed, of animals in photographs. When applied to a few lines of writing, or even a single word written hundreds of years before, the experimenter could determine the sex, health or ill-health, morality, temper, and sentiments of the writer. Drawings and paintings were equally loose-tongued. Doyle wrote:

> I tried it fourteen times, without a failure, upon photographs, in several cases concealing the photograph so that I did not myself know, until the ring had given the circle or the ellipse, what the sex was. It never failed.

Doyle's wide-ranging curiosity soon became engaged with another theory put forward by another contributor to *Light* in a long article published on July 19th, 1919 entitled *Has Nature Her Own Phonograph? A Record Of A Strange Experience.* The anonymous writer detailed the strange experience of neighbours informing him that they had heard an argument in his apartment. The words they heard were verbatim echoes of an argument with a woman in a particular room exactly a year before, from which the neighbours said the "more recent" argument had also emanated. He knew for certain no such argument had occurred – he'd been asleep in it during the time of the supposed argument. He postulated:

> If visual and auditory imprints on the ether can thus apparently be reproduced under certain unknown, subtle conditions, and be recognised by those psychically attuned to

them, Nature may be said to possess her own cinematograph and phonograph. This theory might explain many appearances stated to have been seen in connection with certain ghost stories of a somewhat meaningless type, and would remove the grounds for accounting for the same as due to the agency of discarnate spirits.

Doyle was much taken with the theory of "invisible air records" of former events, and wrote an article for *The Strand* about them that was reported in *Light's* "From the Lighthouse Window" section.

*Light, May 8, 1920*

Sir A. Conan Doyle, in an article entitled "The Shadows the Screen" in the May number of the "Strand Magazine," examines the extremely interesting hypothesis that past events leave a record upon our surroundings which is capable of making itself felt, heard, or seen for a long time afterwards. Sir Arthur, indeed, declares his belief that this is the explanation for many peculiar experiences which have been placed on record.

****

Invisible air records, he says, would explain many things which are otherwise inexplicable. "Men, of strong nerve have been known to be terrified in certain localities without being able to give any reason. Some horror of the past, unseen by their eyes, may still have impressed their senses. One does not need to be very psychic to get the same result on an old battlefield."

****

Sir Arthur adds, "I am by no means psychic myself, yet I am conscious, quite apart from imagination, of a curious effect, almost a darkening of the landscape with a marked sense of heaviness, when I am on an old battlefield. I have been particularly conscious of it on the scenes of Hastings and Culloden, two fights where great causes were finally destroyed and where extreme bitterness may well have filled the hearts of the conquered. The shadow still remains."

****

After relating a case which he considers clearly fits itself into the theory of a form-picture thrown out at a time of emotion, Sir Arthur goes on to say, "Difficult as my hypothesis may seem, we have to remember that the only conceivable other explanations would be either that the man's self was there in front of the fire after a century of spirit life, or that his thoughts in the spirit world concerning an episode in his earth life were so constant and vivid that they conjured up a picture in the room. The latter explanation might be accepted for a single episode, but when it is a constant matter, and when one remembers how many other reminiscences of earth life such a man must have had, it is difficult to consider it seriously." Sir Arthur has boldly faced a complex side of psychic research, and his observations will be found well worth attention.

*

One problem plaguing psychic research was the inconsistency of results, which meant that it could not produce a credible data set that would satisfy the most rigorous scientific criteria. Advocates of Spiritualism excused this by explaining that results were prey to variables – such as the medium's fluctuating ability, or hostile intent among sitters. Some sought to compensate for this gap in credibility by employing mechanistic or technological metaphors. At times, Doyle himself implied a mechanistic view of mediums - in *The Vital Message* he compared the difficulties of getting a good channel to automatic writing to the vagaries of "the British telephone system".

In *Light* on March 20th, 1920, the idea of adding a technological element to psychic research was taken a step further. A "mechanical instrument for psychic communications" was discussed by the Editor of *The Two Worlds,* who described an experiment done in the presence of a strong physical medium, with a planchette. No hands were placed upon the instrument, but a ring of sitters joined hands around it.

Rapidly and firmly the instrument was moved in full light, and scores of autograph signatures of deceased persons were thus obtained. The amount of evidence of identity obtained in a few sittings was enormous.

A month later on April 20th, 1920, in *Mental Telegraphy: The Transmission Of Thought Waves, Light* announced the death of J Howard Williams, sub-editor of The Press Association. Williams, the article said, had previously been involved in telepathy experiments, aided by an "electro-mental generator" which he had invented for "generating thought vibrations." The article then reproduced a letter originally published five years earlier, in which he claimed his telegraphic apparatus had improved success in telepathic communication from a 10 percent success rate to 25 percent.

He wrote:

> In one case a, message of forty words was transmitted and received with only four mistakes... The conclusion I have arrived at is that... by stimulating the brain centres it produces a mental condition that facilitates thought projection.

*Light* added:

> We heard nothing further of Mr. Williams' invention... we are unable to say whether he developed it to a generally practical extent.

A fever of spiritual-scientific speculation abounded. As Einstein's *Special and General Theory of Relativity*, (published in German in 1916 and in English in 1920) gained traction on the public imagination, this also was wheeled into the service of Spiritualists. In a fascinating and beautiful article in *Light* on May 1st, 1920 entitled *Einstein: The Mathematician As A Mystic*, S G Soal noted the possible importance of his theory to Spiritualistic ideas.

> Einstein's theory is significant for psychical research. In its light the psychic will appear as a person whose time and space are abnormal compared with the rest of humanity. The mental phenomena of lucidity, or prevision, whether they occur through incarnate or discarnate personalities, will be conceived as problems of distorted time order and space order — as abnormal modes of separating the four-dimensional complex. We may

even anticipate that from this point of view science will be enabled one day to deal with these phenomena and discover their true philosophy.

With so many claims that Spiritualism was a science or underpinned by science, it was inevitable that the newspapers would demand hard answers to clear questions. On January 7th 1920, *The Evening Standard* published a series of "logical questions" on Spiritualism written by author Newman Harding, inviting Doyle to reply. Prominent spiritualist Ellis T Powell – clearly regarding the questions as facile - stepped in with his own witty replies.

*Light, January 17, 1920*

A CRITIC'S "LOGICAL QUESTIONS" ANSWERED.

I don't know if my old friend Conan Doyle will reply to Mr. Newman Harding. Pending his action, or inaction, I send brief responses. To one or two queries of the absurd type I have replied by counter-questions, equally farcical. I should recommend to Mr. Newman Harding the perusal of some elementary book on Spiritualism, such as Sir William Barrett's 'Psychical Research.' Some slight knowledge of a subject is desirable in all critics thereof.

(1) "What really is a spirit? How is it possible to know one and to understand whether it is the real thing or not?"—A spirit is an individuated personality conscious of its own existence. It may be incarnate (like mine while I am "alive") or discarnate (like the spirits of the "dead"). It is recognised in the same way as other personalities, by visible signs, or, where there is no visibility, by other methods of identification.

(2) "How is it possible to tell bad spirits from good spirits?"—By their fruits ye shall know them.

(3) "Has a spirit a conscience and a soul?"—Yes, it has both.

(4) "What is the difference between a spirit and a ghost?" —Ghost is the old English word for spirit, as in the ancient expression, "the Holy Ghost."

(5 and 6) "Why should it be necessary to get into communication

with spirits through mediums, more especially when these are mostly anything but well educated? Why must spirits and mediums have darkness? Why can't spirits appear and deliver messages in the light? How is it possible to know an honest medium from a dishonest one?" —Why is it necessary to develop the photographic plate in non-actinic light? Why cannot we drink strychnine as a beverage?

(7) "Why do spirits as a rule require tambourines, etc., to play with?" — Why do medical men, as a rule, stand on their heads while being consulted by their patients?

(8) "Are mundane languages also the languages of the spirit world? If so, why? If not, how is it spirits speak in these languages and do not attempt to teach us theirs?" —Mundane languages (that is, conventional sound and sign symbols of ideas) are necessarily used in communicating with mundane intelligence. There is no language in the spirit-world. Ideas flash direct from spirit to spirit.

(9) "Why do spirits wear clothes? Clothes, too, identical in material and fashion with those on earth? How is this material obtained?"—Their apparent terrestrial attire is a means of manifestation and identification. Now we see in a mirror enigmatically, as St. Paul says. We do not know the real nature of the spirit body.

(10) "Why do spirits have similar foods and drinks to those on earth? How are these obtained?"—They don't. But they can, for newcomers, make foods and drinks apparently similar, by the creative power of thought.

(11) "How is it that spirits never have any communications to make that will benefit and advance mankind? Therefore, as spirits are of no practical use or benefit to mankind or the earth, why should we wish to get in touch with them?"—How is it that doctors, astronomers, biologists, and geologists never have any communication that will benefit and advance mankind? The question is less absurd than Mr. Newman Harding's.

(12) "Why do spirits always talk about themselves and their mundane lives"— They do not "always" talk in that way. When they do, they have the same reason as Mr. Newman Harding, meeting an old friend, would have for talking over the good old days and "auld lang syne."

(13) "Why, in the spirit world, judging from the conversations reported, should costermongers still be costermongers, Red Indians still

Red Indians, and village idiots still village idiots, and so on?"—Because survival involves continued personal identity. There are no idiots in the spirit world.

(14) "Why should spirits, according to revelations, live what is practically an imitation of mundane existences? Why be permitted a memory of this world and the life here?"—How can there be survival of personality without memory? It is the essence thereof.

(15) "If the next life is a step onwards, why can't spirits tell us of the different conditions there? Their spiritual senses don't appear one iota in advance. Why?"—See the answers to (5), (6), (7) and (11).

(16) "Has any nation or race ever adopted Spiritualism as a religion, or part of its religion, with success?"—Yes, the British people have adopted a religion based upon the survival of the human personality after death. It has inspired immeasurable devotion and boundless sacrifice. Spiritualism itself is not a religion, but a science.

(17) "If Christianity accepted Spiritualism as part of its religion, what benefits would this confer on this world, apart from helping hordes of charlatans to prosper?"—The doctrine of survival is the essence of Christianity. There is no "if" about it.

(18) "Although sex is necessary on this earth, why is it necessary in the spirit world?"— Sex is a subtle differentiation of personality. The reproductive function is a secondary and ephemeral "accident" thereof.

(19) "Why should the age of 24 years be the golden age to which, in the spirit world, spirits grow or return? If this is so, what is the attitude of a grandchild towards its grandparents, and vice versa? What are the feelings of a mother towards the babe which died at six months, the mother therefore having nothing to do with the bringing up of this infant to the age of 24, and also of the babe which never knew its mother?"—Who is Mr. Newman Harding's authority for the age of 24?

(20) "Why should, and how can, physical relationship on this earth be extended to and continued as spirits? How can mothers and sons here be mothers and sons in the spirit world? If this is so, is motherhood here a dual role producing the mundane son and the spirit son? Again, what were these spirits before the physical life and relationship here? They can't have been the same mothers and sons then, surely?"—Physical relationship is only the corporeal manifestation of spirit affinity. It is the latter which functions here and survives hereafter.

(21) "Is the spirit world the next and final phase? But, as the spirit is immortal, must we not have been in the spirit world before we got on this earth? So, if we go back, don't we return also? Does not this mean an endless alternative of mundane and spiritual existences? If so, *cui bono?"*—We know nothing of this "final" phase. No scientific Spiritualist would affirm that the spirit is immortal, as Mr. Newman Harding does. Survival is one thing, immortality another. The former is proved; the latter is (probably) incapable of any proof susceptible by the human intelligence. Doubtless re-incarnation is a fact in many cases. The young man goes backwards and forwards to college, gaining fresh knowledge and experience every term; why not the spirit, too?

*

Arthur Conan Doyle, gave a shorter reply, originally published in the *Evening Standard*, and reproduced in *Light* alongside Powell's answer.

*Light*, January 17, 1920

Mr. Newman Harding shows the limitations of his knowledge by alluding to the Spiritualist position as if it rested upon the assertions of two men, Sir Oliver Lodge and myself.

Has he never consulted the writings of Sir William Crookes, Professor Hyslop, Professor Lombroso, Dr. Geley, Charles Richet, Dr. Crawford, of Belfast, W. T. Stead, Professor Hare, Judge Edmonds, and so many more?

If he has done so he has no right to state the case as if it rested upon two witnesses; if he has not done so he should consult the recognised authorities before asking long lists of questions which would take a volume to answer.

On examining this list I find that most of these questions are not really questions at all, but assertions, usually false and sometimes offensive. The mentality which can ask, 'How is it that spirits never have any communications to make that will benefit and advance mankind?' on the assumption that the fate of the human race and the present condition of our loved ones who have gone before is of no consequence to mankind, is to me unthinkable.

Is it not evident that the function of higher beings is to minister to our spiritual needs and knowledge, not to invent motor engines or to instruct us in chemistry? We should become automata if we were to allow our world to be run from the outside.

There are only two vital propositions in Spiritualism. These are that personality survives death without a change; the other, that under proper physical conditions communication is still possible.

Professor Hyslop, the highest authority in America, says in his recent work. 'Life After Death': 'Any man who does not accept the existence of discarnate spirits and the proof of it is either ignorant or a moral coward.' I believe that to be a perfectly just dilemma.

As to those questions of minute detail which make up the long catechism of Mr. Newman Harding, their answer is insignificant compared with the importance of the main thesis. A great quantity of information has been gathered and certain conclusions have been formed, but there is latitude for dissent, and no Spiritualist would make such points a touchstone of the truth."

The following is the remark of Mr. Harding's to which Sir Arthur alludes :—

It is all very well for men like Sir Oliver Lodge and Sir Conan Doyle to tell us glibly of a spiritual existence which they can gain access by extraordinary methods which have convinced them that dead relations exist there happily and are quite ready to appear and chat to those they have left on earth, but as the methods are so extraordinary, and the results also, it doesn't help us much.

*

Whether its claims to be a science would ever be upheld, Spiritualism was gaining credibility in the popular imagination. The escapologist and illusionist Harry Houdini, who was to loom large in Conan Doyle's life in the coming years as a vocal critic of Spiritualism, wasn't above changing his plans because of it. On July 31, 1920, *Light* reported that in an interview by journalist Stuart Cumberland, Houdini had been told by "an aura-reading psychic" that an accident would occur to him on June 4th, and that Mr. Cumberland's influence (denoted by a blue aura) would intervene to prevent the disaster.

Houdini was due to perform a stunt in which he took a flying leap from the top of one passing train to another on that day, but on being reminded of the prediction decided not to perform the feat. Houdini reasoned, "If an accident had happened that day the Spiritists would have counted a score, and so I decided to take no unnecessary risks." Nevertheless, since the psychic had predicted that Cumberland's blue aura would save Houdini, Cumberland suspected the psychic would still claim success.

The debates rolled on about scientific Spiritualism, with passion and fervour on either side. Amidst all this, *The Daily Mirror* requested a commission be set up to investigate Spiritualism's claims, in which the great Spiritualist scientists of the day have their evidence reviewed by their peers. Whilst this was not to be easily arranged, another event was - leading materialist Joseph McCabe challenged Conan Doyle to a debate.

McCabe was a fiery and vociferous opponent of Spiritualism, with a strong reputation for incisive debate.

It was potentially a showdown that could, perhaps, land a fatal blow. Both sides awaited it with eager anticipation.

# Chapter 11
## The Need for Energy

Taking a few breaths to pause and look back over the brief years between Doyle's 1916 public announcement of his Spiritualism and the start of 1920, it is humbling to consider Doyle's extraordinary personal trajectory. From being an earnest experimenter, a convert to the cause, a devotee addressing thousands at the Royal Albert Hall, a tireless missionary, a brilliant writer spreading his beliefs with books in the language of the common man, through personal tragedy to communication with his lost son, Doyle's involvement in the movement was complete and all-encompassing. In a few brief years he had moved from dilettante to charismatic defender of the faith.

Yet even this list of accomplishments does not tell the whole story. He contributed to the movement not only deep personal conviction and immense passion, but also his energy to organise and mobilise.

Within a fortnight of the start of 1919, two and a half months after the death of his son, Kingsley, and three and a half months before his address at the National Memorial Service at the Royal Albert Hall, a letter in *Light* showed Conan Doyle turning his attentions to the practical issues of organising this fledgling faith.

*Light, January 11, 1919*

### THE NEED FOR ENERGY

SIR,

One proposition seems to me to be incontrovertible. It is that we who uphold psychic communion are either working upon the most important thing that could possibly engage the minds of men — a thing that throws even the world-war into insignificance — or else we are propagating a mischievous and blasphemous superstition. There is no intermediate position. One or other must be true. We believe, and indeed know, that the first alternative is a solid fact. That being so, the very immediate deduction is that we should live and act in accordance with this belief. It is our manifest duty not to proselytise, since we have no desire to force a benefit upon an unwilling recipient, but to take steps to let the whole world share the knowledge and the happiness which we possess by putting the facts plainly before them, so that if they reject them it is their fault and not ours. To do this we can all work according to our powers. Some can write. Some can speak. These are bound to do so with no thought of self. But the great majority of believers cannot aid in these more personal and strenuous ways. It is for them to provide the money, without which the work is greatly retarded. Nothing can prevent Truth from coming into its own, but the driving force of work and money may contract centuries into years. I am aware that many rich people are whole-hearted believers. I seldom receive a post which does not include some letter containing expressions of gratitude for experiences gained through spirit communion. What are all these people doing to prove their gratitude?

Many urgent things need to be done, and are held back for want of funds. We need not a palatial but a respectable central headquarters. We need allowances for our poorer workers who labour upon unworthy salaries. We need organisation in every county, so that inquirers can get help at their own doors with small local spiritual libraries. Above all, we need a central publishing agency and the cheap distribution of literature. There are many of the splendid early works upon the movement which must surely be out of copyright now. Mrs. De Morgan's "From Matter to Spirit[76]," published in 1863, is a case in point. To read so vital a book as the Life of D. D. Home[77] one has to rely upon a library. That is a book which, published at one shilling, and rather abbreviated, would do great good, for it is the record of the most remarkable human being who has lived within our remembrance. Then, again, there is that most convincing little book which records the early researches of Sir William Crookes. I bought a copy last week and had to pay 12s. 6d. for what is only a pamphlet. Why should people be starved of vital information in this way? There is only one solution, and that is a publishing organisation with young, whole-hearted energetic men to run it, and

---

76 Attributed to Sophia De Morgan, *From Matter To Spirit* was actually written by her husband, Augustus De Morgan, a prominent mathematician and logician. Augustus feared that his reputation and career would suffer were his interest in Spiritualism to become public knowledge, and hence published the book anonymously, and then let his wife take the credit of authorship.

77 Likely referring to *Incidents In My Life*, by D D Home.

enough money to give them the necessary capital. Let us start 1919 with a fixed determination, to prove the reality of our professions, and to leave nothing undone in work or money to carry our wonderful message to a world which is quite ready and even eager to listen.

Yours faithfully,

ARTHUR CONAN DOYLE.

*

Proof of what that energy promised came soon after, as revealed by a *Strand* article reported in *Light* on March 8th 1919. Simply called *Sir A Conan Doyle*, it included Doyle's statement: "I may lead a movement, but there is something ahead which is leading me." The article went on to note that Doyle had "a full programme of activities for the present year and is likely to give several addresses in London in the autumn, but of these matters particulars will appear in due time."

The programme would include addresses in Edinburgh, Central London, Doncaster, Huddersfield, Manchester, Rochdale, Crewe, Glasgow, Portsmouth, Bournemouth, Wimbledon, Wolverhampton, Leicester, Aberdeen, Merthyr, Rhondda, Ebbw Vale, Southport, Blackpool, Preston, Morecambe, Durham, Harrogate, Hanley, East and South-East London, Bristol, Swindon, Lewisham and St Dunstan's, to name some of the venues he visited.

In the April 19th 1919 issue of *Light*, the Reverend Stanley Gordon described in effusive language *Sir Arthur Conan Doyle's Scottish Tour. The Meeting In Edinburgh.*

"Auld Reekie," he wrote, "has had a shock. We had all made up our minds that Spiritualism was a discredited illusion." This he said, had been changed first by publication of Lodge's *Raymond*, and then by Sir Arthur Conan Doyle. He went on to say that Doyle "descended upon us and on Friday evening... the Usher Hall, holding three thousand people, was crowded to hear him." Accompanied by Lady Conan Doyle, who was an "inspiration" to him, "Sir Arthur captivated the audience by his frankness, his straightforward statements and his masterly treatment of his subject."

Laying out his connections with Edinburgh and his previous materialist views, Doyle then spoke on *Death and the Hereafter.* "The audience listened with the keenest interest. Like Oliver Twist, they wanted more," Gordon declared. "Sir Arthur has left a deep impression upon our city... When a man of Sir Arthur Conan Doyle's analytic mind, one who is renowned throughout the world for his competency in weighing the value of evidence and detecting fraud, has studied this subject of Spiritualism and after many years of careful investigation has reached the conclusion not only that the phenomena are real, but that it is his duty to go over the length and breadth of the land proclaiming a new gospel, then Spiritualism has a message for this generation.

The Doyle Effect was also evident at *The Meeting In Glasgow*[78], held in the "vast St. Andrew's Hall", with an audience of around five thousand, who "obtained sitting or standing room, whilst more than two thousand failed to gain admission." Queues had formed three hours before the service, for which (as usual) Doyle gave his services free. "The lecturer, who was accompanied by Lady Doyle, was in splendid form, his powerful voice and clear utterance being heard in the remotest part of the hall," the correspondent reported. The author "pictured in lucid terms facts about the spirit-world made known through Spirit intercourse. The new life, he declared, is one of extraordinary happiness for those who do their duty here. Even death is a perfectly painless process. As the physical eye grows dimmer, the spiritual eye grows brighter as it sees the long-lost loving faces waiting to receive the traveller."

Doyle cautioned his audience that sin received its just reward, although Spiritualism had discovered no hell as depicted by orthodoxy. Taking on a mantle reminiscent of an biblical prophet, he said:

> In the past we have thought too much about Judea and Jerusalem. We have forgotten about Scotland and Glasgow. It is just as much the Apostolic age here as it was nineteen hundred years ago. This morning I myself, with fifteen citizens of Glasgow, went to an upper room, joined in prayer, saw tongues of flame round the room, and felt the wind rushing by our heads[79]. There was not one thing in the Biblical Apostolic room that we

---

78 Also reported in *Light* on April 19th, 1919

79 See Acts ii, 2: "And suddenly there came a sound from heaven as of a rushing mighty wind, and it filled all the house where they were sitting. And there appeared unto them cloven tongues like as of fire, and it sat upon each of them."

had not there. Religion is not dead. It is as living as we who live in this apostolic age.

Doyle answered counter-arguments from orthodox religions: "Are they going to say that the words I speak are inspired by the devil? I make reply that, if the devil took me from the world of materialism and put me where I am now—well, the devil does not know his own job."

The article finished: "There can be no doubt that Sir Arthur's visit has done great good for the cause of Spiritualism in Glasgow."

After the National Memorial Service at the Royal Albert Hall on April 27th 1919, Conan Doyle's Spiritualist profile had risen ever higher. On May 10, 1919, *Light* reported *The British Weekly's* comment:

> The historian and novelist whose books, in cheap translations, may be discovered in the remotest villages of Europe, is a missionary of whom Spiritualism may indeed be proud, for he has every qualification that appeals to the plain man.

In the same issue, F R Scatcherd (editor of the *Psychic Review*) wrote in *The Albert Hall Meeting* of the significance of such a brilliant interlocutor as Doyle speaking for Spiritualism. "Sir Arthur Conan Doyle's 'Sherlock Holmes' is as widely known in Europe as in England," she wrote. "No event will have wider significance in the history of Spiritualism than the accession to its ranks of the creator of that fascinating personality."

*Light* also announced that Conan Doyle would commence a series of three lectures on *Death and the Hereafter* at the Queen's Hall. Similar in content to those delivered in the provinces, they were being given in London because, as the magazine reported, "many Londoners have expressed a desire to hear them."

Commenting on these upcoming lectures in the same issue, Conan Doyle discussed the difficulties he had encountered in arranging the talks. He pressed for action to resolve the administrative problem and revealed just how many people he had reached out to on his gruelling tour of evangelising.

*Light, May 10, 1919*

## ARTHUR CONAN DOYLE ON THE IMMEDIATE NEED

I have recently addressed 20,000 people upon the subject of psychic religion, and altogether since my travels began 50,000 would be a moderate estimate. Wales the North of England and now Scotland are all ripe for a big forward movement.

The weak point is London, and this weakness is due to want of central organisation which in turn is due to weakness in finance. To take an example: if I want to approach any large town in the provinces, I simply communicate with the local secretary, who hires the hall, organises the meeting, and all is simple. If, however, I wish to speak in the heart of the Empire, there is no such simple approach. The suburbs have often arrangements like the provincial towns, but there is no organising secretary or other official whose duty it is to make programmes for London as a whole. If, for example, I were to take the Queen's Hall for a Sunday, if it were available, the whole organisation of the enterprise as well as the work would fall upon my shoulders. This is simply due to the poverty of the central body, who have not been able to afford such an official, though he is absolutely necessary for the movement. The world is waiting for the message, and we must bend all our energies to getting it across.

My suggestion is that such an organising agent be found for the society. If others will aid me in the enterprise I will guarantee from my lectures a part of his salary every year. Surely the thousands who have gained consolation through this movement will not grudge a few pounds for what is vital.

One most important duty which would fall upon him would be the supervision of the distribution of our literature. This should pay its own way handsomely when once it is organised. Glasgow alone sold £200 worth of books and pamphlets last year. When folk go out from a lecture they are in the mood to know more, but with the general boycott which exists, they cannot get the material and it passes from their minds. When a tableful of books lies at the exit they buy most readily, and what they buy is a permanent thing in their families and leads to the complete comprehension of the truth. So far as I can see, there is no supervision of this all important matter. As to the training and segregation of mediums, that also is a most pressing need, but will be easier as the general movement increases.

It is wonderful to see how ripe the harvest is all over the country — but we must rise to the height of the occasion.

Yours sincerely,
ARTHUR CONAN DOYLE.

\*

Doyle's rhetoric was filled with all the urgency and zeal of the convert flushed with the ardour of revelation. An article that appeared in *Light* on May 31st, 1919, with its potentially inflammatory title, *Sir A Conan Doyle On Spiritualism As A Revolutionary Force*, reported on *Nash's Magazine's* serialisation of *The Vital Message*.

The article quoted Doyle's belief that Spiritualism is "most certainly destined to revolutionise human thought and action as none other has done, within the Christian era." He praised the pioneers of the movement who risked their careers, and even their reputation for sanity, by publicly asserting what they knew to be true, revealing the scope of his vision along the way:

> It was they who nursed the system which promises to be, not a new religion — it is far too big for that — but part of the common heritage of knowledge, shared by the whole human race. Perfected Spiritualism, however, will probably bear about the same relation to the Spiritualism of 1850 as a modern locomotive to the bubbling little kettle which heralded the era of steam.

In discussion of automatic writing and its occasional falsities, he showed just how much time he had devoted to his faith:

> It is a profound and most complicated subject, however easily it may be settled by the 'ridiculous nonsense' school of critics. I look at the row of books upon the left of my desk as I write — ninety-six solid volumes, many of them annotated and well-

thumbed, and yet I know that I am like a child wading ankle-deep in the margin of an illimitable ocean. But this at least I have very clearly realised, that the ocean is there and that the margin is part of it, and that down that shelving shore the human race is destined to move slowly to deeper waters.

On June 14th, 1919, the day before his first Queen's Hall talk, *Light* set out Conan Doyle's burgeoning achievements thus far, and that they were making headway, even in London.

We hear great accounts of Sir Arthur Conan Doyle's tour, on which he spoke in Doncaster, Huddersfield, Manchester, Rochdale and Crewe. Everywhere the audience were deeply interested, and so enthusiastic that it was clear the vital message had gone home. The effects are manifest in a great wave of activity and inquiry. From Glasgow we learn that the interest is so wide and deep that the Society there have had to take the Town Hall, which holds 3,000, for their ordinary meetings. Here, in the South, people are more phlegmatic, and London is a very unwieldy centre. But the movement is beginning to show signs of fire and life; the quickening will be sure, even if it is a little slower.

The next day, Doyle commenced his first talk at the Queen's Hall. The full report on the talk revealed Doyle covering much of the ground he had covered elsewhere, but with more rationalised and complete beliefs. It also showed how effective he was at working an audience.

*Light, June 21, 1919*

### SIR ARTHUR CONAN DOYLE IN LONDON.
### ADDRESS AT THE QUEEN'S HALL.

Sir Arthur Conan Doyle, after his triumphant tour of the provinces, made his appearance in London at the Queen's Hall on Sunday last, when he gave the first of three addresses he is to deliver on "Death and the Hereafter." There was a large audience, and the keenest interest was shown in the speaker's convincing statements. Dr. Abraham Wallace presided.

Sir Arthur has a happy platform manner. He talks in an easy, conversational way, but the note of sincerity rings through all his remarks. What he says is intended for the inquirer, and it is good for such a one to hear that the speaker has also had his time of doubt and difficulty before arriving at full belief. When he came out as a young medical man after his university career, Sir Arthur was, he admitted, like most young medical men, a materialist. In those days the most foolish thing to him seemed to be Spiritualism. Then one of his principal patients took an interest in table-turning, and asked him to join in his experiments. He did so, and got the usual stupid messages. He did not proceed much further, but was interested enough to read up the subject in several books; still he was very hard to convince. At last he came upon two books which impressed him very much — one "The Life of D. D. Home," the other Sir William Crookes' book, giving an account of his experiments.

Home's phenomena were wonderful, and were never questioned. There was no miracle recorded in the New Testament which he did not do, short of raising the dead. He floated over a street seventy feet high; in the presence of Lord Lindsay, Lord Dunraven, and others he swept round a room, writing on the wall as he went. Never once as a medium was he questioned, and his powers were displayed before Robert Chambers, the publisher, Thackeray, and other good witnesses.

Finally, Sir Arthur became entirely converted to the phenomena. He said to himself: "I know these things are true; what the meaning is I do not know." Presently there came the war. People began to look more earnestly into their beliefs. It was then, among all the misery in the country, that he felt if only it could be proved that life went on after death it would be the biggest thing in the world; it was the one moment in the world's history when it was most needed. It suddenly came upon him; he saw the relation of one thing to another. He saw the purpose of all the things that seemed foolish. He saw that all these phenomena were simply a telephone bell ringing to call attention to the messages. They were the signs of the new revelation sent by God simply to impress a generation which could not be impressed in any other way.

What were the messages? They had been coming through in all parts of the world, and they purported to be from the dead. Wherever they came they were extraordinarily like one another. They contained an entirely new philosophy; it came in many different ways, but it was always the same. That was a very strong argument for its truth. Having convinced himself of the truth of these messages, he wrote a little book on the New Revelation.

The result of that book was that a large number of people wrote to him asking what they should do. He received many heartbroken letters. He discovered a very good medium. Having tested her, he sent all these people on to her, and then he used to ask them to write to him again and tell him exactly what had occurred. He received letters of the most remarkable description.

A little time ago he had a discussion in the London papers on Spiritualistic phenomena. He undertook to convert the whole lot of them if they would each send a representative to his house. Seven sent representatives. He showed them a pile of letters—-twenty-six in number—replies concerning the medium; twenty-four reported successes and two failures.

The Churches, Sir Arthur concluded, could not afford any longer to ignore these things. There were now 352 Spiritualist churches in Great Britain. They had not come to weaken the Churches, but to strengthen them against materialism, which was their real enemy.

Sir Arthur Conan Doyle was frequently cheered during the delivery of his address.

*

The reports on the second and third talks show Doyle working the crowd again, and reveals how the word was spreading in the heart of London.

*Light, June 28, 1919.*

SIR ARTHUR CONAN DOYLE AT QUEEN'S HALL.
THE SECOND MEETING: LORD GLENCONNER PRESIDES.

SIR ARTHUR CONAN DOYLE'S second meeting at the Queen's Hall

on Sunday morning last was even more numerously attended than the first, and this in despite of the disadvantages under which the meetings are held, notably the fact that they have had, perforce, to be held in the mornings, and at a time of the year when the sunny weather provides such strong counter-attractions to indoor gathering. Moreover, after his first meeting, Sir Arthur, with characteristic outspokenness, had pointed out that his subsequent addresses would be practically repetitions of the first, and this it was feared would also act as a deterrent. It was clear, however, that his frankness had produced no ill-results, but rather carried out his idea that his message should, as far as possible, be delivered to fresh ears each time, for we could not fail to notice the absence of many persons who were present at the first meeting and whose places were taken by others.

The chair on this occasion was taken by LORD GLENCONNER, who was accompanied by Lady Glenconner and their son, Mr. David Tennant. Lady Doyle, whose devoted support of her husband in his mission is not the least noteworthy part of it, was also amongst the audience as on the previous occasion.

Lord Glenconner's speech as Chairman was of more than passing interest, as it embodied a statement of his own attitude towards Psychical Research and that more popular and larger exposition of its principles which comes under the head of Spiritualism. We hope to supplement the present brief summary of it with a fuller report next week.

THE CHAIRMAN said that he was glad of the opportunity to be present on the platform not only to support Sir Arthur Conan Doyle in the work he had so courageously undertaken, but also to say a few words on a subject that was at present exercising the minds of the people. It was a subject which had interested him for some years, and during the last three years had been brought very forcibly to his attention. Only by a solid and careful accumulation of facts tending to show that mind could work independently of the bodily organisation could the scientific materialist be met on his own ground. It was this work which the Society for Psychical Research had patiently undertaken. The value of the Society's labours was inestimable, and he would like to see it working under the aegis of the Church, for the aims of both were in the same direction – the destruction of materialistic thought. He deplored the opposition of the Church towards the attempt to prove by evidence that conscious communication between the two worlds was possible. As a Scot, he was proud of his national Church. One of the most prominent ministers of that Church was a member of the Society for Psychical Research, and he could speak from his own knowledge in saying that amongst the smaller country churches there were intelligent ministers who were awake to the importance of the subject and studying its literature with an open mind. Adverting to the attitude of those scientists who condemned or criticised without investigation or after a mere perfunctory examination of the claims of psychical research, the chairman referred to the contrast provided by the example of Dr. Crawford of Belfast and other distinguished experimenters who had given sometimes fifteen or twenty years to a study of the subject before making any public statement. Such men were scientists indeed: might their tribe increase!

Sir Arthur, early in his address, affirmed that the messages he had received from the other world meant the abolition of the fear of death. There was, he said, an etheric body which St. Paul called the spiritual body, meaning not the spirit, but the body in which the spirit was. Scientific discoveries had shown that the physical body was permeated with ether, and a French scientist had made an important discovery when he demonstrated that there was a difference between the ether surrounding the body and the ether in the body.

The body was permeated with "bound ether" even to the smallest tissue, and if his (Sir Arthur's) body disappeared, there would still remain a mould of his body standing in the place of the physical body, but exactly like it, and this body was indestructible. At the moment of death this etheric body – this spiritual facsimile of the other — passed over. It disengaged itself until it found itself looking at its own body.

Conditions in the other world were remarkably like our own raised to a higher sphere, more beautiful, ethereal, and infinitely more happy. It was a "rest cure" after the trials of this life. Here man knew his worst; there man knew his best. It was a life of congenial work, which gave opportunity for the inherent capacities of man. There was family life, where only those in sympathy drew together. Spiritualists knew that this was not a dream.

For fifty years the Church had talked of "diabolism" instead of being alive to the truth of Spiritualism and bringing that truth into its own fold. If the Established Church accepted the doctrines stated it would get fresh dynamic power which would carry on Christianity. If it did not it was doomed. Nothing could live against truth.

\*

In his third talk, Doyle went on to explain more of the events and phenomena of the séance room, all the while filling in the detail with scientific hypotheses that would make sense to the common man. The final talk, too, was a massive success.

*Light, July 5 1919*

### SIR ARTHUR CONAN DOYLE AT QUEEN'S HALL.
### FINAL ADDRESS: VISCOUNT MOLESWORTH PRESIDES.

Sir Arthur Conan Doyle delivered the last of his three addresses on "Death and the Hereafter" at the Queen's Hall on Sunday last. The lecturer was in splendid form, and his remarks were constantly interrupted by applause. Though in substance the same as the previous addresses, Sir Arthur introduced some new matter. For instance, he supplied a trenchant reply to criticisms contained in an article in the Press by Mr. E. F Benson. Lord Molesworth, who presided, said: — "I feel it a great honour to preside here this morning and to have the pleasure of introducing Sir Arthur Conan Doyle as a lecturer on Spiritualism. It is a subject which deals with spirit communion and the continuity of life in the great hereafter. I am very glad to be associated with Sir Arthur in this great crusade. As one who has been personally convinced, I am very glad of the opportunity of marking to some extent my gratitude for the comfort and hope that I, or I should say we, have derived from the researches of Sir Arthur Conan Doyle and other great authorities. Sir Arthur's name is well-known to you. He is entitled to be listened to with respect, and on this subject I might even say with reverence."

Sir Arthur Conan Doyle, referring to the fact that the present was the last of his meetings in London, said that from the considerable correspondence which had reached him the effect of the presentation of the truths of Spiritualism seemed to have been to bring conviction and comfort to a large number of people. He believed in his heart that it was the religious teaching that came from Spiritualism which would prove to be the greatest thing the war had left behind it.

Dealing with the darkness of séances, Sir Arthur said that this was peculiar to the phenomena séance, which depended on etheric causes. Ether was a transmitter of light, and if the ether was so engaged, it was not available for the transmission of psychic power. Wireless was governed by the same laws: it was known wireless messages could be sent further at night than by day, because the ether was not engaged in transmitting light.

"Why are spirit powers not used to locate missing people?" was a question often asked. The idea that a sailor, drowned in mid-Atlantic, who knew nothing of mediums or of Spiritualism, should convey information as to his drowning, was preposterous. It was like asking a man to send a telegram from a village where there was no telegraph office. "But that psychic laws can be extended and used for the detection of crime, I have no doubt whatever," said Sir Arthur, "and they should be used more than they are. But we must not ask for the impossible."

The lecturer made a spirited reply to a recent article by Mr. E. F. Benson. Reviewing what he described as the "extraordinarily convincing tests obtained through the clairvoyance of Mrs. B., he said that he had sent the letters containing the particulars to Mr. Benson, because the latter had said that "mediumship was an odious trade." He sent him the whole forty-six letters, and Mr. Benson examined them and published an article in reference to them. In this, when speaking of successes, he had childishly put the word in inverted commas, but when alluding to failures the word was printed in the ordinary way. That was not decent controversy at all. (Applause.) Mr. Benson's explanation was that what was told to the sitters was the result of thought reading, and he expressed this opinion in a cock-sure way. In saying that he was only throwing dust in the eyes of the world.

"Thought reading," the lecturer proceeded, "is when I have a definite idea in my mind and another person is receptive and I convey the thought of, say, the ace of spades into his brain. If I do that I, consider I have done well. In that sense thought reading does exist. But to take it for granted that in thirty-seven cases out of forty-six the medium could look at people and take out of their brains the knowledge of their friends, incidents in their lives, as well as their names — that has never been proved in the world, no, never." To give thought reading as an explanation for what had occurred was a perfectly preposterous thing. Granting the existence of thought reading, it would not cover the facts. One lady who visited the medium said she had to write to a number of her relatives before she established the correctness of things told to her. The medium certainly could not have got that information by any process of thought reading, because the facts were unknown to the sitter. Other cases were quoted where it was shown that the medium, instead of following the thoughts of the sitter, corrected those thoughts where they were in error. The results achieved by the medium were most astounding. "Either Mr. Benson is not a man to appreciate evidence," said the lecturer with some warmth, "or he has read the evidence most carelessly." Referring to the tone of arrogance in the remarks, Sir Arthur added, "There is a mental insolence about them which I very greatly resent." (Applause.)

Dealing with the allegation that a certain medium had been prosecuted by the police, and that this was something which reflected on her character, Sir Arthur said: "Every medium in England is liable to be prosecuted by the police. It is due to the rotten state of the law. There is not an early Christian, not an apostle, not St. Paul, who would not have been up at Bow-street if he had been alive today." (Applause.)

In conclusion the lecturer asked what was Christianity going to do about Spiritualism? Were the Churches going to take his volume of evidence and digest it, or were they going to stand aloof and call it diabolism? If they did not admit the truth of the revelations, sooner or later a Church would rise which would displace them.

*

Throughout 1919, *Light* reported on Doyle's continued fundraising and evangelism. On July 19th, his overseas influence was noted by a quote from the pages of *La Revue Spirite*. On August 9th, *Light* commented on the donations to the LSA Memorial Endowment Fund for founding a centre for the London Spiritualist Alliance, recognising Doyle's special place among Spiritualist evangelists: "The list below includes the subscriptions specially devoted to furthering the efforts of Sir A. Conan Doyle."

Meanwhile, Conan Doyle pushed for a consolidation of Spiritualism's position with a suitable headquarters.

*Light, August 16, 1919*

### A CENTRAL INSTITUTE FOR SPIRITUALISM

We have received the following letter from Sir Arthur Conan Doyle:—

By a coincidence I have received two letters in the last few days showing how other nations are building up worthy temples to form central points for the great spiritual movement now going on all over the world.

One was from the National Spiritualists' Association of Washington, in America, and it says: "The erection of a splendid and commodious National Memorial Temple is now receiving liberal donations. That Temple, with its administration building, library, reading room, seance rooms, record vaults, auditoriums for conventions, meetings and Lyceum, will indeed become a world benefit."

The other was from Dr. Geley, in Paris, and describes how, at 89, Avenue Nial, a great establishment is being formed through the enlightened liberality of M. Jean Meyer, where every conceivable aid to the student of psychic matters will be available.

The small results attending your own appeals are disheartening compared with these great foundations, and it is the more surprising since the whole world admits that Great Britain is now leading the way in this tremendous religious evolution. I trust that the fact only needs to be stated in order to induce some of those who have themselves gained consolation to come forward and help to erect that which might bring so much consolation to others.

It has been suggested that I should appeal in the general press, but surely that would be a humiliating course to take.

ARTHUR CONAN DOYLE.

\*

*Light* reported Doyle's doings enthusiastically, including a July 19th announcement that "Sir Arthur Conan Doyle has done a fine stroke for the public good by his attack on food profiteers" in the post-War environment.

The following extracts from *Light* show how much of his energy was dedicated to the cause.

*Light, August 23, 1919.*

"The Challenge of Spiritualism" is the title given to an interview with Sir Arthur Conan Doyle in the "Daily Chronicle" of August 13th.

The interviewer, Mr. Charles Dawbarn, writes: "There is something so eminently sound and wholesome about Sir Arthur Conan Doyle, something so British about the immortal literary figure that he has given us for our perpetual joy that he would advertise any creed. Sure we are that nothing but sincerity and a desire to serve humanity lie at the bottom of his missionary efforts for Spiritualism."

*Light, September 20, 1919*

A proposal to invite Sir Arthur Conan Doyle to make a lecturing tour of Australia and New Zealand is being considered by Australian Spiritualist societies. The difficulty that has to be overcome is that of finance.

*Light, September 20, 1919*

Sir Arthur Conan Doyle's lectures on "Death and the Hereafter" at Portsmouth on September 6th, and at Bournemouth on September 12th were overwhelming successes. At the Portsmouth Town Hall and at the Winter Gardens (the largest hall in Bournemouth) he broke all records for attendance.

A friend who was present at the Bournemouth lecture heard a stranger in the crowd that was surging to the doors say in complaining tones, as he struggled for admission, "Anyone would think it was Tetrazzini."[80] Surely a fine tribute to a

---

80  Luisa Tetrazzini (June 29, 1871 – April 28, 1940) was an Italian coloratura soprano of great international fame.

Spiritualist address.

Another friend who was present writes, "Sir Arthur was in splendid form, and the applause at the end was tumultuous." The effect of the meeting at Portsmouth has been that the small local Spiritual Temple has had to give place to the Portland Hall, the largest hall in Southsea, seating 1,600 people.

*Light, October 4, 1919*

In the "New Statesman" of September 27th a contributor, J.L.M., writes on "The Vogue of Spiritualism." He opens with the following passage : "On a glorious summer afternoon in a seaside resort on the South Coast I observed a crowd, attacking the doors of a stuffy public building. Curious to know the attraction which was powerful enough to draw them from the coolness of the beach I joined them, and after some difficulty managed to obtain standing room at the back of a large hall packed with people. I discovered they were there to hear a missionary with a new gospel — Sir Arthur Conan Doyle on Spiritualism."

*Light, October 11, 1919*

SIR A. CONAN DOYLE AT WIMBLEDON

The Wimbledon Spiritualist Mission has engaged the large King's Palace Picture Theatre in Wimbledon for the four Sundays in October for special local propaganda, Sir Arthur Conan Doyle kindly lent his valuable assistance by taking the first meeting on the 5th inst. The hall accommodates eight hundred people, and every seat was sold. A large number had to stand, and many were turned away. Owing to the railway strike Sir Arthur had to motor all the way from Crowborough.

He was in splendid form, riveting the attention of his audience from first to last; speaking with telling effect on his great subject, "Death and the Hereafter." His analogies were very helpful, and one could feel that they struck right home. The audience was most enthusiastic.

Mr. Ernest Beard followed with a short but very useful address.

This Wimbledon enterprise has aroused considerable opposition, as was to be expected, the Church party taking the Wimbledon Theatre next door for the same dates in order to hold counter meetings. It is doubtful whether they can arouse the same enthusiasm for their opposition, and produce the same power and sense of exaltation as was so distinctly felt at the King's Palace last Sunday evening. Sir Arthur stipulated that half the profits of the meeting shall be given to the L.S.A. Memorial Endowment Fund, which was willingly agreed to.

The other meetings in October will be "admission free".
R. A. B.

*

On October 25th 1919, *Light* announced rather breathlessly: "As a rule we do not give to Sir Arthur Conan Doyle in 'Light' anything like the space necessary to convey an adequate idea of his tremendous activity or his magnificent work in our cause. If we did there would be no room for any other matter." In this case, however, they decided to make an exception, stating their deep appreciation for all he had been doing. The magazine went on to call him "the Knight of Spiritualism" and described his talk the previous Sunday in Leicester as "a wonderful triumph... One journal describes him as a fiery evangel sweeping through the Midlands."

To the outside observer, it appeared there was a cult of personality building up around the man. He even inspired adulatory poetry. A poem written by a Mrs Mildred Gentle appeared in *Light* on November 15th 1919. "There are now many," the magazine noted, "who feel grateful for the consolation he has given," before giving a short extract from her work, called *To A.C.D.*:

> The clasp of God's hand incarnate, the music ineffably sweet
> Of a still small voice in the darkness giving halt to the stumbling feet.
> A dawning sense of freedom, of respite from the quest,
> A breaking away of the shadows; the glimpse of a mountain crest.

> Life's road winds over the hillside, and the path is full of light,
> And ever fresh gleams of glory are bursting into sight.

I speed on my way rejoicing; holding the record true:
God's in His heaven, and heaven is here, and a prayer in my heart
for you.

Other Doyle-related interests and occurrences were also reported by *Light*. During the War, Doyle had paid a visit to Australian troops on the front, and in a report in the November 8th 1919 issue, this was alluded to in an address to the Institute of Journalists by a Mr Bean, the Australian Official War Correspondent. His words in many ways convey the glamour Doyle's name carried.

As soon as the "Diggers" knew "Sherlock Holmes" was visiting them they gave him...a memorable welcome. But before they knew he was the famous novelist they took him sometimes for Marshal Haig or Marshal Foch, according to their ideas of the significance of his impressive uniform. For Sir Conan Doyle, although the most modest and genial of men, had arrayed himself in his uniform of deputy-lieutenant of an English county. He admitted he did this with the idea that it would be useful when passing sentries. And so it was.

It was somewhat disturbing... when strolling along with Sir Arthur to note that he was not returning the salute of the "Diggers."

"Bless me, they are not saluting me!" said Sir Arthur.

"But they are!"

"Why?" asked Sir Arthur.

"What do you expect with those things on?" said Mr. Bean, indicating the uniform.

After that Sir Arthur saluted, but in a half-hearted way, not because of want of feeling, but because of his modesty. Later on he stood with Mr. Bean in front of the grave of an Australian. A steel helmet and rifle were on the mound of earth. The heart of the genial Sir Arthur was flooded with pity. "Here is one, at all events, who deserves a salute," he said simply, and stiffened himself and saluted with all his warm soul behind the act.

The romance associated with Doyle seemed to resound in every part of his life. On November 22, 1919, *Light* reported how at a talk to 2,500 people in Aberdeen, Doyle "spoke for ninety minutes without a pause... and every point of his remarks went home." The gushing report told how he "referred to his first association with Aberdeen, forty years ago, when as a young student he was on his way to join a Peterhead whaler, on which he had spent seven of the happiest years of his life. That he would ever live to address a representative meeting of Aberdeen citizens, he said, would have seemed at that time beyond his wildest dreams."

In fact, Doyle spent less then a year on the whaler in a near-fruitless search for a whale population that had nearly been hunted to extinction, but the expedition's halo of glamour was no less bright for it.

With the year drawing to a close, the energy Doyle had promised at its outset showed no sign of abating. On December 6th, 1919, a small announcement appeared in *Light* which caused a frisson of interest throughout the ranks of Spiritualists and materialists alike.

> Negotiations are being carried on for a public debate to be held early in the New Year between Sir A. Conan Doyle and Mr Joseph McCabe, to take place in the Queen's Hall. Mr Horace Leaf also is arranging for a debate in Edinburgh or Glasgow with Mr. Cohen, Editor of "The Freethinker".

Joseph McCabe was an excellent debater with an incisive mind. The announcement ensured that there was plenty more for Spiritualists to look forward to from the man who had become one of the most vocal spokesmen of the movement.

In the meantime, Doyle commenced a series of Spiritualist articles called *The Uncharted Coast* in the Christmas Number of *The Strand*. *Light* also reported Doyle's reflections on how the nature of Spiritualist phenomena had changed in a letter in the *Daily Mail*.

*Light, December 27, 1919.*

## THE LINE OF SPIRITUAL ADVANCE.

Sir A. Conan Doyle, in the course of a letter in the "Daily Mail," last week, makes some interesting reflections on the spiritual evolution from cruder phenomena, to finer and more intellectual proofs. He says : —

"In the early days of this movement it was foretold by Mrs. de Morgan and others that the line of advance would be from the crude material phenomena, common in those days, to the finer and more intellectual proofs which the human race would become more fitted to receive. This prophecy has, in the course of the last fifty years, been amply justified. The spirit rap, levitations, and even materialisations have become far less common. The evidence in these directions has been given, and this stage appears, to be closing down. On the other hand, we have never before had such an outburst of the finer phases of spirit intervention, of spirit photography, of inspirational addresses, writings, and paintings, and very especially of that clairvoyance or 'discerning of spirits' which Saint Paul counted among the most valuable of spiritual gifts.

"In writing this letter my object was, however, to point out some of the more intellectual proofs of spirit intervention which may appeal to those minds which recoil from grosser manifestations, only justified by the necessities of the material age in which we live. Of written inspiration much might be said, for no philosophy that has appeared has such a literature as has grown round Spiritualism. To those who imagine that the inspirational messages are of small intellectual value I would name only two recent books: 'Claude's Second Book[81]' (Methuen) and 'Letters from the Other Side[82]' (Watkins), which contain the very essence of spiritual knowledge, and, incidentally, a good deal of prophecy, in the case of the latter book, which has been literally fulfilled since the time the messages were taken. If those two books are not indeed inspired, then what are we to think of the transcendent intellectual qualities of those two ladies; whose hands were used to produce the script?"

\*

---

81  By L. Kelway-Bamber.
82  By H Thibault.

So, with Conan Doyle looking back on the past 60 years and its latest developments, the decade that had been marked by unprecedented horror, destruction, upheaval and loss came to an end. The Roaring Twenties had begun. To mark the New Year, and to show that his promised energy was still as vital as at the old year's outset, Conan Doyle wrote *A New Year Message* for the *Sunday Express*, quoted in *Light* on January 3rd, 1920:

> I look upon religion as the basis of all society, and truth as the basis of all religion. Therefore the recognition of truth concerning our destiny is the most important thing in the world. My wish for the New Year is, therefore, that people shall set aside foolish incredulity and shameful levity and shall seriously examine with honest and reverent criticism the enormous new revelation which has been sent us recently by God, realising that His methods are not as ours, and that there is neither small nor great in His sight. The last two great creeds came the one out of a camel driver's tent, the other out of a carpenter's shop.

In the new year Doyle continued his tour of talks up and down the country and wrote for the *Strand* and any other publication he could evangelise in. So, we see in *Light* the following engagements and events reported:

*Light, January 10, 1920*
Sir A. Conan Doyle in the January "Strand Magazine," in the second part of his intensely interesting series, "The Uncharted Coast," writes, "So far have we advanced that of the eighty or ninety cases carefully detailed in Dale Owen's 'Footfalls,' published in 1859, we find now, sixty years later, that there is hardly one which cannot be classified and understood."

*Light, February 14, 1920*
Sir A. Conan Doyle's forthcoming engagements are, 16th, Durham, where he will be the guest of Bishop Welldon, 17th, Harrogate, 18th, Hanley. We understand that, with his family, Sir

Arthur will visit Australia in the autumn.

*Light, March 4, 1920*
Mr. Charles T. Williams informs us that Sir A. Conan Doyle is to lecture in East and South-East London early in April.

*Light, March 4, 1920*
Sir A. Conan Doyle, On February 17th, at the Deanery of Durham, delivered a remarkably convincing address on Spiritualism to a party of guests invited by Bishop Welldon, who presided. The latter, in introducing the speaker, said it was impossible at this time of day to regard Spiritualism as something to be laughed out of court.

This last point was not one the materialist Joseph McCabe could agree with. The date for their debate, announced on 6th December, was set for 11th March.

Many Spiritualists hoped Doyle would bring all his energy to bear in making an undeniable case for their religion, while exposing the barrenness of the materialist position.

In a whirl of activity, Doyle continued to spread the word, reasoned with preachers and argued at materialists before he arrived at the Queen's Hall to face one of his most eloquent critics.

It would turn out to be a fascinating confrontation.

## Chapter 12
## The Great Debate

Joseph McCabe was in many ways the polar opposite of Sir Arthur Conan Doyle.

Small, lightly built and fast talking, McCabe was a willing controversialist with a ready wit. Self-educated, he was renowned for his ability to quickly understand and explain abstruse matters in plain English.

Born in 1867 in Macclesfield, Cheshire, he was the second son of William Thomas McCabe, a weaver and draper and his wife, Harriet Kirk, a milliner; both poor but respectable Roman Catholics.

Educated at a Catholic elementary school, he later trained as a Franciscan friar, was ordained a priest in 1890 and in 1895 became rector of St Bernardine's College, Buckingham. However, in 1896 his growing doubts led him to abandon his post, his order, his church and his religion.

From then on, McCabe worked as a freelance writer and speaker, becoming the most industrious and influential campaigner in the free thought movement throughout the English-speaking world.

He was a founder of the Rationalist Press Association in 1899, served as a director until 1902, and became an honorary associate in 1908.

McCabe claimed to have written more than anyone else alive. He certainly produced thousands of articles, hundreds of books and booklets, and dozens of translations and pamphlets under his own name and several pseudonyms; he also gave thousands of lectures and took part in hundreds of debates all over the world. A polyglot and a polymath, he mastered several languages, natural and social sciences, theology, philosophy, economics, and above all ancient, medieval and modern history.

He developed into a hardline atheist and a devastating controversialist. This, then, was the man against whom Conan Doyle was matched on March 11th, 1920.

Anticipation for the head-to-head was piqued in the preceding month by a talk McCabe gave in Glasgow.

Light, February 14, 1920

## SIR A. CONAN DOYLE'S GHOSTS, MR. MCCABE'S PLEASANTRIES.

Mr. Mccabe has for some time now disposed of the Holy Ghost, and he has now turned his attention to the ghosts of this mundane plane, who apparently have been causing him some uneasiness. However, he seems to have satisfied his own mind, and made a bold effort to try and satisfy the minds of his hearers, that the ghost idea is a delusion and a snare.

He set to work by informing his hearers that Sir A. Conan Doyle had remonstrated with him for misleading the people with his teachings, and thereby causing great harm. However, Mr. McCabe thinks he is going to get his own back when he meets Sir Arthur in debate in London shortly. He is going to point out to Sir Arthur the heinousness of his crime in telling mothers that they will meet their children after death.

Table-rapping, tilting and moving were all explainable by conjuring. Knocks and sounds were due to abnormally developed joints of the limbs.

He divulged to his hearers a great secret when he stated that the so-called messages purporting to come from the spirit world through the medium to the recipient were produced by a wireless system between the recipient and the medium, who caught the thoughts of the recipient and passed them off as coming from the spirit world. He left his hearers in the dark as to how medium and recipient are attuned.

Then he opened an attack on spirit photography, which was, he declared, due to trickery. His idea of a spirit photograph was that of the effect produced when a person shifts your camera when taking an object.

Mr. McCabe smiled profusely as he went from stage to stage, ousting ghosts and exposing their pranks at every turn. The McCabeites greeted his conquests with laughter.

In his eagerness to conquer in other fields of thought, Mr. McCabe has evidently overlooked the most vital point in the study of man. If he leaves out the spiritual side of man, he is not studying man at all, any more than a person can study astronomy without the stars. He stated that man was a chemical machine. But can chemicals think? To me chemicals can no more think than the batteries of a telephone system can talk.

To convince a man who does not want to be convinced is a most difficult task. Nothing will convince such an individual that "death does not end all," till he passes through the physical change called "death." and finds to his great consternation that he is none other than a despised and rejected ghost.

*

*Light* hoped the Doyle-McCabe debate would mark a new phase in Spiritualism's onward march, remarking in an editorial of March 13th:

> The Conan Doyle-McCabe debate will have taken place before our date of issue... hazarding a guess, we should imagine that it will prove that Spiritualism and psychic research are now no longer on the defensive, but are able to take a challenging attitude towards Materialism and Sadduceeism in all their forms.

When it came, the debate was lively, well mannered and did not contain a single mention of hidden wirelesses. Thanks in part to McCabe's eloquence and mock-adversarial style, it was an entertaining evening, with both rationalist and Spiritualist parties cheering points well made.

McCabe's theatricality complemented Doyle's easy amiability. The verbatim account of the debate shows how McCabe relished playing to the audience, "submitting" his "evidence" to their "grand jury" in a kind of cod-legalese.

A long list of leading Spiritualists attended, including Lady Doyle, Viscount and Viscountess Molesworth, Dr. Ellis T. Powell, Mrs. de Crespigny, Mr. H. Engholm, Miss Scatcherd, David Gow and many others.

The order of play was simple: McCabe to start with an opening speech of 40 minutes, Doyle to set out his stall thereafter for the same length; 15 minutes apiece for McCabe and Doyle's replies; each to have a final 15 minutes to sum up. The Chairman, Sir Edward Marshall Hall was chosen for his neutrality. It was his job to start the proceedings and sum up at the end.

McCabe's opening statement set the tone of his attack with a poetic flourish showing that materialists, too, were well aware of the mysteries of the Universe and their effect on the creative mind.

> Long ago in the early history of man it was noticed that there was a shadow, a coloured reflection of oneself, seen on the ground or in the water. From that germ early man a million years ago developed the idea that there was a twofold personality in the individual. As time went on creeds were formed, and priesthoods evolved this idea until at last it became the germ of another world—an immortal world, generally placed in the sky.
>
> I do not wonder at that early speculation of primitive man. I do not wonder that it persisted during hundreds of thousands of years of human life. I do not wonder even that when man's mind rose to the height of philosophy he still retained that belief in his immortal personality. What was that world in which our fathers lived even three hundred years ago? A narrow world, a toy world, compared with the universe that we know today. It was a world bounded by unscaleable walls—those "flaming walls of the world," as they said in the older times. Beyond those narrow walls of this world were boundless spaces, in which the imagination of man could create endless legions of spiritual beings.
>
> Three hundred years ago those walls of the universe fell, and man found himself living on one tiny speck in an illimitable material universe. The mind of man began to change. Where were those spiritual worlds of which earlier ages had dreamed? ...During the last hundred years there has been happening what has happened in every development of civilization since the world began—the mature mind of man, the maturer knowledge of man, dissolving all those old religious illustrations and religious creeds...
>
> ...Millions are fast falling from this dream of an eternal home, and just then there comes this rapping on the walls of the universe, this Spiritualistic movement. Just when men are

beginning to wonder if at last religion is doomed, there comes this portentous phenomenon we are discussing in the shape of Spiritualism. I do not wonder that my opponent takes it to be a new religion, a new revelation.

After this beautifully presented opening McCabe pointed out the great difference between Spiritualism and older religions. Unlike any previous religious movement in the world's history, he said, Spiritualism was "born of fraud" and based "to an alarming extent on fraudulent performances". Even the great mediums like Eusapia Palladino had been caught cheating on numerous occasions – the rest of her sittings, he said, to appreciative laughter, were "not found out".

McCabe also attacked a claim by Doyle that fifty professors in great seats of learning around the world had examined and endorsed Spiritualism. He cited others who regarded Spiritualism as "an affront to science" and lampooned popular ideas of the afterlife as "an asylum for the feeble-minded." He charged Sir Oliver Lodge and fellow Spiritualist scientists with having their thinking clouded by grief and challenged Doyle to provide the names of ten university professors who had "endorsed or defended Spiritualism" within the last thirty years.

He next turned his forensic eye on the medium D D Home. Home, a famous medium of the previous generation of Spiritualists, was regarded by Doyle and many others as the greatest physical medium ever to have lived. He was credited with extraordinary powers, including levitation. He was said to have once famously floated out of a window two storeys up and into another room during a séance in front of reliable witnesses.

"Home was the ablest and most profitable adventurer that ever appeared in the Spiritualist movement," McCabe pronounced, analysing the testimonies of the levitation witnesses. "The supposed levitation of Home was the most hollow piece of charlatanry in the whole history of Spiritualism." He pulled the eyewitness accounts to pieces. One witness described a shadow cast on a wall by Home as he came in through the window, yet a look at the almanacs showed there would not be enough moonlight for such a shadow to be cast. A windowsill 19 inches wide with a balustrade ran on the outside of the building between the two rooms. Why, then, was Home supposed to have levitated between them?

Next, McCabe mercilessly deconstructed the Spiritualist experiences of Doyle and Sir Oliver Lodge. Of the latter's account in *Raymond* of a Spiritualist's description of an at-the-time unknown photograph of Raymond, he pointed out the skilful vagueness of the medium.

In nearly every single detail that medium is right, whatever the details turn out to be. He could be in the open air or not; he could have a stick or not: the medium is not sure. This is offered to us—these details almost infallible where they are definite, always indefinite where they are not infallible—are offered to us as a sign of supernatural power on which to base our belief in immortality.

Amidst loud cheers, McCabe summed up his opening statement:

Whatever other witnesses there may be, you will find... that distortion of judgment, that blearing of vision, which occurs whenever a man enters that wonderful world, that world of almost unparalleled trickery in the history of man... Let us leave that cloudy, misty, disputable, misleading world, and let us concentrate upon this earth upon which we live.

Now it was Doyle's turn. He immediately gave a list of eminent scientists who supported Spiritualism. The audience cheered as he announced, "They have not been to one seance, like Mr. Clodd, or to two or three, like Mr. McCabe. Many have studied for twenty or thirty years, and been to a hundred seances. When it comes to people, who have never had any practical experience, simply because they think and reason so, arguing against men who have taken the trouble and done the work, then I say they are out of court."

Fraudulent mediums, he called "hyenas". But he did not generalise one medium's fraud into a general rule. Instead he divided mediums into the *jet black* ones who deceived for their own gain, and the *snow-white* ones who never did.

Sometimes, he conceded, even respectable mediums deceived, perhaps because their powers had failed them, as Palladino had done, but that did not disprove all the phenomena she had produced. She was thus a grey medium. He insisted some mediums were always genuine.

D D Home was one such, and he was beyond reproach. He "never took any money for anything he did. He showed his powers in all lights." Regarding the state of the moon and whether it provided the backlighting to Home as he floated in through the window, this was irrelevant. "If you saw a man floating in at a window, and there was a light behind him, you would not ask yourself whether it was a street lamp or the shining of the moon. You would be too much occupied in thinking of that man floating in." All that was left of McCabe's evidence was assertion and mudslinging.

Some mediums certainly committed fraud when their powers deserted them; Sir Ray Lankester exposed the medium Henry Slade in London, Doyle acknowledged, but Slade was later examined in Leipzig by Professors Zollner, Schriebner and Weber. During one examination "a great screen of aspen wood five feet away was shattered from end to end by psychic force. Zollner said that the fracture was against the grain of the wood, and that two horses could not have done it. It is as if these invisible forces, by this tremendous exhibition of power were saying: 'Well now, is *that* fraud?'"

Doyle had experienced hundreds of phenomena over the years; others throughout the country had experienced similar numbers. The single cases of evidence numbered "tens of thousands". To cheers, he declared: "Imagine the cumulative evidence of such cases. That is what our opponents will never admit — the enormous cumulative evidence of all these cases."

He recounted the séance given by Mr Evan Powell where his own son had materialised to him, describing binding the medium to ensure no trickery was involved.

"Presently, after many physical phenomena which were very striking, a voice came quite close up to my face. Both my wife and I cried out that it was my boy. He began to talk, and talked in a voice and manner quite distinctive about a private matter. When he had talked he put his strong heavy hand — he was a big fellow — on my head, and pressed my head forward as solidly as possible. He assured me that he was happy, and I can assure you that he left me a good deal happier than he found me." Others present confirmed his account.

Doyle spoke of a séance where his brother Innes had materialised. He gave compelling evidence from other researchers, including photographs of ectoplasm. Citing the long research of Dr Crawford in Belfast, he finished with a flourish:

"I will now merely ask you whether Mr. McCabe is in a better position to give an opinion as to what this force is than a man who has devoted five years of his life in a laboratory under test conditions to working at it?" The room broke into cheers, and Doyle went on: "I hope I have made you realize that Spiritualism is not quite such a slight and humorous thing as Mr. McCabe has attempted to make it out to be."

McCabe dismissed Doyle's evidence, disputed the validity of the Professors' names supplied, since none of their works were cited - and added that some of them were never Spiritualists. To the laughter of the audience, he added:

> Now I find that in this long list of I don't know how many distinguished men there are, so far as I can hurriedly count, just ten professors mentioned in the entire book. Ten University professors, and of those two are not University professors.

So the debate went on, with McCabe criticising Doyle for failing to answer on their own terms the challenges he had thrown down.

McCabe discredited more of Doyle's evidence, including, to the audience's delight, the picture of an ectoplasmic face manifested by Marthe Béraud: "In one of those very photographs in Sir Arthur's book the ghost is a true picture of President Wilson, cut out of a French illustrated paper, and stuck with paste on the medium's breast."

In reply, Doyle pointed out further inaccuracies in McCabe's criticisms, and gave a striking assertion about D D Home. "There are altogether on record some fifty or sixty cases of levitation on the part of Home. He used to fear that people might think they were hypnotized, and so as he floated round the room he wrote his name above the pictures. That was told by Carter Hall, the editor of the Art Journal, a most excellent witness."

He added new evidence – the sighting of visions in a crystal. "I asked the editor of the Morning Post to be good enough to come over. He came and saw what no one could help seeing — these visions succeeding each other in the crystal." The editor admitted to seeing these experiences, denying that any trickery could be involved.

McCabe's final attack was pithy and to the point:

> I decline to accept any revelation which rests in any large degree upon mediums like Marthe Béraud, and Home, and others. I prefer to study the world, and to study the world in that natural light that shines above our heads day by day. (Cheers.) I prefer to cling to this life, to this human nature that we do know so well. I stand here respecting to the uttermost the sincerity of Sir Arthur Conan Doyle, but I stand here with the same sincerity to say that this movement is one vast, mischievous distraction of human energies from the human task that lies before us today. (Prolonged cheers.) I say that within the four corners of this world in which you live you will find inspiration for all the human conduct you can conceive.

In his final speech, Doyle charged McCabe with failing to understand the work done by Spiritualists. McCabe was a man of moral courage, but the whole case against Spiritualism presented by him was superficial and had been "got up" for the purpose of the debate. He reiterated his view that his evidence was strong and clear.

To cheers, he cited the consolation Spiritualism had brought to "thousands and thousands" of people, then finished:

> If I am here tonight, it is simply because I deeply feel the absolute importance of trying, as far as one man may, to remove all those barriers which stand between suffering humanity and this great knowledge which is pouring out week by week, and month by month, but which is still held back by honest, well meaning men who cannot adapt their minds to a philosophy which, if they admit it, is a negation of all that they have been preaching during their whole lives.

The Chairman then closed the meeting, after votes of thanks given by the speakers. The verbatim account notes: "The meeting closed amid cheers."

The whole was reported in a simple and straightforward report in *Light* on 20th March 1919. It did not go into detail because the verbatim debate would be published a few weeks later.

Doyle, however, clearly felt some frustration.

*Light, March 20, 1920*

## LETTER FROM SIR A. CONAN DOYLE.

Sir A. Conan Doyle writes: —

I have no desire to re-open the Queen's Hall debate in print, but as Mr. McCabe denied certain facts I am bound to show that they actually were facts.

The first point concerns the Professors who had, as I stated, accepted our view, some limiting the acceptance to the phenomena only, and some going the whole way with us.

Mr. McCabe challenged me to produce ten names. I produced a list which I said contained forty names. He, after a casual examination, threw it down on the table with the assertion that as far as he could see, it contained only ten names, two of which were not professors. As a fact the list contained forty-two names, and Mr. McCabe simply bluffed the audience when he pretended there were only ten. The names are: —

Great Britain. — Professors Lodge, Crookes, Barrett, Mayo, Challis, de Morgan, Henslow.

America. — Professors William James, Elliott Coues, Denton, Mapes, Hare, Hyslop, Hyde, Corson.

Continental. — Tornebom (Sweden), Zollner, Carl du Prel, Weber, Scheibner, Seiling (Germany), Grimard, Richet, Reichel, Maxwell (France), Gigli, Chiaia (Naples), Schiaparelli (Milan), Brofferio (Milan), Lombroso, Armicis, Ermacora, Finizi, Pictet, Marghieri, Pio Foa, Forro, Morselli, Geresa, Falcomer, Sans Binito (Barcelona), Ochorowicz (Warsaw).

These furnish forty-two names in which I have not included men of science like Dr. Crawford, Myers, Russel Wallace, Varley, and many more who do not happen to have had posts in a University. Of course, the list is by no means complete.

On a second point of fact, Mr. McCabe questioned Lord Lindsay's account of Home's levitation, and put forward the supposition that Home stepped from balcony to balcony outside — so far as one could understand what his supposition was. He quoted the beginning of Lord Lindsay's statement, but he suppressed the end, which surely he must also have read. It runs:—

"Lord Adare then went into the next room to look at the window from which he had been carried. It was raised about 18 inches, and he expressed his wonder how Mr. Home had been taken through so narrow an aperture. Home, still entranced, said, 'I will show you.' Then with his back to the window, he leaned back, and was shot out of the aperture head first, with the body rigid, and then returned quite quickly."

How does this fit in with Mr. McCabe's theory of the balcony? As a fact there was no balcony.

Surely, I did not exaggerate when I said that the evidence for this event was clearer than that for many of the historical occurrences which all the world has agreed to accept.

\*

An article on the following page did not share Doyle's frustrations. In *Spiritualist v. Rationalist,* Spiritualism was the new kid on the block, come to sweep away old-fashioned ideas of a purely physical universe. It was quite a claim, considering the scientific / rationalist world view on which the materialist arguments hinged was only a few hundred years old. The article proclaimed, "It was more than a contest between two opposing systems of thought. It was the age-long conflict of an old and settled order against a new and unsettling one." The forces of materialism were "embattled" as were the conservative elements both inside and outside the church which were "gathering to resist the incursion of a new idea."

The article argued that Rationalism was useful "within its own sphere", but spoke of it in the past tense as if it were a spent force, "It aimed to make an end of prayers and incantations as a convenient substitute for sanitation and social reform. It protested against the idea that the victims of poverty and social injustice should be drugged into submission to their lot by the promise of compensation in some future life of which there was (as the Rationalists considered) no evidence whatever." Rationalism had a necessary intellectual function to fulfil that would help human evolution, but its "one especial defect" was that it "carried too far its contempt for the affections." That's why "Spiritualism was called into being," a thought system baffling to Rationalists - "a kind of hybrid in which the intellect and the emotions, the mind and the affections, were inextricably mixed up together."

Meanwhile, the *Pall Mall Gazette* was reported as contrasting the "bluff, big and breezy Sir Arthur" - who seemed more readily to fit into the mould of the Materialist, while "the slight figure and keen, incisive tones of Mr. McCabe seemed to represent the opposite."

On March 27th, *Light* reported the Rev. Walter Wynn, a confirmed Spiritualist, as saying at an address at the Delphic Club that he could find no single refutation of any fact brought forward by Doyle. "Mr. McCabe simply postulated fraud in every case." But the problem of the world "was not whether Spiritualism was a religion, but whether its phenomena were not shaking to the ground the dogmas of the Church regarding the after-life."

The last surviving witness to the famous D D Home levitation, Lord Dunraven, wrote into the *Weekly Dispatch* to clarify the famous events on the night of December 16th, 1868 at Ashley House, Ashley Place. He had gone back to his original notes, laid out in a letter to his father. The key events were described dramatically in the interactions between the four men present, himself, Lord Crawford (then Master of Lindsay), Mr Wynne (Charlie) and D. D. Home:

> "He (Home) then said to us. 'Do not be afraid, and on no account leave your places'; and he went out into the lounge.
>
> "Lindsay suddenly said, 'Oh, good heavens! I know what he is going to do; it is too fearful.' Adare: 'What is it?" Lindsay: 'I cannot tell you; it is too horrible! Adah says that I must tell you; he is going out of the window in the other room, and coming in at this window.'
>
> "We heard Home go into the next room, heard the window thrown up, and presently Home appeared standing upright outside our window. He opened the window and walked in quite coolly. 'Ah,' he said, 'you were good this time,' referring to our

having sat still and not wished to prevent him. He sat down and laughed.

"Charlie: 'What are you laughing at?' Home: 'We are thinking that if a policeman had been passing and had looked up and seen a man turning round and round along the wall in the air he would have been much astonished. Adare, shut the window in the next room.'

"I got up, shut the window, and in coming back remarked that the window was not raised a foot, and that I could not think how he had managed to squeeze through.

"He arose and said, 'Come and see.' I went with him; he told me to open the window as it was before, I did so; he told me to stand a little distance off; he then went through the open space, head first, quite rapidly, his body being nearly horizontal and apparently rigid. He came in again, feet foremost, and we returned to the other room.

"It was so dark I could not see clearly how he was supported outside. He did not appear to grasp, or rest upon, the balustrade, but rather to be swung out and in."

Lord Dunraven, referring to the above, says: —

"I make no comment except this. Rigorously speaking, it is incorrect to say, as I think has been said, that we saw Home wafted from one window to the other. As to whether he was or was not, I am concerned only to state the facts as observed at the time, not to make deductions from them."

Such accounts could never fit McCabe's world view. At a talk *On The Dangers of Spiritualism* later reported in *Light,* he announced, "A member of the audience at the Queen's Hall said to me as I left, 'What a painful surprise you will have when you pass over!' If Sir Oliver Lodge is right in what he depicts in 'Raymond,' and also Sir Arthur Conan Doyle, I think it will be like an asylum for the feeble-minded, and I cannot say it will be a pleasant surprise for me to find myself in that world without the rationalistic weapon to exterminate myself when I am tired of it."

By April 17th, the *Verbatim Report* of the debate was available from *Light*'s offices. The argument between Doyle and McCabe was far from settled, and shots at each other rumbled on throughout the 1920.

*Light, June 5, 1920.*

## SIR A. CONAN DOYLE AND MR. McCABE.

The Rationalist Press organ, "The Literary Guide," prints in its June issue an article by Sir A. Conan Doyle in reply to Mr. McCabe. It is chiefly concerned with the latter's comments on a booklet containing the names of a number of men of distinction who have supported the Spiritualist position. It was quoted from by Sir Arthur at the public debate in the Queen's Hall, and Mr. McCabe took strong exception to some of its statements. Sir Arthur in the present article writes:—

"In the course of my remarks at the debate I expressly said, in connection with the booklet, that there were one hundred and sixty names in it of people of high distinction, many of them of great eminence. On counting the names in my own copy I find one hundred and sixty-four, so I have not been inaccurate. The history of the little book is that it was compiled by Mr. Charles Hyde, a Spiritualist in the United States, and that when a copy reached me I added such names as I could remember. This accounts for the fact that a number of American Senators are included, whose names are unfamiliar to Mr. McCabe and probably to the British public, but who none the less have a claim to be people of distinction. This also accounts for the fact that Sir Oliver Lodge's title is wrongly set forth. Americans are naturally less familiar with our details, just as Mr. McCabe is unfamiliar with American Senators. The fact of the authorship is stated in the book and the reason of the inaccuracy evident. Since we all know who is meant by Sir Oliver Lodge, the use of the mistake by Mr McCabe is a good example of the sort of niggling criticism which he applies to Spiritualism. To argue thus is to argue like a barrister with a brief, not like a broadminded, earnest man who seeks truth at all costs. Mr. McCabe is so absorbed, for example, in the fact that the provincial American printer has blundered over the exact, title of Professor Challis that he has no space or thought for the fact that this gentleman said of Spiritualism: 'The testimony has been so abundant and consentaneous that either the facts must be admitted to be such as reported, or the possibility of certifying facts by human testimony must be given up.' That one weighty sentence is worth all the clever skirmishing of Mr. McCabe."

In a rejoinder Mr. McCabe says, "Sir A. C. Doyle's long and courteous article leaves my criticism intact."

\*

In the June 12th edition of *Light*, the article *Mr Joseph McCabe On The Warpath* reviewed his latest book, *Is Spiritualism Based On Fraud?* which McCabe insisted was a "damning indictment of Spiritualism," claiming to subject the evidence of Sir A. Conan Doyle to a drastic examination.

*Light* was dismissive, declaring it doubtful whether a detailed analysis of the book was "worth the trouble". It went on, "There are some things which Mr. McCabe cannot yet see, and some things which he has still to learn. These things are obvious to those who have graduated in both schools—the Secularist and the Spiritualist. We cannot wait for him to arrive; our business is to go on, and leave him to gyrate gracefully in the circle he has set for himself until he is tired of it."

On July 10th, 1920, *Light* reported on further criticism from the outspoken materialist, Edward Clodd.

Sir A. Conan Doyle writes in the "Daily Graphic" (June 28th): "Mr. Clodd has, in your columns, ruled me out of the Spiritual controversy on the grounds that an anonymous critic in 'The Times' has said that I 'cannot grasp the principles of scientific investigation.' Is Mr. Clodd prepared to agree that if a newspaper critic condemns materialism as a fallacy it is therefore a fallacy? One must be in desperate straits for an argument before one adopts such a one as this, and I should feel that it was ruled out by all 'principles of scientific investigation'."

Others stepped in on the side of Doyle. In a long article, A. Hunter gave a detailed account of attempts by members of the army to replicate phenomena in Dr Crawford's experiments with Kathleen Goligher by attempting to raise a table with their toes, as McCabe had claimed had been done. The attempts ended in utter failure, and this, Hunter claimed, discredited McCabe's analysis of Goligher's methods.

Looked at in the cold light of day, it is clear that those like McCabe determined not to believe, would forever continue not to believe, whilst those like Doyle and readers of *Light* who were committed to the cause would continue undeviating on their ways, too.

Though the Doyle-McCabe debate didn't provide the knockout punch either would have liked, it was in many ways a wonderful culmination of Spiritualism's growth in confidence during and since the Great War. In Doyle, Spiritualists had a powerful and eloquent champion, whose skill with language was equalled only by his certainty in his faith. It confirmed Doyle not only as a popular fighter for his beliefs, but as an evangelist, a missionary and an important figurehead for the movement.

Doyle's beliefs were sharpened, tempered and hardened in the criticism he received for his views, and the opinions of materialists that he was deluded served only to make him more adamant.

The Doyle-McCabe debate points to the journey ahead for Doyle. He would take on all comers and with his calm and steady reasoning and unshakeable faith, he would overcome.

Had anyone imagined Doyle's energies might be flagging after his long round of travelling and speaking, an article in the May 1st 1920 issue of *Light* scotched any such thoughts. The article was an account of his talk at Coulson Hall in Bristol.

Its final paragraph laid out the next part of his spiritual mission:

> In the course of his remarks Sir Arthur said that looking out into the world and seeing the misery of the bereaved, he remarked to his wife, "If we two could only convey this thing across to the public it would be well worth giving the remainder of our lives to it." His wife agreed. That was three years ago, said Sir Arthur, and during those three years they had done little else (applause). He proposed to go to Australia and New Zealand and America, and after that to continue his work in this country.

Conan Doyle, then, would take his mission beyond the shores of Great Britain to the furthest-flung parts of the Empire, and to her closest ally.

It was perhaps not surprising that he should first visit Australia and New Zealand with his message of consolation. Those countries had also lost the flower of their manhood in the Great War. They were ready to hear his message.

Whilst he was there, new communications from England would set him on a course disastrous to the high reputation he had built up in the preceding years. For now, however, it was time to celebrate his extraordinary achievements as a Spiritualist.

## Chapter 13
## Departures

The Australian Spiritualist Societies' invitation to Sir Arthur Conan Doyle to make a lecturing tour of Australia and New Zealand was first mentioned in the 20th September 1919 issue of *Light*.

By mid 1920 the preparations had been made for the champion of Spiritualism to take his message of solace across the world. For the many appreciative and grateful members of the Spiritualist community, a token of their regard for him seemed in order.

In the article *A Farewell Luncheon To Sir A. Conan Doyle* on 3rd July 1920, *Light* noted that "Sir Arthur and Lady Doyle have been approached on the subject, and cordially accede to the proposal" of a farewell luncheon. Those interested were asked to communicate with the Luncheon Committee at the offices of *Light*. "Spiritualists will welcome this opportunity to meet Sir Arthur and to mark their appreciation of the wonderful work he has been doing throughout the country." The charge per head would be 7s and 6d.

Just a week later on 16th July, *Light* announced great interest being shown in the proposal. The luncheon would be held at one o'clock at the Holborn Restaurant, Kingsway, London, on Thursday, July 29th.

"There is no doubt that Spiritualists will rise to the occasion and make this gathering a representative and historic one," the magazine noted, and hoped that mediums would be "present in force", along with those who had benefited from Doyle's wonderful work. "The Knight of Spiritualism" would receive their appreciation for his "unselfish and magnificent efforts to spread this great truth." Seating was restricted to 250, and *Light* cautioned, "there may be a difficulty in accommodating all who desire to be present".

The prediction proved accurate. By the 17th July issue of *Light* all tickets had been sold. "Letters of appreciation are pouring in, and applications for tickets have quite exceeded the most sanguine expectations of the Committee." Meanwhile, the great and the good of Spiritualism would be present, including George Berry, president of the Spiritualists' National Union and Ernest W. Oaten, vice-president. The Reverend G Vale Owen would pronounce the Grace and Dr Abraham

Wallace would preside. During the luncheon an illuminated testimonial in the form of a scroll would be presented to Doyle.

The following week, *Light* was still receiving "fruitless applications" for tickets. Those who had bought theirs early could "congratulate themselves on their promptness," while those who had missed out could console themselves that those present "will constitute the most representative body of Spiritualists that has probably ever been gathered together in this country. In one way and another every Spiritualist Church, Society and community will be represented."

After a succession of dismal wet days, the morning for the Farewell Luncheon arrived in a blaze of sunshine. Echoing the comment on the weather for the Albert Hall Memorial Service in which the snow was interpreted as Nature's sympathy for the event, *Light* reported "a single day of summer sunshine intervened most fortunately for this occasion."

After the Rev. G. Vale Owen pronounced grace, Mona Street presented Lady Conan Doyle with a "magnificent bouquet composed of roses and arum lilies, decorated with ribbons representing Spiritualist colours."

*Light* dedicated 2 full pages to coverage of the event.

*Light, August 7, 1920*


THE FAREWELL LUNCHEON TO
SIR ARTHUR AND LADY CONAN DOYLE.
An Enthusiastic And Representative Gathering.
Presentation Of Illuminated Address. A Dramatic Episode.


Thursday, July 29th, 1920, must inevitably become a historical date in Spiritualism, for it marks a great occasion: On that day there was held at the Holborn Restaurant, London, an enthusiastic Farewell Luncheon to Sir Arthur Conan Doyle and Lady Doyle prior to their departure for Australia. That is its outer significance. But in a deeper sense it marks a unity and a power in the Spiritualist movement which cannot fail to have most important results. The occasion, too, showed the instantaneous and overwhelming response to an invitation to do honour to a loved and distinguished leader. This response, indeed, was so enormous that it taxed the genius of a born organiser like Mr. Engholm to cope with it.

The Royal Venetian Room at the Holborn Restaurant seated 280 representative guests gathered from every part of the United Kingdom. So many who wished to be present had to be refused that, as Mr. Engholm said in the course of his speech, it would have been possible, had time permitted, to have taken and easily filled the Albert Hall. As it was, it was impossible to find seats for the members of the London Press, who had to be entertained in an adjoining room, from which they emerged when the speeches began.

Sir Arthur Conan Doyle was responsible for a highly dramatic moment in the proceedings. In the course of his fine speech he unexpectedly asked all those present who could declare positively that they had been in communication with the dead to stand up. Practically the entire assemblage rose to its feet. Sir Arthur confessed that even he was surprised at the response to his invitation, adding, "It is the most wonderful sight ever witnessed in London."

After the toast of "The King" had been proposed from the Chair and duly honoured, the Chairman, Dr. Abraham WALLACE, gave the toast "The health of Sir Arthur Conan Doyle and Lady Doyle." He said: —

"My Lords, ladies and gentlemen,—It is owing to the foresight and energy of our friend Mr. Engholm (cheers) and those associated with him on the Committee that we are present here to-day at this kind of Agape, or love feast, to do honour to our distinguished friend and beloved fellow worker, Sir Arthur Conan Doyle, as he is going to leave us in a few days, accompanied by his wife, to cross the seas and tell the people in Australia and New Zealand what he is doing in this country and to carry with him his splendid message."

Referring to his own visit to the United States last winter, the Chairman said he was sure that Sir Arthur would receive a fine reception if he went to California. After some allusions to the work of Dr. Alfred Russel Wallace and Sir William Crookes he remarked that history had always shown that every intellectually honest man or woman who had devoted sufficient time and attention to the subject emerged from the inquiry as a firm believer in the spirit hypothesis, just as Sir Arthur Conan Doyle had done.

He associated Sir Arthur with four of the greatest investigators whose memory he (the Chairman) cherished— F. W. H. Myers, Richard Hodgson, James H. Hyslop, and that great soul, William T. Stead—

remarking in parenthesis and amid cheers, that he was glad the Bureau Mr. Stead established was still in existence and was in the hands of his distinguished daughter. Some of Sir Arthur's critics knew him only as a writer of history and of detective and other stories and did not realise that he was a scientific man. They were ignorant of the fact that he was a medical student in Edinburgh University at a time when the University had the largest medical school of the world, and was at the very zenith of its fame, with a professoriate unequalled in any other centre of learning. He was trained not only in methods of exact science but in medical psychology, and hence was well qualified to become, as he had become, a perfect psychical researcher. Sir Arthur had shown his powers not only as an attractive lecturer, but as a great debater in supporting the claims of Spiritualism, especially when he had to deal with the studied misrepresentations of so-called Rationalists. In the future he would be known not only as a great writer, lecturer and debater, but in an unique sense as a great missionary of Modern Spiritualism. And now, accompanied and supported and encouraged by his gracious partner, Lady Doyle, he was about to go to the Antipodes, as one of the greatest benefactors of our English speaking race, bearing messages of comfort and joy to our Colonial brothers and sisters who had suffered bereavement, as we had, through the Great War. He (the Chairman) therefore asked his fellow Spiritualists of England, Ireland, Scotland and Wales—for he understood all these countries were represented there that day—to drink to the health of Sir Arthur and Lady Doyle. The toast was enthusiastically honoured.

SIR ARTHUR CONAN DOYLE'S SPEECH.

Sir Arthur Conan Doyle, who on  rising  received a great  ovation, said:—

I cannot address this audience in conventional terms. I must call you friends and comrades. We are comrades in the greatest mission that folk ever set forth to do in the history of the world. That mission is to convey to the human race that the time has come when we must uncover once again those old foundations upon which religion was originally built, which have become so overgrown by the jungle of theology that they are lost to sight. Our mission is also to turn faith into knowledge; it is to abrogate as far as one can all terror and fear of death, and incidentally it is to open up entirely new fields for science. I do not think I exaggerate when I say that all these purposes put together constitute the greatest mission that man could undertake.

In pursuing that mission we are met by that usual storm of criticism and abuse which is very excellent for us. I would not have it otherwise. But our object is, while profiting by that criticism, while making sure that every link in our chain is true, none the less to fix our eyes upon our distant object, and to go forward unflinchingly, feeling like the Psalmist, if the Lord is with us, what matter who is against us?

I was touched by what you said of my wife. It is very easy for me to do this, because I love adventure, I love travel, I do not object to contention in a good cause-— (laughter)—but my wife does make sacrifices. It is she who has to break up her household, part with those of whom she is so fond. She who has to take the children from school, she, in fact, who has to break up all those domestic felicities which are dear to a lady.

She does it because she had encountered in her own person those consolations which she would stick at nothing in order to convey to others. (Cheers.) It would indeed be hard for me if I differed in any way from the way in which she looks at these matters. Fortunately she has shared my knowledge, shared my experiences, and is not only well abreast of me but very often she is in front.

It is now some three years since I started this campaign and determined to devote the remainder of my life to this work. (Cheers.) It struck me, if one could get people together face to face, one could get past all those jocosities and misrepresentations in the Press which have tended to blur and obscure this subject. Once you get people into a hall, they cannot get out; there is no escape. There you are able to go into the length and breadth of it, so that the whole picture opens, and at last I think they begin to understand what it is we are trying to do. I have put up beside my bedside a large map of England and Scotland, and have put a red splotch wherever I have spoken. I am glad to say that now Great Britain has assumed a highly eruptive aspect. (Laughter.)

What I have always found is that it is not my lecture that does the good, but the local discussion, ventilation and arguments in the Press. We always have those good, unwilling friends who come forward at once to make a row. I know them all; they are all the same in every place you go to. There is always the materialistic gentleman, who insists upon his right to eternal putridity. (Loud laughter.) There is the gentleman who has such a deep respect for the Bible that he has never even examined it and knows nothing about it. He approaches with Deuteronomy in one hand and Leviticus in the other, and he is a very violent attacker, but not, I find, very difficult to evade. But it is the spiritual ferment which is created which I think may do some good in Australia, not my poor remarks, but the fact that the subject is brought prominently before the people, and that a certain percentage do recognise how enormous it is, and how intimately it concerns every one of themselves. It is in the personal application that our strength lies.

I have been asked, "Why Australia?" Well, I thought I had done for the present my work here. I had very flattering invitations to go to America, but our great chief[83] has already covered that ground and has produced just that discussion which I have wished to see. Australia is remote, is somewhat neglected in some matters by lecturers particularly, and it seemed to me that the Spiritualists there, from what I heard, were scattered if fairly numerous, very anxious to have a lead and to have some means by which they could come to a head. They thought I could help them and I was very glad to try. They have done such splendid work for the Empire. Both Australia and New Zealand have shed their blood so lavishly. In proportion to their numbers there are just as many desolate homes there as here, and it seemed both to me and my wife if by any exertion on our part we could bring a little comfort such as we have sometimes been privileged to do here to these great imperialists over yonder, it would indeed be a privilege for us to try to do so.

I made them understand that we do not go out there to address or bolster up any sect. This subject is much too great for that (hear; hear). We go with a wonderful message applying to every man, woman and child in the world, and we are going to talk straight to the Australian public. The whole world at present needs comfort. That is what it needs. It is worried and flurried and it has got a little bit peevish in consequence. What it wants is comfort. We have got the comfort to give. So far as I can see we are the only people who have. We have got it and we bring it not with vague assurances, not with conflicting facts, but with positive knowledge and absolute personal experiment and experience. That is what is wanted now; something much more solid and definite than in the past. We can tell them that the dead are very near us, that the

---

83  Sir Oliver Lodge had performed a tour of the USA in 1920.

veil is very thin, that they are most accessible. My wife and I counted up yesterday and made a list of eleven departed friends and relatives with whom we have spoken together face to face, hearing their voices, not through any table or writing mediumship or anything that could be criticised, face to face hearing their voices, and talking as we would have talked with them if we met them in this world. What we tell our friends over there is what we have heard from the lips of the dead and what must therefore be true. No such direct message has ever been given before, and in spite of every opposition we will get it across, or try to, to those bruised hearts for whom God meant it.

The more one studies it, the more one reads of the subject, the more one realises that it is the same message which came two thousand years ago and which was so mangled and obscured by the stupidity of man that it has been lost during all these centuries. When I read the New Testament, with the knowledge that I have, it is to me as if I was reading some palimpsest upon which God had written knowledge, and then mankind had written over it, but behind all that human script still you get a glimpse of the Divine message. I was reading the other day a book about the catacombs, the tombs of the early Christians. The writer was a Canon of the Church of England. He said in some examples, talking about the Scriptures, "these people seem to have been talking to the dead!" This is what they did in the first century. Here we are in the twentieth century, and we are talking to the dead. But what Church is there that obeys that apostolic example? What Church is there which actually practises that communion of saints about which they talk so glibly? It is only on our shoulders that that mantle has fallen. The human race has gone round, I will not say in a circle because it would be a slur on the providence of God to imagine that for twenty centuries the whole human race could be left to wander as a lost man wanders in the desert, coming back to the place where he started from. Rather would I say that it is an ascending spiral by which you reach a point having a great resemblance to the point below, where you gain possibly that knowledge forgotten below, but where you add to it all that science, all that civilisation has given in addition, and so raise the whole race to a higher level. (Cheers.)

What has happened to our race is that we have reared a structure which is too high for the foundations on which it is built. What we need is to underpin, examine, and restore those foundations. German wars and Bolshevism, every horror that we know of, has come first from the fact that we have been building on foundations of sand and pretending that it was rock. To me the religious aspect of this question is everything. (Hear, hear.) I am interested, as every intelligent man must be, in the psycho-physical powers which have come incidentally to us and which curiously enough have put us into the position of knowing a great deal more of matter and its possibilities than ever the materialists have known. I naturally am deeply interested also in our conversation with the dead. But, after all, that is personal. In any case we will meet them in a few years; it is not the essence of the matter. The essence of the matter is the high teaching, the religion, the philosophy, what it is that the dead tell us. For the first time has been given a description of the Universe which is adequate, logical, which carries us forward, gives us something to hope for, makes us realise that it is indeed not only an all-powerful but an all-good God. This is the real New Revelation which casts a searchlight from heaven down upon the darkened roads of earth.

I must get back from these general large subjects to this, particular gathering which you have so kindly organised for us. This gathering includes every shade of Spiritualism from what I may call the Fathers of the Church down to these little children who, when most of us have passed away, not into rest, I hope, for we are not that sort (hear, hear), but when we are digging away on the other side of the tunnel, these little kiddies will carry on the tradition and remember what they have seen and heard today. I am honoured by the presence here of very many distinguished Spiritualists—journalists like David Gow and John Lewis, all-round splendid workers like Oaten and Yates, Blake, and so many more that it would become a little invidious if I went on to mention them. But especially I would mention Oaten, because he has been my comrade in many a scrap. I look upon Oaten as half bull-dog and half apostle. Every form of activity, from editing a paper to going off in a trance, from building a church with his own hands, which he did, down to arguing with a Chief Constable—every form of activity comes alike to him. He is the kind of boy we want in our fighting line! I cannot help mentioning the name of Percy Street, another man of exactly the same type and a glorious fighter for Spiritualism. As for Harry Engholm, in him we have had thrown up at last what we needed—a great organiser.

The way Mr. Engholm organised the McCabe debate and the way in which he has now organised this luncheon—to give the two occasions in which I was personally concerned—show that he has extraordinary capacity in that direction.

I greatly esteem it that many mediums and many great authorities on the subject are here. I would mention, first of all, a very old friend, Mr. A. P. Sinnett. I knew him first in 1885. He was one of the first men to turn my thoughts strongly to things of the other world. At that time he had written the "Occult World" and he explained Theosophy as no man before or since has ever explained it. He made me understand it, and that was no small feat (laughter). I have always carried an affectionate feeling for him and his cult, and I recognise that there is no difference at all of any import between us, that we are simply dealing with the next step while he, more far sighted but perhaps a little more vague, can see rather further into the new country.

But especially am I complimented to-day by the presence of a large number of professional mediums (cheers). I speak most deliberately when I say that in these days of sorrow those men and women who have got true psychic power and use it for the benefit of the public are absolutely the most useful members of the whole community (cheers). Those are the people whom our barbarous laws cause to live always in the shadow of the police. That they endure for the sake of the comfort they give and the knowledge they have. They have also to endure the jeering of a most ignorant Press. But the thing which they should not be called upon to endure is that absolute want of responsibility on the part of the Spiritualists who use them in the heyday of their strength and then forget them when, in the course of waning years, those wonderful powers, like all other powers which are partly physical, have disappeared and gone. It is a disgrace to us and enough to bring a curse on our movement—our treatment of the old mediums.

I have told you that my wife and I have come into contact with eleven of our dead and have talked to them. But I want you to give me something I can carry with me to Australia. I am going to carry the beautiful souvenir which you have given us, but I want something else. I want every man and woman in this hall who knows and can swear that they have been in touch with their departed dead kindly to stand up.

(The vast majority of the company immediately rose in their seats.)

I believe that is the most wonderful demonstration that has ever been seen in London. I do not think in my whole life I have ever seen anything more dramatic or extraordinary, because, believe me, I never dreamt there would be such a general response. Once again I thank you in my wife's name and my own for all your extraordinary hospitality. You send us forth in good heart, and if we do not do well on the other side your hands at least are clean. (Cheers.)

The illuminated address was then presented by Mr. H. W. Engholm, following which the Rev. Walter Wynn proposed the toast, "Spiritualist Societies Here and Overseas," which was responded to by Mr. Ernest Oaten, but a report of these and the rest of the proceedings must be deferred until next week.

Sir Arthur and Lady Doyle's three children—Masters Dennis and Malcolm and Miss Jean Doyle—were present among the guests.

*

The following week, *Light* carried the response at the Luncheon to Doyle's speech.

*Light, August 14, 1920*

### THE FAREWELL LUNCHEON
### TO SIR ARTHUR CONAN DOYLE.
Presentation Of The Illuminated Address
And Subsequent Speeches.

Mr. H. W. Engholm, in presenting the illuminated address, said that this part of the function which he had to carry out as ambassador of the Luncheon Committee, was to him the most delightful thing he had ever done in connection with the Spiritualist movement. He had had a great deal to do with Sir Arthur in his work, having been at many of the meetings he had addressed, and he was struck by the fact that Sir Arthur retained his old keen, critical faculty. He said that for the reason that on one or two occasions men well known in Fleet-street had remarked to him, "Since Sir Arthur Conan Doyle took up Spiritualism he seems to have gone off at the deep end!" (Laughter.) They meant by that to imply that anyone who went in for a study of this great subject must lose his critical faculties and become involved in fantasies. "Only the other day," Mr. Engholm proceeded, "I was talking to Sir Arthur on a question dealing with a spirit photograph, and I was rather inclined to believe it was the real thing. To hear Sir Arthur take up one point after another in the picture and examining it critically, give his verdict upon it, showed me that Sherlock Holmes is still with us. (Hear, hear.) But we have in him a spiritualised Sherlock Holmes—that is the difference. (Cheers.) The address he was presenting represented a token of esteem, not only from all present, but from the Spiritualists of the whole country, for the signatures might have been multiplied in thousands. Judging by the applications received to attend the luncheon, he felt that in other circumstances they might have taken the Albert Hall and filled it. He hoped, nay, he felt almost sure he was safe in prophesying that when their good friends Sir Arthur and Lady Doyle returned, they would have the Albert Hall in which to welcome them. He hoped then he might propose himself as organiser. (Laughter and cheers.) The illuminated address was then handed by Mr. Engholm to Sir Arthur

The Rev. Walter Wynn proposed the toast of "The Spiritualist Societies Here and Overseas." He said he would have liked to see every Christian Church represented there that day. It seemed to him that the fundamental mission of Sir Arthur Conan Doyle was essentially Apostolic and Christ-like. He believed that not only in Great Britain, but throughout the world, there was a consciousness that Sir Arthur represented a rising current of thought in the human race. Because he believed that Sir Arthur Conan Doyle was carrying an essentially Christian doctrine to the ends of the earth he felt honoured to be present that day to wish him and Lady Doyle God-speed. (Cheers.)

Mr. Ernest W. Oaten (Vice-President of the Spiritualists' National Union) said he did not know which half of him they wanted to see—the bull-dog or the apostle — (laughter)—but, at any rate, it was an honour to be asked to represent the Spiritualist Societies of Great Britain and Overseas. Theirs had been an onerous task. They had been carrying a burden when persecution was heavy and obloquy was undeserved. They had everywhere proclaimed the truth when the whole movement was in the wilderness. For fifty years they had carried it upon their backs, and he rejoiced to-day that, the pioneers had done their work so faithfully that the movement was now ringing throughout the length and breadth of the world. (Cheers.) He rejoiced in being there that day because Sir Arthur Conan Doyle had been a unifying force in their movement. He had brought together all branches and all phases in a spirit of fraternity which would, he trusted, be perpetuated in the future. When Sir Arthur decided that he ought to give his message to the world, he (the speaker) was lucky enough to drop across him. Sir Arthur was looking for work, and he (the speaker) found him some. (Laughter.) He was sometimes asked what the Spiritualist Societies were doing. He replied, "The same thing they have been doing for fifty years—developing mediums, without whom there would have been no Spiritualism." Let them realise that fact. In a thousand places they had been faithfully developing circles, year in and year out, in order that the psychical faculties which men possessed should be unfolded for the benefit of the world. During all that time they had had much to endure. A good deal of persecution came to them from the theologian who, in his zeal for the truth he loved, was jealous lest its value should be underrated. Perhaps he was justified in his doubts. At any rate, the theologian was beginning to learn at last that Spiritualism was not, and never had been, the foe to religion. It was the firmest rock upon which religion could be built, and it would stand when all other speculative matters had dropped into the limbo of the forgotten past. On the other hand, science had treated them with cold frigidity, and that despite the few brilliant names of those who had stood on their side. But, at least, they had been enabled to put science in this position, that whether she wished it or not, she had had to extend the boundaries of her investigations. (Cheers.) They had opened up new fields to be explored, had brought new worlds into the compass of man's intellectual concept. They were, he claimed, the friends of both science and religion, which would subsequently become one. The Spiritualist movement formed the strongest ground upon which they could meat and join hands. He believed that presently this nucleus of Spiritualism would form the solid basis of a world religion. Let them pool their resources, and out of that which was obtained, they should at least have enough truth to guide the world with greater certitude and greater facility than it had been guided in the past.

They were continually being asked how Spiritualism concerned past teaching, how it squared with history a long way back. Might he say that although that was important, it was not the most important matter. The point which mattered was what was going to be the relation of Spiritualism to the future. The past could not be altered, but the future could be made. They were out for a greater religion, a greater future, and they believed they could build it best by close association with those benign and living ones who had been their source of strength in the past, the source of their inspiration in the present, and would be their hope in the future.

Their attitude towards the whole world was, "We do not mind what you believe, believe what you like. Our business is, what do you know?" Let them bring it in and pool it into a common fund for humanity's benefit. It was in that spirit that the Spiritualist Societies to-day were facing their tasks of great magnitude, with a consciousness of angel guidance and spiritual inspiration. They knew they would win.

He had pleasure in responding for some three hundred Spiritualist Societies in the United Kingdom, and in giving Sir Arthur and Lady Doyle their kindliest greetings and heartiest send-off. Might they do as much work across the seas as they had done in England, and might they return rejuvenated and even strengthened for further work. (Cheers.)

\*

The text of the address handed to him underscored the high esteem in which he was held by his fellow Spiritualists:

> We, the undersigned, present at the Farewell Luncheon to Sir Arthur Conan Doyle and Lady Doyle, desire to record our feelings of admiration, and affectionate regard towards them both.
>
> To you, Sir Arthur, we offer our gratitude for the heroic and self-abnegating work you have carried on so long as the missionary of what you have so well termed the "New Revelation," the message of spiritual consolation and enlightenment divinely inspired at the beginning of the new epoch of the world's history.
>
> To you, Lady Doyle, we offer our tribute of appreciation and regard for the noble way in which you have supported your

husband's work, always at his side with true devotion to him and to the cause he so devotedly serves.

We wish you both every happiness and success in your journey to Australia and New Zealand, there to carry on the great mission to humanity, and earnestly hope that we may give you all our congratulations on your return.

Our good wishes and most, affectionate thoughts go with you.

The afternoon was a triumph, demonstrating how central Doyle had become to the movement. Mediums who attended also revealed its impact on other planes.

"In conversation with some of them afterwards," *Light* reported, "a record of impressions they received was given. A common feature distinguished these accounts." One psychic spoke of seeing "a golden archway, "another described it as "a magnificent rainbow," a third as "a luminous cloud," and a fourth as "a golden horse shoe." *Light* added, "These impressions were communicated individually, immediately after the guests arose."

On August 7th, 1920, *Light* published a valedictory letter by Sir Arthur Conan Doyle which summed up his aspirations for Spiritualism, wished well to the friends he left behind – and in typical Doylean style, also grappled with the practical matter of fundraising.

*Light, August 7, 1920*

## THE NEEDS OF SPIRITUALISM IN THE METROPOLIS.
### A MESSAGE TO THE READERS OF "LIGHT" FROM SIR ARTHUR CON AN DOYLE.

I am, I think, one of the oldest readers of LIGHT, as well as a member of the Council of the London Spiritualist Alliance, of which that journal is the organ, and on my departure to Australia I want to say a few words regarding both.

Each represents the fruit of long years of faithful and self-denying work on the part of many men and women. Some have now passed on to higher service; others, old and worn, are veterans who have done their part and of whom no more can be reasonably expected. Still others, at the centre of things, are doing their best and hardest to steer the Alliance and LIGHT safely through narrow and perilous channels, so that they may be gradually adapted to new times and conditions. It is a piece of work that has required and still requires immense pains and patience. Not easily are old traditions broken with and old methods outgrown. These are the natural results of many years of the trials and tribulations of the Spiritualism of an older day, when any rash step, any precipitate movement, might have proved disastrous to a subject that had a host of enemies and was an object of popular scorn. The changes and adaptations call for the greatest tact and forbearance, as well as skill and courage.

We — I am speaking not only for myself — want to see the Alliance and LIGHT emerge to the position of the leading centre and the representative journal of Metropolitan Spiritualism at least, and thoroughly equipped to carry out the great work that lies before them. I want to ask for them the support of everyone who has the interests of the movement at heart, not only as an acknowledgment of all they have done, but of all they may, with such support, still achieve. I understand that LIGHT has collected something over £4,000 towards a desired £10,000 to provide house accommodation for the Alliance and itself. Even the main sum is little enough in these days, and the remaining few thousands could be added if only one or two of the wealthy friends of the movement could be induced to be generous. The starting of a pension fund for veteran workers is also a separate but a most pressing need. Many who are not rich in this world's goods are sacrificing their strength and leisure and giving of their best to help the movement forward, but they look to their richer brethren to uphold their hands, remembering ever what dross worldly wealth must ever be compared to great progressive movements of the Spirit.

I leave England with many regrets at even a brief separation from you all, although I depart on my mission to Australia full of hope and courage with regard to what lies before me. I am confident that on my return I shall find that further strides have been made, and that Spiritualism has won measurably nearer to its true position as a world-force, carrying a message of hope to humanity at large. Above all, we must be charitable

to each other's opinions, and, whether we be Unitarian or Trinitarian, unite upon the one essential point of spirit return and communion.
ARTHUR CONAN DOYLE.

*

Before his departure, Doyle continued lecturing, writing articles and fulfilling his missionary work in Britain. At another talk in Exeter on August 4th entitled *Death and the Hereafter,* he laid out his faith once more:

> After reading as much as any man has ever read on this subject in print and in manuscript," declared the lecturer with conviction, "I have not the faintest doubt of the next world. I know exactly what is going to happen to me when I die. I know what I shall find. I know the details. Yet, if you will believe me, I have not got a credulous mind. On the contrary, those who know me best are aware that I have a critical mind, and that it takes a great deal of time to convince me.[84]

In *Light* of August 21st, 1920, the following announcement appeared.

> Sir Arthur Conan Doyle sailed for Australia by the steamer "Naldera" on Friday, August 13th. In deference, it is understood, to Sir Arthur's wishes, only relatives and a few personal friends were present.

A letter soon followed.

*Light, September 11, 1920*

A LETTER PROM SIR A. CONAN DOYLE.
Religious Discussions On Shipboard.

Sir A. Conan Doyle writes as follows from S.S. "Naldera," under date August 25th:—

---

84 *Light,* 14th August, 1920

"It was stated yesterday that 'Never since the P. & O. Company was founded has there been so much religious discussion upon a ship.' It is not rancorous discussion, but rather the clearing up of difficulties.

"Last night I addressed two hundred and eighty first-class passengers, with Parsees, Mahomedans, Buddhists, and men of all persuasions, including the Christian Bishop of Kwang-Si, a most excellent prelate, far more human and broad minded and intelligent than most ecclesiastics. It was a classic sea, for we could see the island where St. Paul was driven by Euroclydon to the south of Crete.

"All went excellently. On Friday I am to address the second-class passengers—in the Red Sea in August!—so I will have a warm time, in fact it is a bad case of Sweated Labour. But it is worth anything, for I find the whole world yearning for knowledge and not knowing how to get it, or how to distinguish the true from the false. We want more philosophy and fewer phenomena now, though the good medium is still the necessary starting point."

*

There was no stopping Doyle.

## Chapter 14
## Future Controversies

Conan Doyle's missionary work in Australia and New Zealand would be the start of a series of projects and missionary tours to take him around the world. It would be the next leg of his great spiritual adventure. For now, we leave him at the height of his powers, respected as a great thinker, an honest public speaker and the possessor of an incisively critical mind.

Throughout the 1920s there would be a shift in public perception of him. Deep controversies would rage. Already in *Light* of the previous four years, some of the seeds of those controversies had been planted. Doyle's relationship with his close friend and at times most vociferous detractor, Harry Houdini, would come to the fore in the following years.

Houdini had already become a subject of discussion for Spiritualists. He'd started off as a fake medium, but in later years had repented and taken it upon himself to expose fraudulent mediumistic techniques. Many couldn't let go of the idea that he had genuine powers.

An article from *Light* of March 1st 1919 entitled *Houdini, Medium or Conjurer?* argued against *Light*'s official position that Houdini's extraordinary feats of manifestation were the result of legerdemain.

The author, Mr J Hewat McKenzie confidently attributed to Houdini "mediumistic powers of a transcendent character." He rationalised that Houdini "does not wish the public to know that some of his work is due to spirit agency, for an announcement of this kind would be badly received by a music-hall audience. Legal processes might also be entered against him, and the disturbing mental forces which would be aroused during his performance would possibly militate against any successful demonstration of a psychic nature." He finished with a plea to *Light*: "I... trust that if opportunity arises *LIGHT* will decide to examine Houdini's manifestations on behalf of itself and its readers."

Houdini was also taken to task by *Light* for his claims against Spiritualism. An article of February 14th commented drily:

> Mr. Houdini, the illusionist who escapes from locked cells and closed tanks, makes some pretty confessions in the 'World's

Pictorial News' of January 31st ult. He was a bogus medium because he was young, poor, and newly married. There is no spirit manifestation he cannot reproduce or improve. Well, we suggest he might produce a psychic photograph of a recognisable face on the fifth plate of a sealed packet of twelve.

Another element in which Doyle would become increasingly interested was Spirit Photography. The Crewe Circle, run by William Hope, was a group of amateur photographers who had begun to manifest unusual and unearthly imagery. In their photographs, alongside living subjects, the faces of loved ones would often appear – the latter apparently never having been photographed in such poses during their lifetime. It was uncanny, and Conan Doyle's investigations into the subject were the basis for his classic work *The Case for Spirit Photography*.

Doyle was already looking into the phenomenon, as a *Light* article from August 23rd, 1919, showed:

> Sir Arthur Conan Doyle replied in last week's issue of "Truth" to the doubts cast by that journal on the genuineness of the spirit photograph of his son obtained at Crewe on May 31st. After giving details of the manner in which the photograph was taken, Sir Arthur sums up with the remark, "The results are complex and mysterious, but they need earnest and sympathetic consideration, not indiscriminate and ignorant abuse."

A further article, from January 1920, showed Doyle grappling with the problem of Spirit Photography again, this time criticising the probable fraudulent process by which it was produced:

*Light, January 10, 1920*

"SCREEN" MARKS IN PSYCHIC PICTURES

A correspondent in France raises an interesting question with regard to the stipple marks or "screen" marks mentioned in a letter of Sir A. Conan Doyle's which accompanied the publication of a psychic photograph representing his son who fell in the war. Sir Arthur, as quoted by our correspondent, attributes these to a probable transfer of a screen picture from an illustrated magazine; and our correspondent takes up this point and shows that similar "screen" marks have appeared on *moulds* of a materialised "double". The clay showed similar "screen" marks as if the impression had been made through cambric. (pp. 124 and 198 "Exteriorisation de la Motricité," De Rochas.)

This is attributed by some experimentalists to an invisible protective psychic screen, and good reasons are for the hypothesis. Till, however, the process actually employed by the operators on the other side is much more elucidated, all these hypotheses seem too much like guesswork. The data are still insufficient.

Our correspondent suggests that "spirits have kept us too long in the dark as to this matter, which touches closely the proofs of their identity." That is so, and useful experimental work could be done in that direction. If automatists would devote their attention to getting *precise* and exact *matter* of this description and would retain the personal communications for those to whom they are specially addressed, automatic writing would stand higher in general esteem than is the case to-day.

*

Doyle was a man of deep passion and conviction, who once he had made his mind up on a matter would stick to it. He was a man of imagination and brilliance, warm-hearted and sometimes unsubtle in his thinking.

All of these traits contributed to perhaps the most famous, or infamous of the matters he investigated, the case of the Cottingley Fairies. It took a long step forward whilst Doyle was in Melbourne on his Antipodean tour.

Doyle had been made aware in May 1920 by F R Scatcherd, editor of *The Two Worlds*, that a pair of girls living in the village of Cottingley, Yorkshire, had produced extraordinary photographs of themselves playing with little woodland spirits. Unable to meet them due to lecturing commitments, Doyle had left investigation of the girls, Elsie

Wright and her cousin Frances Griffiths to Edward Gardner, a building contractor and senior member of the Theosophical Society.

The negatives already produced were sent to Kodak, who affirmed they had not been tampered with, though Kodak added that the images could be faked without tampering. Harold Snelling, an expert on fake photography declared the pictures genuine. That was enough for Doyle. The girls, then, had photographed real fairies.

The investigation sought further evidence in new photographs.

In Melbourne in September 1920, Doyle received a letter from Gardner confirming that the girls had taken three new photographs. The news was a matter of great excitement to him as he continued his Australian tour. It confirmed that his instinct on the matter was right. When he had first been approached about the photographs in May, he had coincidentally been considering the tradition in some cultures that children could see fairies. He was told of the Cottingley images just as he completed an article for *The Strand* on this exact subject. Several factors combined here to make the news more powerful. Doyle believed the news was Providence at work once again; it was certainly what Jung would have called Synchronicity.

It is also interesting to consider whether, since Doyle's father had painted fairies and died of mental illness, he felt this new materialisation in some way exonerated his father.

In Australia, Doyle's reputation as an ethical and brilliant thinker on Spiritualism was at its high point.

In the years to come, his judgement would be strongly questioned. All the way through a far more difficult decade, Doyle would stick to his faith with unshakeable firmness.

Those events, however, are for another book.

This one is near its end.

# Afterword

In the introduction to this work, I asked the question, *how could Arthur Conan Doyle, the man who invented the ultra-rational Sherlock Holmes, believe in séances, mediums - and even fairies?*

I have not, I admit, fully answered that final clause, though I think the development of his thinking to take him to that point is clear to see.

Doyle started as a young, inquisitive doctor in the 1880s seeking to know everything he could about the world, and later became the inspired author exploring wonderful and extraordinary possibilities and phenomena that sparked his brilliant imagination, his scientific curiosity and his religious instinct. Further on, he was the dilettante who experienced strange and inexplicable phenomena but was comfortable enough in his world of fame and wealth to leave them at that. Then the upheaval of the Great War, the deaths of friends and family members caused him to seek pattern in the chaos and to find a reason for the orgy of destruction ripping Europe apart.

Thus, his trajectory changed.

Afterwards he was, successively, the toe-dipper announcing himself to the world as a Spiritualist and seeking to integrate his belief with Christianity; the writer of *The New Revelation* communicating in popular language his own beliefs and conversion; the prophet of an entire movement who spoke to thousands at the Royal Albert Hall; the grieving father who spoke face-to-face with his dead son; the tireless evangelist spreading the word to every part of the United Kingdom; the brilliant debater who took on some of the fiercest critics of the age; and finally, a missionary seeking to convert the entire world.

Of the influence of his early rejection of Catholicism which left a "spiritual vacancy" at the centre of his being, of his father's mental illness which led him to question the nature of personality and the soul, of the consolation that his father's soul may have been intact and only his body had let him down, of his belief in divine intervention and his soft-hearted rationalisation that Spiritualism was sent to the world to transfigure the pain of loss from The Great War, and of the loss of friends and family - not least his son - it is impossible to quantify how much each strand fed into his increasing commitment to believe. Yet in this book, I believe I have tracked his development, thanks to that extraordinary magazine with which he was so closely associated, *Light*.

And what of that moment in 1887 in Southsea when the two great strands in his life coincided - the publication both of his first Sherlock Holmes novel, *A Study in Scarlet*, and the letter in which he announced himself to be a Spiritualist? How should it be understood? My view is that Sherlock Holmes was the fruition of a long line of materialist thought that had developed over years. His Spiritualism was a seed newly planted that would grow and fruit later and, given the chance, would have supplanted the former. At that moment, the two modes of thought existed side by side, one mature, the other newly growing.

I am sure Doyle's faith was one reason he tired so soon of Holmes's materialistic world view and tried to kill him off at the Reichenbach Falls. Yet, at the same time, Holmes gave Doyle financial freedom and security. There is a tension in that relationship, but not necessarily a contradiction. And it is certainly not a paradox.

Who, then, was Sir Arthur Conan Doyle? In the June 19th issue of *Light,* David Gow wrote *Three Character Sketches* of the most important leaders of the Spiritualist movement, Sir William Barrett, Sir Oliver Lodge and Sir Arthur Conan Doyle.

Of Doyle, he wrote:

> Sir Arthur is a many-sided, rather than a complex, character. That his mind is one of a creative quality is manifest from his books and the fact that he is the progenitor of a character that rivals Sam Weller as a theme of popular allusion. His intellect is more of the capacious than the subtle type. A hard saying, perhaps, when one considers the play of subtlety in the Sherlock Holmes stories. But these things are hardly characteristic. His mind has an amplitude that has nothing in common with the fox and ferret types, although it may be large enough to include them. With the large mind goes the large heart—greatness of soul. He is too big to be quite understood by his little critics. All they can see, as a rule, is a small part of his mind. Here is the man who wrote the Sherlock Holmes books and other popular stories, and who believes in Spiritualism. That it puzzles them is

not surprising, seeing how small is the knowledge on which their judgments are based. Sir Arthur put only a relatively small part of himself into his books. Even the "History of the Great War," a monumental book involving a colossal amount of work, did not exhaust his mental resources. To-day, he stands before us as one who has a great message to deliver, and will deliver it, cost what it may. He belongs to the prophets, the "forth-speakers," which the world has had always with it, and for which it has always stones. Even so, it has always a respect for anyone of its citizens who shows himself, in its own phrase, a man, and Sir Arthur is a man all through, with all the manly virtues.

That is why, except amongst the homunculi, bred in studies or monasteries, even the man who rails at Conan Doyle with his lips, respects and admires him in his secret heart. Mr. Valiant-for-Truth, I have heard him called. Yes, he is a fighter, and that of the bull-dog type. I think of him more as Mr. Greatheart, who was not only a doughty warrior, but a royal helper and a friend to all the afflicted and oppressed. It has been said of him that he is a "bonnie fechter." He is also a benefactor—a lover of his kind. Knight errant and Knight Templar, he seeks high adventure in spiritual causes. If he does not, like Don Quixote, tilt at windmills, he may occasionally level his lance at "windbags"— and though he pierces them adroitly, one may feel that they are unworthy of his steel. Let me round off my story in the phrase of Chaucer: He is a verray parfait gentil Knight.

David Gow.

*

END

# Appendix A.

## Further Adventures in the World of *Light*

This appendix provides a flavour of the preoccupations and discussions of the readers of *Light* during the year that Conan Doyle went public in 1916, and looks at the attitudes of Spiritualists toward different aspects of the psychical world.

It shows that many of Sir Arthur Conan Doyle's interests overlapped with those of *Light,* as a writer of fiction, a scientist, a man set on his own religious path and an explorer into realms of the unknown. It starts, as it should, with ghosts.

## HAUNTINGS

*Light, January 1, 1916. Page 6*

### A TRIO OF GHOST STORIES.

To readers of LIGHT stories of hauntings are more than mere sensational anecdotes. When well-accredited they serve as part of the great mass of records that testify to the spiritual nature of mankind. If it is a gloomy and forbidding department of the region of human psychology it is chiefly because it is not yet properly understood and woven into the fabric of spiritual science.

The following stories, which we give in brief form without the usual literary embellishments, are all represented to be true by their original narrators.

The first relates to an old country house, which, after remaining empty for some years, was purchased by a gentleman whose name must not be divulged. It had previously belonged to a man of title who had gone abroad after the sudden and mysterious death of his wife—a beautiful woman whom he had taken from the ranks of professional singers. An old servant—a gardener—was allowed to stay on. This man, in showing the new tenant over the house, exhibited a strong desire to pass one door, but being obliged to yield in the end, disclosed a beautifully furnished boudoir decorated with fresh flowers. The gardener pleaded that the room might not be disturbed. It belonged, he said, to his late mistress. Since her death it had been his consolation to keep the room as though she still lived in it. His appeal was granted.

One day the new tenant saw the gardener with his ear to the door of the room. When asked for an explanation he answered that he could hear his mistress singing the same song she had sung when she had last occupied the room. On going to the window both the gardener and his master saw a fair woman sitting at the piano singing. Suddenly the voice broke into a cry and the apparition vanished. At the same moment they became aware that another man had been attracted to the spot, a man who fled when aware that his presence was discovered. The gardener turned and pursued him, crying out that it was the murderer of his mistress. The master followed in time to see the man stumble on a narrow bridge and fall into the ornamental water that bounded the park. He was unable to swim. The gardener at first refused to attempt to rescue the drowning man, but eventually tried to do so—apparently in obedience to the desire of his mistress whose spirit he seemed to see. He plunged into the water, but failed to effect his purpose and both were drowned.

The story lacks something because of the absence of details, but it was related some years ago in a high-class weekly as being a true one.

The next tale gains something in definiteness from a hint of the locality—the neighbourhood of Tottenham Court Road. Mr. G. R. Sims has told the story, describing it as the case of an apparition which appears on a given date every year. On this particular date the form of a man is seen in a certain room apparently engaged in washing his hands. A lady artist who once occupied the room beheld the apparition and complained to the landlady, who protested against the suggestion that she should take a week's notice, the tenancy being for a longer term. When a solicitor was called in she admitted that other tenants had made the same complaint on previous occasions—always on that particular date—and had not remained in the house afterwards.

Some years ago classic Oxford was excited concerning the story of a local apparition, which had a curious peculiarity. In walking, only that portion of the body from the knee upwards was visible. It appeared as though it were wading through the floor of the hall in which it was visible. When an architect was taken over the building he pointed out that the floor had been raised some eighteen inches since the place was first built. The ghost was walking on the original floor. We have only the newspaper account to go upon, and no details are vouchsafed, so that we can only repeat the story under reserve, although it is stated in the journal that the reality of the apparition has been " triumphantly vindicated " against the scientific sceptics of Oxford.

*

## PSYCHIC THEORIES AND TECHNOLOGY

At the start of the 20th Century ideas about the mind and technology were changing. Freud's 1899 *Interpretation of Dreams* provided a ready-made repository for unexplained phenomena: The Unconscious.

In *Light* for January 1st 1916, an article on *Psychic Phenomena And The Subconscious* reported the psychic investigator J Ernest Hunt's view that psychometry and clairvoyance "were in essence subconscious faculties... manifested in rudimentary form sometimes spontaneously and very often without any reference whatever to discarnate spirits."

Technology, too, was advancing. As early as 1858, a trans-Atlantic telegraph cable had been laid between Britain and the United States. A letter to *Light* on July 7th, 1917, took an apparently critical view. A correspondent signing himself "Reverend Boanerges Martext" (the first name means "Sons of Thunder" the second means "blundering preacher") warned that the telephone was "one of the most pernicious agencies ever devised by Satan for the destruction of souls". He quoted chapter and verse to prove his point, to hilarious effect. Though obviously a spoof, the piece highlighted the march of technology since Bell's very first telephone call, made in 1876.

Technology's advance was moving at ever-faster pace. Marconi had proven it possible to send Morse code via the airwaves, making unseen remote communication possible. Orville and Wilbur Wright had flown the Kittyhawk in 1903.

By 1916, aircraft raining death from the skies. An article in *Light* on November 24th, 1917, bemoaned that fact that "for the third time in the last six weeks the speaker booked for a Spiritualist mission in which I am interested has asked to be excused because of air-raid conditions." The writer went on to argue that this was behaviour "unworthy of a Spiritualist" exhorting his confrères to "show more courage", adding: "Surely we who preach that there is no death should not fear death!"

People saw analogies in technology. If the wireless provided a metaphor for spirit communication, and aircraft for how new spheres for exploration were opening, then what meaning lay in the phonograph, which enabled one to capture the living voice of a person and play it back even after they had died?[85]

Perhaps technology could even provide objective proof of spirit activity. An article in *Light* on January 16th, 1917, *The Phonograph And Psychic Research*, discussed how the phonograph could prove that spirit investigations were not hallucinations, by recording rappings and voices.

A similar approach was taken to another, older technology, psychic photography, as this extract from an article in *Light* from April 15th, 1916, shows:

> Psychic photography is very much in the air just now. In our last issue Dr. W. J. Crawford gave an account of a remarkable flashlight photograph taken by himself in the course of his investigations in physical phenomena. It revealed the presence of what for want of a better term we have to call the "power" or "psychic fluid" used in the production of the physical manifestations at the séances he describes... Perseverance in this line of experiment may have extremely valuable results in establishing the genuineness of a branch of psychic investigation that has hitherto suffered by the undue eagerness of some of its followers...

The logic in Psychic Photography was clear. If a spirit could move tables to communicate, how much easier would it be for them to manipulate light, or the chemicals on a photographic plate?

Arthur Conan Doyle was to become a great advocate of Psychic Photography, later having his own picture taken with spirits, and

---

85 See Chapter 10, *Of Spiritualist Science*, for the discussion "Does Nature Have Her Own Phonograph?"

intervening on the side of Mr William Hope during the Hope Controversy in the 1920s . Most famously, he would endorse as genuine the images of the Cottingley Fairies.

## SÉANCES

Séances were central to Spiritualist practice and worship. This is an excellent account of one séance originally performed in 1856 in the presence of Scottish publisher, Dr Robert Chambers.

*Light, June 3, 1916*

### DR. ROBERT CHAMBERS
### ON PHYSICAL PHENOMENA

The following description of a séance, held at my house thirty years ago, is taken from a letter written at the time by Robert Chambers to a friend interested in Spiritualism, who kindly allowed me to copy it. The medium was a servant who lived six years in my family. Beside Dr. Chambers there were three guests present. I do not give their names at length, for some have left this world, and the mention of them in this connection might not be agreeable to survivors. For the same reason a few words here and there are omitted. Their place is marked by points.

### DR. CHAMBERS' ACCOUNT.

As soon as we were settled after tea, raps were heard within the table, and the spirits were consulted as to our relative positions in the circle, which being adjusted to their content, we proceeded to converse in the usual manner... We found that the spirit of Captain M., the husband of Mrs. M., was present. He was first recognised by his characteristic knock...

At my suggestion he was asked to make himself sensible to her at this moment. At the same time the lights were removed, all but that of a low fire, in order that the medium should see him, should he become visible. The girl then declared she saw the spirit (describing him by recognised traits [I remember that one of these was the scar of a cutlass wound on the cheek.—S. E. De M.]) standing in a raiment of black velvet, fringed with gold, beside his widow, and preparing to touch her. By and by, as we sat in breathless silence, Mrs. M. said she felt something cool and soft touching her head. Now he was kissing her under the chin, as he used to do in life. Some of the company said they saw lights playing about her face. Her hands shook and twitched about the table where they rested... I asked if I might be favoured with some sensible proof of the presence of the spirit. The servant then said she saw Captain M. come along behind the circle to me. Now he was at my side. Now he was putting his hands on my head. Mrs. — — and others professed to see my face illuminated. For my own part, while perfectly prepared for some peculiar feeling, I was sensible of nothing beyond a cool aura on my hands below the table, if even that were real. After some other experiments of the kind I was led by something in the conversation to put the question: "Can I be informed of any means by which I might gain greater patience under irritating thoughts and circumstances?" —a complaint I have lately been suffering from, and of which I have the grace to be ashamed. The answer was: "Do not study too much," Mrs. De Morgan repeating the alphabet. This is very remarkable, for it is my belief that a studious life is a cause of irritability. I had, moreover, expected a religious answer instead of one so rational as this.

It then occurred to me to test the reality of the noises by requesting that they might be transferred from the table to the panelling of a bookcase against the wall five or six feet distant. After a little time they began to be heard against that panelling, and we carried on some conversation with them in that situation. Thus it became quite certain that there was no trick in the case. Whatever else may be fallacious, the noises are a verity. It took some time to get them back to the table. We then endeavoured to get the spirits to move two pieces of paper into contact on the table, but they declared that for the present this was a feat beyond their power...

Believe me, dear Miss D., very sincerely yours,

R. CHAMBERS.

*

## THE BRITISH EMPIRE

In any survey of the world of Light, it is impossible to ignore the influence on society and psyche of Britain's position at the heart of an empire.

Conan Doyle frequently referred to the exotic in his writing. In the Sherlock Holmes novel *The Sign of Four*, a long-standing grievance over the theft of treasure during the days of the Indian Mutiny brought grisly murder to the suburbs of London. With a mysterious entity able to climb through tiny apertures, commit murder and leave bizarre footprints, the story also had a cryptozoological bent. *The Speckled Band* (Doyle's favourite Holmes story), *The Five Orange Pips*, *The Valley of Fear* and other works such as *The Captain of the Polestar* and *The Parasite*, to name a few, also included the foreign and the outlandish as central to the plot.

*Light, January 22nd, 1916, page 30.*

## A SOUTH AFRICAN GHOST STORY

The following story is forwarded by a South African magistrate who vouches for the good faith of the narrator, whose name he gives us in confidence:—

In the summer of the year in which the events narrated took place, I was out of health, and, my husband being ordered to this district from the Transkei, I came here with my children in my travelling ox-waggon. Our house being unfinished, we were rather in a difficulty. Captain B— rode across from Tylden one day, and told me that there was a small cottage unoccupied on the farm T—, four miles from the camp, and that he would put in some troopers to whitewash and repair it, when it would be at my disposal. So we moved there, travelling with a Cape cart and two horses, which were driven by a Kaffir.

The cottage stood amongst thick mimosa woods on the bank of a spruit. It consisted of three rooms, in a row, with doors opening between, each room having also an outside door.

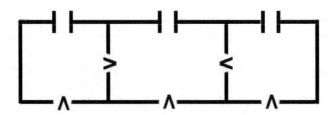

This is a plan of it. My children occupied the room on the right, and that on the left. The one between was used as a sitting-room, and was provided with a very heavy dining-table. On the night of our arrival, a clear moonlit night it was, we were struck by the behaviour of the horses in the stable. They shrieked and screamed and dashed about, and in the morning their Kaffir groom reported that they were covered with foam and perspiration, as though they had been ridden all night. I myself walked across to the stable and saw the plight they were in.

The next day my nurse arrived from Queenstown. This day we noticed that my dog, a very self-assured animal as a rule, was obviously stricken with terror. He crept about, hiding under beds and trying to shelter in our skirts. This went on all day.

The nurse had a bed on the sofa in the sitting-room, and I slept alone that night. It was bright moonlight, and the window had no blind, so that my room was fairly light.

All at once I saw a white figure enter the room, and cross it to the chest of drawers, upon which it leant. I thought it was my twelve-year-old daughter, who had a habit of sleepwalking, and I called her three times loudly by her name in order to wake her.

As soon as I spoke, the figure turned and came swiftly towards me. It had its back to the light, but nevertheless I could see every detail of its countenance. It was awful. Red furious eyes blazed in a pasty-white, coarse-featured face, and a mass of red hair framed all. This dreadful apparition swept forward and bent over me and the appalling face was thrust close into mine.

I lost consciousness, and knew no more for I know not how long. When I came to myself, I remembered all, and hastened to strike a light. I was terror-stricken, and lay for a long time afraid to put out the candle.

At length I did so, but no sooner was the room dark than the dreadful being was there again. As she crossed the room I noticed that she passed between the foot of my bed and a large armchair which I knew to be pressed up close to the bed. I knew then that the appearance was not mortal.

The night dragged past somehow, and great was my relief when morning came.

At breakfast, I met the children and the nurse, but such a dread was upon me that I could not bring myself to speak of what had occurred. I asked the nurse how she had slept. She said, "Very well, but what a strange habit your servant has of tidying the sitting-room in the night."

I said, "Does she do that ? "

"Yes," the nurse said, "and makes such a noise about it too. She came in dressed all in white. She banged the furniture about, and moved this table against the wall. Afterwards she moved it back again."

After breakfast I tried to push the heavy table, but I could not lift or move it an inch.

We were forced to spend some weeks in that dreadful house, and many and strange were the happenings we witnessed. Our strange guest would come sometimes and throw about our possessions with such a clatter that it seemed everything must be smashed ; but nothing was even scratched. At times the children would dash screaming into my room, terror- struck at what they could not plainly tell. On the day my travelling-waggon arrived the kitchen happened to be crowded with troopers, so the Kaffir driver of the waggon said he would sleep in the waggon. Late at night he came dashing across to the kitchen door, beating upon it and screaming for admittance. They did not open at once, and when they did the poor man was found in a dead faint on the threshold.

Afterwards he told us his story. He was sitting on the waggon-box smoking, when he noticed the oxen, which had been left tied to the "trek-tow," begin to drag at their ropes and to bellow and groan. Then he saw what he took to be a little flame flashing to and fro amongst them. Suddenly a figure which he described as exactly like the one I had seen (and whose visit I had mentioned to no one) came to him in the waggon. She swept stormily once or twice up and down its length, and then came close to him and thrust her horrible face into his, just as she had done to me.

One evening we were all together in the sitting-room, when we were horribly startled by someone close by—indeed, amongst us as we sat—clapping hands violently together, and then giving utterance to a long, terrible shriek. My eldest daughter, who was twelve years old at the time, remembers this distinctly.

We learned that a Miss R— had died recently under suspicious circumstances on the neighbouring farm of —, some distance away from the cottage she had elected to haunt. The Kaffirs of the neighbourhood told us that not one of them would dream of approaching the cottage after dark, for they all knew of the awful lady who walked there, and who seemed possessed of a demon of uncontrollable rage and desire for revenge.

Some years later we returned to the Transkei and passed near —, where the T— family was murdered by the Kaffirs at the beginning of one of the wars. Here was a Dutch farm, and we alighted from the waggon and went to ask for a glass of milk. We passed the tree under which the T—s were sitting when the Kaffirs swooped down upon them and killed them all. The old Boer woman was very kind and intelligent, but her daughter had a strange, vacant look, staring at us all the time we were there and not uttering a word. I was told afterwards, when unfortunately it was too late to question the people, that this girl had been visited by the awful spectre of —, and had never been since in her right senses.

In Komgha, some ten years after my experience at —, I went to a large picnic got up by a number of us to beguile the tedium of the little village. At lunch time I noticed a child sitting alone, wearing a big sunbonnet. I went to ask her what she would take, and bent down to look under her bonnet. I recoiled with a feeling of horror: the child's face, with its red hair, its large flat features and pasty complexion, was the face of the ghost!

So profound was the impression made on me by this occurrence that for days after I felt troubled and uneasy. I learnt afterwards that the child was a Miss R—, the younger sister of the girl who had died years before at the farm in the Eastern Province.

\*

# THE GREAT WAR

With the Great War, previously unseen numbers of deaths prompted families across the country to seek news of their departed loved ones in séances.

A superstitious vein ran through the country. Newspapers published reports of astrological forecasts and omens. In 1914, the Reverend A Calderbank reported witnessing a naval battle in the sky. The discussion of Calderbank's Phantom Fleets rumbled on in *Light* for years, with those offering a supernatural source for the vision countered by those with a materialistic explanation, as in this article:

*Light, January 1, 1916.*

## PHANTOM FLEETS.
## THE VIEWS OF A FRENCH PSYCHICAL AUTHORITY:

Commenting on the vision of a naval battle in the skies, seen by the Rev. Father Calderbank, of the Franciscan College, Cowley (an account of which has appeared in LIGHT), M. C. de Vesme, in an article in the Paris "Annales des Sciences Psychiques" for November-December, mentions that he wrote to Father Calderbank for confirmation. It will be remembered that the Hon. Ralph Shirley, in the "Occult Review," suggested that the vision might have had reference to the naval engagement off Heligoland which took place some days after; Father Calderbank, in his reply to M. de Vesme, expresses a different view. He writes:—

In reply to your question, I have to say that the account published by Mr. Shirley is correct in its entirety; his idea, however, that it was intended as a prevision of a naval combat appears to me to be unfounded. That which took place, was in the nature of a mirage...

The whole phenomenon is, I think, capable of a perfectly natural explanation. I think that the atoms of watery vapour can in certain conditions act in the same way as the atoms of mercury upon a mirror, that is to say they can reflect and project, although I cannot pretend to be able to give an exact scientific explanation on this point.

M. de Vesme quotes an instance of projected vision, an account of which was given in "Der Hansfreund." The incident, we are told, took place near Ujest, a department of Gross-Strehlitz, Silesia, in 1785:—

On January 27th, between three and four o'clock in the afternoon, some fifty persons saw a body of infantry, disposed in three ranks, and led by two officers, carrying red banners, marching towards them. The first line halted and fired in the direction of the spectators, though no sound of firing was heard. A thick smoke then enveloped the ranks, and when this had cleared away the infantry soldiers had given place to mounted hussars.

On February 3rd, about eight o'clock in the morning, this vision was again seen by some four hundred peasants. One of these, bolder than the rest, mounted a horse, and galloped towards the phantom army, but on reaching the spot which they had seemed to occupy, he found no trace of them, though his companions who remained behind saw him surrounded by soldiers in various uniforms.

On the 15th of the same month this scene was again witnessed by some thirty people. General Sass had sent a detachment of soldiers to that neighbourhood. The officer in charge of the detachment rode up to the ghostly troops and presently a mounted officer detached himself from their ranks and came towards him. They both saluted. The Prussian officer then asked the other who he was and what he wanted, but got no reply. He drew his pistol and was about to fire, when the whole vision disappeared.

M. de Vesme suggests that the spectacle was due to a meteorological and optical phenomenon, and supposes that the mounted figure which rode up to and saluted the officer was really the latter's own reflection. He also refers to an incident described by M. Flammarion in his book on "The Atmosphere," where three people of Verviers saw an army in the sky, and so distinct was the vision that they were able to recognise the uniforms of the artillery regiments, and could distinguish a cannon which had a broken wheel and was about to fall over. This took place in June 1815, the year and month of the battle of Waterloo.

*

PROPHECIES OLD AND NEW.
The turmoil in Europe also caused the classic occult texts to be reconsulted.

*Light, January 1st, 1916.*

## THE PROPHECIES OF NOSTRADAMUS

The correspondence in the "Observer" last month on this subject included some interesting letters by Mr. Hamilton Minchin and Mr. W. Gorn Old, to which we have not been able to refer previously for want of space. Mr. Minchin quoted the concluding quatrain of the prophecies, which is as follows:—

Le grand empire sera par Angleterre,
Le pempotan des ans plus de trois cens:
Grandes copies passer par mer et terre,
Les Lusitains n'en seront pas contens.

("The great empire shall be with England—The all-powerful for more than three hundred years—Great armies shall pass by sea and land—The Portuguese will not be pleased therewith.")

Mr. Gorn Old gives the following as translation of two of the quatrains:—

One shall arise who shall cause the god of the infernal Huns to live again, the terror of mankind. Never were greater horrors nor more evil days than those that shall come to the Latins by this scion of Babel.

*

New prophecies of the end of days and earthly destruction abounded.

*Light, January 8, 1916*

## REMARKABLE WAR PROPHECIES

The number of prophecies concerning the war... continue to increase rather than diminish. Our Paris contemporary, the "Psychic Magazine," for the 1st and 10th October, deals with some interesting predictions attributed to German seers, contained in a collection of prophecies published by. M. Grobe-Wutischky. Here is a psychic communication published before the war by M. A. Bussler in "Zentralblatt für

Okkultismus " (Vol. 4, p. 462):-

Italy takes the part of France and turns against Austria. Denmark receives English troops, and takes part with several divisions in an invasion of Schleswig. The only faithful ally of the Emperor William is the Austrian Monarch, Francis Joseph. But Austria is obliged to send a great part of her army to the South-East, where the Balkan States are preparing an invasion; another detachment of the army must guard the Italian frontier. The first great event will be an unlooked-for defeat of the German army on the South-West. Germany will be defeated at sea.

Russia will get East and West Prussia and Posnanie (Pomerania?). Silesia will revert to Austria, who will have to cede Galicia to Russia and Bosnia to Serbia. The central States of Germany will regain their independence. Alsace-Lorraine and Hesse will become French, Hanover English, and Mecklenburgh a tributary State of Russia. Prussia will only consist of the provinces of Brandenburg and Saxony.

Another prophecy given by R. Knapp in the periodical "Zeitschrift für Okkultismus und verwandte Gebiete" for December 3rd, 1908, points to terrible events in the near future, and on January 12th this statement is amplified as follows :—

War will break out when least expected... Germany will become so small that its inhabitants will be able to retire into a single town. There will be epidemics, such that the birds in the air and fish in the waters cannot live. German ships will go to Asia and China. The conqueror himself will be ruined. We see these events coming, but cannot tell at what time they will happen.

Reference is also made to a prediction well known in Hanover, which winds up with these words:—

After the battle there will remain so little of the German Empire that one will be able to take it all in at a single glance from the top of a tree...

- Translated by D N G

*

## FORTUNE TELLING, THE LAW AND THE WAR

British psychics faced the dangers from the authorities.

On January 22nd, 1916, *Light* reported briefly on the prosecutions of two mediums tried for fortune-telling – still a crime under the Witchcraft Act of 1735 and the Vagrancy Act of 1824. It went on to recommend that "every family have its own home circle and develop its own mediums," and that societies should exert a strict supervision over the phenomena given at their meetings. In this way mediums would be protected from persecution.

*

## THE ANGELS OF MONS

Perhaps the most famous psychic event of the Great War were the visions of the Angels of Mons.

Between 22nd and 23rd August, 1914, in the early weeks of the war, British troops at the Battle of Mons were outflanked by the German Imperial Army. Forced to retreat, they marched without break for days and nights, some even sleeping on their feet.

During this period, soldiers reported visions of phantom cavalrymen who disappeared into thin air.

At the end of September 1914, author Arthur Machen's short story, The Bowmen was published in the London Evening News. The story tells of the ghosts of bowmen from the Battle of Agincourt intervening to defeat a German division.

Written in the first person, the story was misunderstood by some readers to be a true account of events on the battlefield. Over the following 6 months the story ran away, combining with tales of the visions of phantom cavalrymen and direct lies from nurse Phyllis Campbell, who had been posted on the Front, and who later happily admitted "I have seen no vision, but in my heart I believe that the Captains of God are leading the Allies to Victory..."

Claims for Angels of Mons phenomena variously included:

• The sighting of a shining row of beings standing between the opposing British and German forces.

- The appearance of St George to British troops.
- The discovery of German bodies with arrow wounds.
- A shining luminous supernatural cloud intervening at the vital point of the battle of Mons.
- Angels fighting on the side of the Allied forces.

Sermons across Britain cited the Angels of Mons as evidence of Divine Providence, and Arthur Machen's attempts to quell the story even led some to accuse Machen of a lack of patriotism.

The controversy rumbled on throughout the War and long after, and even included an early example of a now-familiar conspiracy theory: that British Military Intelligence had spread the story as a propaganda exercise.

The case gave birth to countless attempts to explain what such sightings could mean and how they could have happened, with no less a commentator than distinguished scientist Sir W F Barrett stepping into the discussion.

*Light, January 15, 1916*

## SIR W. F. BARRETT ON HUMAN SURVIVAL
## AND THE MONS VISIONS.

...As regards the reputed "visions of angels" at Mons and elsewhere on the battlefield in France, he [Barrett] sees "nothing inconceivable in certain soldiers possessing the clairvoyant gift which undoubtedly exists among some people." He then gives the following letter which has been sent to him. It is from a soldier whose arm was shattered in the retreat from Mons, and who is now in hospital at Brighton; and was addressed to the writer's nephew :

I will be able to relate to you some wonderful things of my experiences whilst in France and Belgium, of glimpses into hell and glimpses into heaven. It was no uncommon thing for tens of thousands of Germans to be repulsed, or even put to flight, by, as it seemed, only three to four thousand of us; the hosts of heaven seem to intervene on our behalf. The wounded on the battlefield were attended by white-clothed nurses—the angels of God. This will seem incredible to you, but nevertheless it is a fact, as I myself am a living witness of some of these visions. Everybody did not see these angels, but quite a few of us did, and I am sure had it not been for the protecting hand of God and His angels none of us could have lived through such a hell."

The value of such testimony Sir William finds difficult to estimate, "for we must," he says, "of course allow for the widespread influence of imagination and suggestion, and of hallucination arising from some illusion of the senses."

A spirit sighting also occurred among British Imperial Indian troops, with *Light* reporting on January 22nd 1916, that Sikh soldiers had seen battlefield visions of Guru Govind Singh:

These accounts are by no means the Indianised versions of the tales told about St. George appearing before the British troops at Mons. Many of the Sikhs who tell of their experiences do not know a word of English and never heard that their British comrades had seen visions of their patron saint. The statements of the Sikhs, therefore, refer to an experience all their own.

According to one account, Guru Govind Singh—who lived in the 17th century and who infused the martial spirit into the Sikhs —appeared on the battlefield riding a beautiful white charger with a long flowing tail. He wore a resplendent aigrette[86] fastened to his turban-which waved above his head like the "white plume" of Navarre, a veritable oriflamme to his followers. It may be recalled that the Guru is invariably depicted in Sikh annals and shown in old paintings riding a white horse and wearing a large aigrette. One of the favourite names by which Sikhs of this age remember Guru Govind Singh is "He with the aigrette."

According to a second version, "the photo of Guru Govind Singh" was the only thing that the Sikhs, advancing in a bayonet charge, saw to their "right, left, and front." The words quoted are from the account given by Subadar (Indian Major) Sardar Narain

---

86  Head-plumes of the egret, used for adorning a headdress.

Singh, of the 14th Sikhs, who received six bullet wounds while engaged in action in Gallipoli, from which he has recently recovered. He says that the vision of Guru Govind Singh appeared before the Sikh soldiers just as the bugle sounded "March" and they brandished their bayonets. He declares that he cannot explain in words "the spirit this holy sight infused in us. It emboldened us to march on, piercing through the abdomens of the enemy, unmindful of the havoc being wrought by the horrid machine gun. We shouted 'Sat Sri Akal' ('God is Timeless'—the battle-cry of the Sikhs), and chanted the 'Shabads' (hymns) of 'Halla' (attack) as if ours was a nuptial procession. Those among us who fell wounded or dead we minded never, as the only thought before us was devotion to the Guru who was so omnipresent in the march, and adherence to Government."

\*

## THE SÉANCE AND THE SOLDIER
Soldiers as much as any other section of society were attracted to Spiritualism.

*Light, January 15, 1916.*

## THE DIRECT VOICE.
## A REMARKABLE EVIDENTIAL SÉANCE:

"M. E.", an officer of Engineers, now at the front, sends us the following notes of a sitting with Mrs. E. Roberts Johnson on the evening of December 14th, 1915 :-
It had rained all day and was a dark, gloomy afternoon when I set off in the car to cover the twenty-seven miles which I had to travel before reaching the residence of Mrs. Johnson. I had not seen her for over eighteen months, for on the outbreak of war the army claimed me and I had to abandon what I believe would have been a most interesting and important series of sittings with one who, in my view, is undoubtedly the premier voice medium at the present time.
At seven p.m. five of us took our seats in the drawing-room. Mrs. R sat

on Mrs. Johnson's right, and I on her left; my brother sat next to Mrs. R and Mr. E sat between my brother and myself. The sitters, except my brother, were the same I had been accustomed to meet at Mrs. Johnson's in the days before the war. The trumpet having been placed in the centre of the circle, the séance was opened with a little singing and a prayer. We had not long to wait before we heard tapping on the furniture in the room, followed in a minute or two by the voice of Mr. Duguid greeting us in his usual cheery fashion. He commented on the war, and said that he thought the end was now in sight. We then heard the trumpet being moved about and each of us was touched by it in turn. This was the prelude to one of the best and most convincing sittings I have ever had in my life. I cannot give every detail, as the major part of it was of a private nature, but I will give such of it as may reasonably be published, any names given being naturally fictitious. Addressing my brother, Mr. Duguid said the spirit friends were assisting him to carry on my work in my absence - a matter of which none but my brother and myself had any knowledge. Turning next to Mrs. R he assured her that she had no need for anxiety about certain matters which she judiciously kept to herself. Her brother, Mr. E, thereupon wanted to know what secret it was that she had kept from him, but was stopped by Mr. Duguid with the remark, "Man, thy name is curiosity." My own particular friend, "Silver Star," came next, and from that moment to the end of the séance never let a minute pass without keeping me assured of her continued presence by touching me on the arms, hands, or knees. She said that she had not left me during my twelve months of work in the firing line but had been with me all the time. She had evidently been busy on her own account too, for she had learned to speak very good English since we last conversed together. Mr. Duguid explained that she was a powerful guide and that I might place great reliance on her help in time of need. I asked her if she could give me any information about a small wicker table in a collier's cottage, but was interrupted by a peal of laughter and the statement that she moved the table to let me know that she was there.

This was good, for I had not completed the question or referred to the movement when she broke in with this explanation. To make the matter clear I may say that after the heavy fighting at Loos in the end of September we had dropped a mile or two behind to recuperate, and one morning as I rolled off the bed in a collier's cottage in which I had been billeted I noticed a small wicker table, which was within, I believe, about six feet of me, dancing about for no apparent reason. I should have forgotten the incident had not an unexpected communication reached me a few hours later which made a pleasing and very marked change in my military career.

Next Mr. E was greeted by an old friend who had recently passed over - and here I may remark that all the friends who manifested gave their names distinctly and, if there was the slightest doubt, added their late address so clearly as to leave no room for continued incredulity. This friend assured Mr. E that he was not dead but came to his (Mr. E's) house as usual on Sunday nights, and he gave an intensely natural description of their meeting on the Sunday night previous.

A voice spoke to my brother saying, "I am John Berry, you know my son." My brother said he did not call him to mind. " Oh, yes, you do; I kept the grocer's shop at the corner of High-street." "I think," said Mr. E-, "that you should be addressing me. I knew him very well." Mr. Berry apologised for his mistake, adding,"Tell my son I look in to the business every day and it is going on all right."

"Silver Star" spoke again, and when I referred to her as "little girl" she corrected me and said she was not little but was quite tall, and had very black hair and eyes." I see you in the deep black holes with the wires. I am with you and help you." (This rather astonished me, for I had made no mention to any of my friends of this part of the work which falls to my lot at the front.) She then proceeded to describe what she had seen as the result of my laying wires in the "deep black holes," but as it was somewhat gruesome I changed the subject. Next, some near and dear relatives came and spoke to Mrs. R, but I refrain from giving details. Only those who have been present at such meetings can know of the intensity of happiness they create. A brother of ours who had long passed over talked to us as only a brother could; he told me that I had many very powerful spirit friends who helped me and kept me safe. We next heard a bugle, and I recognised the call of a certain unit, followed by a voice, "I am Bugler Dennis, and I want to thank you for your kind help and thought. I am all right now. Good-night." It brought a lump into my throat, for it had pained me to see him go down in the second battle of Ypres.

A friend of Mrs. R played a little on the piano behind me, but scarcely spoke. An uncle and a grandmother came and talked with my brother and myself. "Silver Star" again manifested, and I said that I often wished when in the trenches that I could see her. She promised she would try to show herself with the help of "the old woman." Mrs. Johnson here interjected, "What old woman?" and was comforted by the reply that it was the old woman who dwelt downstairs at the house where I lived in France - "the old woman that wears a funny cap."

Here again I got a surprise, for I had hardly given this woman a thought. I may say that when out of the trenches I am billeted in a partly ruined house in a town which is near the line, and is continually shelled. The old woman has taken refuge in this house, and my servant bargains with her on my behalf for hot water and other odd comforts, such as needle and thread which a woman can provide, so I seldom see her personally. "Silver Star" saw my wrist watch with a luminous dial, but would not touch it as it might "burn her," but she read the time correctly. Mr. Duguid now interposed and said that the power was done. I thanked him for having given me such a happy and memorable sitting, and he in turn complimented me on my devotion to Spiritualism, remarking that it was our strong belief in the great truth which ensured the success we had had.

There were fourteen different voices in all, seven being for myself. Every one of them was clearer and louder than our own voices. I go back to the front with a sense of pleasure and happiness which only such communion could create, and I cannot but express my sincere gratitude to Mrs. Roberts Johnson for her kind thought in arranging the sitting when she heard I was at home on a short leave, especially as she was not in perfect health at the time.

*

## PSYCHIC WARFARE

For many, the heightened consciousness which came with fighting on the Front led to what they could only describe as a psychic sense. Once again the extraordinary conditions of war appeared to be revealing new aspects of what it was to be human. Precognition, spirit visitation and telepathy were just some of the effects soldiers reported.

Light, February 19, 1916

## THE PSYCHIC SENSE ON THE BATTLEFIELD.
## VISIONS AND PREMONITIONS AT THE FRONT.

In "Brotherhood" for February Mr. W. S. Hendry relates a conversation he had with a wounded Tommy whom he had successfully treated for acute rheumatism contracted in the trenches. In the course of the chat, the soldier declared that though he and his comrades saw and heard nothing of the Angels of Mons, they experienced when in the firing line an awakening of the psychic sense—coming events often casting their shadows before. He said:—

In the trenches or going to them we "feel" what is ahead of us quite plainly. It is common to hear our pals say, after the event, "I knew that would happen"; but it is equally common to hear predictions that we all see for ourselves come true in a few hours or days. For instance, one day our company was moving up to relieve the firing line. The ambulance wagon was behind us. A pal says to me, with a nod towards the wagon, "it's following us to-day, it will be taking me down to-morrow"; and it did, for he was wounded. Another says, "I know when I'm hit I'm killed"; and it is so. Another, I remember, one night told us he was to be sent home. We laughed at him, but he said he felt certain he was to be sent home wounded; and in a few days he was. On another occasion our company had to take a position, and we got through the first lap without a single loss; as we took cover for a little, I said to some near me, "We're all safe so far." "Aye, aye," a pal answered, " I knew we would be, but it's the next lap I fear"; and before we had got through the next part he was down. My own experience was curious. I had been weeks in the trenches and nothing had happened to me, till one morning I took my place with a queer feeling—a certainty that something was going to happen to me that day. I scrutinised keenly every possible source of danger, but could see no more reason to account for it than there had been on previous days. However, within a few hours I was carried off wounded in several places.

That is the psychic sense we develop, and it is commonly reported that Joffre has it keener than anyone else. He knows the result of the battles before they take place, and is always ready for emergencies!

Thus Mr. Hendry's soldier, and the story connects curiously with statements made to us by two officers who called at our office during a brief stay in London before returning to the front. Both testified to a certain quickening of the interior sensibilities experienced by many soldiers engaged in the trench warfare. Prevision of death was quite frequent, and Colonel — related that several of his brother officers had the experience of seeing the apparition of some comrade and afterwards learning of his death. The other officer, who is attached to the Royal Engineers, told us of escapes of soldiers from what appeared to be certain death. There were no cases but what, on the face of them, appeared to be due to quite natural causes, but the experience was so frequent as apparently to defy the law of chances, and this created a general impression of providential care. He told, for example, how in one instance a body of men were saved from a barbed wire trap by the moon emerging from a cloud just in time to reveal the danger. There was nothing extra-natural in this; it was the continual repetition of such things, he said, that provoked the idea of a watchful Power. In his own case, however, he had remarkable evidence of direct interposition on his behalf from the unseen world. From a third officer we received, indirectly, a similar record of personal psychic experiences.

*

## HYPNOSIS

*Light* magazine was in many ways an almanac for the many different and strange phenomena that so fascinated and inspired Conan Doyle. That Doyle's imagination blended with real-life events and effects is reflected in novels like *The Parasite*, in which a hypnotist from the West Indies takes control of a man's life and makes him her slave.

Conan Doyle had attended a display of hypnosis in 1889 in Southsea, in which he witnessed men being stuck to the floor, dancing like ballerinas, having pins painlessly thrust through their arms or suddenly falling asleep in a post-hypnotic trance. No surprise that the same unaccountable subject should appear in *Light*.

This account from *Light*, March 4th 1916, of the effects of hypnosis echoes the type of stories loved by Doyle, and also leaves the reader with fresh mysteries to consider – mixing as it does the possibility of an Out

Of Body Experience or spirit vision with the unexplained phenomenon of Hypnotic Control:

A Russian lady tells a curious story of her experiences with one of her domestics, a young chambermaid, who suffered from some nervous affliction, for which the lady treated her hypnotically. Among much that is of the usual character, the following circumstance may be of interest to those who imagine that the will of the operator wholly dominates that of the subject. The girl was put to sleep in the customary fashion, and told that she was not to get up until eight o'clock, and that she was not to do up the apartment in her charge. These orders were given in the usual authoritative manner. Notwithstanding this, the maid continued to rise early, and go about her work in the hypnotic sleep, returning to bed when finished, and awaking naturally at the appointed time. Somewhat puzzled, her mistress ordered her more emphatically to remain in bed, and sleep until eight. In the hypnotic state the girl then flatly told her mistress, "I shall sleep until eleven." " You only need to sleep until eight." "I shall sleep until eleven." Curious to know the result, the lady waited until eleven, and then proceeded to awake the girl, with the following result:—

"It is time to get up," I said, when my watch indicated eleven o'clock.

"I shall sleep five minutes yet," replied Varia, firmly.

"But it is exactly eleven o'clock," I told her.

"According to your watch, but, according to the sun, it is five minutes from eleven."

"But where do you see the sun? Your window looks north."

"I see the sun. The walls do not prevent me." I sat down, keeping my eyes on my watch. In five minutes Varia said : "Awake me. Breathe on my brow, on my eyes." She then awoke, instantaneously recovering her timid and piteous expression of face.

This experience showed the lady that her subject, while in the hypnotic sleep, became clairvoyant, and, having received some disquieting news regarding the health of a relative, the following effort was made to utilise the gift:—

"Could you tell me how N— is ? "

"Leave me for an hour and I shall try to go and find him and I shall see N—. I shall go to his house."

I returned in an hour and made some passes, as observed that the sounder she slept the better she spoke.

"Do not be uneasy, the lungs are only partially affected. There is no abscess. He will get better." (In the sequel her diagnosis and prophecy proved to be correct, in spite of the verdict of the doctors.) Having finished her task, she said: "I am tired; I must sleep now." This phrase, "I must sleep" my servant repeated each time she accomplished what seemed a more or less difficult task.

Varia's ideas while asleep were changed entirely from those she entertained in her ordinary condition, and she spoke in a superior and critical fashion. In her normal state she was somewhat narrow in her sympathies—a result, perhaps, of her peculiar training.

*

INTERSTELLAR TRAVEL AND VISITING ALIEN SPIRITS

In *Light*, on January 8th 1916, this small notice appeared, prefiguring the modern preoccupation with UFOs and all things from other planets:

— Are the planets inhabited, and, if so, are their inhabitants men like ourselves ? ...Many readers will be familiar with the works of Eva Harrison, who is called by the spirits "Love-light," and whose husband, "Light-bearer," was, before his death last year, the medium of their small circle. In her latest book, "Wireless Messages from Other Worlds" (Fowler, 2s. 6d. net), she introduces us to visitors from Mars and other planets, and even from the constellation Orion! They come in the spirit, leaving their material bodies behind, and tell us many things that are not yet to be found in manuals of astronomy. The reader will accept the facts and the teaching or not, according to his temperament and his previous knowledge of psychic and scientific matters; but he will in any case admit that the book is marked with those qualities of earnestness and sincerity which are happily so characteristic of workers in this field.—S.

*

## THE SIGNIFICANCE OF DREAMS

In *Light*, hauntings jostled alongside deaths and dreams in a vast nebulous world in which significance piled on significance. The following article by W. Ilfracombe is a fabulous account of the way in which the Spiritualists at the start of the 20th Century sought to connect all unexplained phenomena together. At the same time that Jung and Freud were offering their takes on the nature of dreams, the readers of *Light* were equally fascinated by their meanings.

*Light, March 11, 1916.*

## THE WHITE FRIAR.
## A CLAIRVOYANT'S STORY.

A few years ago, when dining with my friends, Mr. and Mrs. A— (whose name, which is well known, is in the possession of the editor of LIGHT), I saw standing behind the chair of the former the figure of a monk. His head was bent down so that his cowl nearly covered his face, but I could sense that he was very jealous for his charge, and wished to protect him from all unfavourable conditions or environments. He did not, however, seem conscious of the presence of others in the room, much less that anyone could see him. Later I asked Mr. A— if any other clairvoyant had seen a monk in his surroundings. "Yes," he replied, adding that several had done so. Then he was interested to hear that I also had seen the friar, who, he said, was a character well known in history.

On another occasion, when Mr, and Mrs. A— and their little girl were returning home after an evening spent with friends, the child suddenly spoke in an awed whisper to her mother: "There is someone following us in the road and watching us all the time."

The mother looked back, but could see no one, and said so.

"O yes, mother, indeed there is, and he is dressed in a long white robe with a hood at the back, and a cord round his waist; can't you see him? See, he's there." (She pointed in the direction.) "Now he has crossed the road and is standing by that tree, still watching us."

A year later, when the Angel of Death had visited the home, and mother and daughter were left alone, the former had a dream, so exceedingly vivid that she felt it to be a real experience and not merely a dream. Anyway, it is like a continuation of the incidents related above. In this dream Mrs. A— was walking on a road in a beautiful country, when someone came running towards her, who said, "Your husband has been calling for you; he so needs your presence. Won't you go to him?"

"Tell me where he is, that I may go," was her reply.

"It is a long way, but if you go straight on you will find him."

The way was indeed long, but the pilgrim felt neither weariness nor fear as she hastened her steps and travelled (as it seemed) hour after hour on a road which appeared to be interminable. At last, however, she came to a steep hill, which she ascended. On a plateau at the top were a great many monks, all habited in white, and all busy building some kind of edifice. Addressing the one nearest to her she asked for her husband, feeling sure that he was somewhere in the building. "You have-no business here," was the response; "go away."

"I will not," she retorted. "I must find my husband; what have you done with him?" At once all the monks turned towards her and commanded her to return the way she had come. Ignoring them, she walked round the building and found a door open at the hack. Entering, she ran along a passage, feeling there was no time to be lost. At the end was a cell, to which she felt magnetically drawn, and there she found her dear one - robed in white like the monks outside; the little furniture there was in the cell being also white. Mr. A— was sitting with his head in his hands as if in deep meditation, and did not at first perceive his wife's presence; but on her exclaiming, "Dearest, I have found you at last," he looked up. Recognising then who the speaker was, an expression of deep and lasting love came over his face, but to her amazement and horror he, like the monks outside, told her to leave, for she must not be with him now. In great distress the wife knelt down beside him, begging him to remember their old love and not send her away, for she was sure he needed her now as much as ever he had done. Then, finding that the monks had discovered her presence in the building, and were not only calling to her but coming to compel her to depart, in an agony of emotion she pleaded with him to order the monks away, and to tell them she was his wife and therefore had a right to stay with him.

Her last remembrance was of seeing him standing and holding up his hand to motion the monks away, saying simply, but with a power and authority which all felt bound to obey, "She is my wife. Leave us."

\*

## COMPENSATORY VISIONS

The extraordinary happenings occurring in the world in 1916, the visions and psychic phenomena alongside awful destruction for many implied huge changes to come. This article is a fabulous combination of religious, mythical and spiritual thinking. The voice of the prophet sounds loud and clear.

*Light, March 11, 1916*

### THE SPIRITUAL SIGNIFICANCE OF THE HOUR

On Sunday afternoon last, at the Higher Thought Centre, 40, Courtfield Gardens, S.W., Mr. W. Tudor Pole delivered an address on the subject mentioned above.

...Mr. W. Tudor Pole, referring to the prophecy of Jesus concerning the rising of nation against nation, earthquakes, famines, and troubles, and to his saying that these would be the "beginnings of sorrows," said that the passage would be more correctly rendered, these events are "the beginning of the pains of a new birth." If a thousand years hence we could look back on the history of the present time as we could now look back at the great crises of the past we should be able to recognise much more clearly the immense significance of the ordeal through which the world is now passing. He had recently talked with an officer just returned from the front who had taken part in some of the worst phases of the fighting, and who had told him that before going into battle he had passed through a strange mental and spiritual experience. It was as though all material conditions and events had fallen away from him. This had been followed by a vivid sense of the elemental facts of existence; it was as if he had become a child again. A great wind seemed to rush through his consciousness, followed by a great calm and interior illumination. When the Knights of the Round Table sat in conclave, it would be remembered, there was a rushing wind that filled the room, and in the peace that followed there shone a great light, a great illumination, in which came the vision of the Holy Grail. Mr. Pole then related a personal experience in Palestine at the time when the near approach of the war was casting its shadow on the world. As he sat under the stars in a state of deep depression there came, as it were, a searching wind around him, and yet, strange as it seemed, within the wind where he sat there was absolute quiet. And then he heard a sound of thunders as though the whole world were splitting to pieces. At last, amid the gloom that fell, there dawned a great light in which the world seemed to be bathed and he became conscious of a Mighty Presence which told him of some of the terrible things to come and gave him help and comfort with regard to the events which were to befall. The lecturer then dealt with the cleansing and spiritualising processes of the world-war, and its effects in expelling the things which had so long stood between humanity and a sense of those infinite and eternal laws in obedience to which alone lay its true happiness. An interesting discussion followed.

*

## THE CURSE OF THE MUMMY
## AND THE POPULAR IMAGINATION

The mysteries of ancient cultures and their magical rites were a source of deep fascination to the Edwardians. Conan Doyle had been intrigued by Ancient Egyptian attempts to preserve the dead for a physical afterlife and had early in his career dedicated two stories to the idea of the magic around mummification and Egyptian rites.

Doyle's 1891 story *The Ring of Thoth*, written in the same period as the Holmes stories *A Scandal In Bohemia* and *The Red-Headed League* explores a theme which will be familiar to filmgoers – the obsession of an immortal Egyptian High Priest with his long-dead lover.

The 1932 film *The Mummy* contains many echoes of Conan Doyle's story, as does the Indiana-Jones-on-acid tales of the more recent *The Mummy* franchise.

The mummy idea combines many of the preoccupations of readers of *Light* wrapped up in one neat package. The possibility of an unseen power at work, the possibility of a life after death, of occult knowledge, the ghoulish and the macabre, of exotic lands – and also, in the article below, a curse that might have caused mass deaths

In one aspect, the *Mummy of Evil* story can be regarded as a classic example of the way in which random events take on a meaning after the event. In another, how rumour builds on rumour to make a perfect folk tale.

The story goes that the mummy of the High Priestess of Amen-Ra became an infamous artefact because of the bad luck it brought.

Stories around the case included a mutilation, a series of suicides, a claim that a photographer who photographed it was shocked to see that the face on the picture was completely different to the real one and that the photographer, too, committed suicide.

After a string of such terrible mishaps, it was sold to an American collector by the British Museum, who travelled with it on a ship bound for America. The ship they departed the shores of the UK on was none other than RMS Titanic...

The article below is a reader's response to an interview with the British Museum's Dr Wallis Budge, the pre-eminent Egyptologist of his day, who denied any knowledge of the sarcophagus and its mummy.

*Light, September 30, 1916*

THE SO-CALLED "MUMMY OF EVIL."
A DIFFERENT VERSION OF THE STORY:

Miss E. Katharine Bates writes us that she is much puzzled by the statements in regard to the "mummy of evil" and the quotation from Dr. Budge, of the British Museum, which appeared in our issue of the 9th inst., and which were taken from an article by Marion Ryan in the "Weekly Dispatch." Miss Bates gives the following account of the matter:—

Let me tell you that I know at first hand about the mummy case in the

British Museum, presented by the late Mr. Douglas Murray many years ago. There was never any question of this containing a mummy. He was advised to offer it to the Museum because of the many misfortunes which happened to him and several of his friends whilst it was in his possession. Mr. Murray, whom I knew personally quite well, spent an afternoon with me at the Lyceum Club and told me the whole story of his acquiring the case in Egypt and what happened later. It was in the early 'sixties that he (then a very young man) and two young men friends spent a winter in Egypt for shooting, &c. During one of these expeditions he left his dragoman in Cairo, and told him to keep an eye upon anything really worth buying in the way of antiquities. When the trio returned, this beautiful mummy case was one of a few valuable purchases made by the dragoman. Douglas Murray told me that, for some unknown reason, he felt at once a repugnance to taking it, and as his friends rather reproached him for not having shared his spoils with them, he proposed that they should draw lots. To his disgust the mummy case fell to him. Now comes the only part of the newspaper accounts which Mr. Murray did not endorse. The papers used to say that his arm was shot off by one of his Arabs. This was not true, but he did lose his right arm very shortly after taking over the case. He was out duck-shooting one day when the gun he was carrying burst and shattered his arm so badly that it had to be amputated in Cairo. He described the agony he suffered in the journey to Cairo in those days. On their way home one of his companions died and one or two other misfortunes occurred which he began to attribute to the mummy case, thinking the High Priestess might resent its having been removed. Anyway, he told the story to a Mrs.—, a well-known literary woman, a friend of his, whose name I had better not give. She begged him to let her have it, and unwillingly he consented after warning her, but she thought it was all superstition and coincidence combined. The following year it was again in his hands. Mrs. — had experienced two very marked calamities since she took it to her house, and declined keeping it longer.

Then it was that a friend suggested its being presented to the British Museum, on the ground that such an institution could hardly be affected by the loss of an arm or money or friends. He agreed to do this, but on meeting an old friend, a Captain W—, in town and telling him of his resolve, the latter tried to dissuade him, and failing to do so, begged that the mummy case might be sent to him in Hertfordshire for a week, so that he might copy some of the decorations and paintings, promising to take every care of it, and to make all arrangements for its going direct to the British Museum if desired. Mr. Murray complied with this request. Within six months Captain W— had committed suicide. Mr. Murray wished a photograph (still to be seen) to be taken by an eminent photographer before the case was sent to the Museum, and this was done. The young man who was ordered to convey the case in a cab to the photographer's committed suicide very shortly afterwards, and a few months later the man who took the photograph died (I cannot remember if this death also was suicide).

In December, 1901, I was staying in London with an acquaintance who was then a Theosophist. One morning she invited me to accompany her to the British Museum and try to find this mummy case, having heard that it could be identified by the photograph which was fastened outside. I could not go that morning and she returned at lunch time, having spent several hours in a vain search. It was then arranged that Mr —, a well-known Theosophist, should go with her. (I had left London by this time.) I understood that Dr. Budge consented to join the party, that he located the case – although the photograph was inside, not outside— and that my acquaintance Mrs. K—, was allowed to climb up some steps and make a sketch of the Priestess from an upper angle. (She wrote several sheets to me about this at the time.) It had been said that the photograph when taken showed an entirely different face from the painting on the front of the case. Mrs K— (an artist herself) did not agree with this but wished to see if it might look very different from some other angle of vision. Her conclusion was that the face in the photo and that on the case were essentially the same.

Now, as Dr. Budge was present (she would hardly have been able to get the steps otherwise) I cannot understand his apparently ignoring altogether this special mummy case presented by Mr. Douglas Murray, for in the statement quoted in LIGHT he only speaks of two mummies, one of which belonged to Mr. Ingram and the other to an Englishwoman who does not appear to have given it to the British Museum at all!

The Douglas Murray case I saw for myself years ago, in the room the centre of which was filled by the glass case containing the prehistoric man with reddish hair.

As Douglas Murray - a most upright and honourable gentleman - told me himself all about his adventures with the mummy case and its final consignment to the British Museum, I shall continue to believe in the truthfulness of the narrative. I am sure if he were alive he would not object to his name appearing in connection with the matter.

I have frequently heard the tale about the "Titanic," but never believed it. It seemed unlikely that the British Museum would sell such a valuable specimen which had been presented to them.

*

### THE DEEP TRAUMA OF THE WAR

It is fitting to end this Appendix by focussing on the massive significance The Great War held in people's minds. The deep shock that struck this generation led some to believe that this was indeed the "end of days" or that it could only be explained with reference to Spiritualism.

Just so with responses to the new ritual brought in the year after Armistice Day, the Two Minutes Silence.

*Light, November 15, 1919.*

### THE GREAT SILENCE.

On Tuesday last the British peoples throughout the world paid a deep and touching tribute to the Glorious Dead. In the "Daily Mail" of that date appeared the appended letter from the Rev. Walter Wynn. It is instinct with fine thought, and its publication by this great daily on a day of such national importance is a significant fact.

*

*To the Editor of The Daily Mail.*

SIR,—Many thousands of mourners will live through today with sad hearts. They will feel deeply grateful to our beloved King and his people for an act of reverent memory, but they will not be seen in public thoroughfares, if they can help it! Not even a congregation in any sacred edifice will watch their tears. In silence, as deep and solemn as that into which the heroes have seemed to pass, the bereaved will probably be unseen. "In the Central deeps of our being we are all alone," said F. W. Robertson. But some of us will know the truth of Goethe's immortal words: "Here eyes do regard you, in Eternity's stillness."

And it is because I know that the heartache of millions would be relieved if they believed with certainty their sons were living, I ask for your valuable space to say I know that my son, Rupert Wynn, is alive. I know this as the result of long investigations. He is happy. He is near me. He, and millions of the departed, will witness the nation's fitting tribute to their heroism in sublime moments of hush and reverence.

These words are not written in any spirit of controversy. What Carlyle called a "scientific certainty" is as bread and wine to our hearts. I write only in the hope that my confidence may enable tears to be wiped away in numberless homes and inspire the sorrowing ones to say concerning the departed—"They live."

WALTER WYNN,
Author of "Rupert Lives!"

***

In the same issue of the "Daily Mail" appears this striking letter, the signature to which we imagine hides the identity of one of our well-known correspondents:—

"SIR, — The Great Silence will also, be a great séance — the greatest and noblest ever held. Forty-six — or more — million people will be engaged in sending a gigantic thought wave to the other side. Will it burst the barrier between the two worlds, and shall we get a reply?"

"B."

*

# Appendix B.

## People and Organisations in this Book

### People

**Ball, Henry,** (1861-1931). A local architect in Southsea whom Conan Doyle befriended while he lived there in the 1880s. Ball was a prolific designer of Victorian municipal buildings. Doyle regarded Ball as a dedicated seeker after truth very much in his own mould, and for a while considered him as a prospective match for his sister, Connie. It was with Ball that Doyle performed some of his earliest psychic research.

**Barrett, Sir William F,** (1844-1925). A highly effective practical physicist, renowned for the discovery of the silicon-iron alloy known as "stalloy". Barrett was a fellow of the Royal Society of London, the Royal Society of Edinburgh and the Royal Dublin Society. He was knighted in 1912.

Barrett's interest in psychical research came from experiences with mesmerism in the 1860s. He was interested in thought transference, rappings and object movements which he witnessed in good light with two unpaid mediums. He also investigated poltergeist activity. Following a talk with E. Dawson Rogers in 1876, he took up the latter's suggestion that leading scientists and scholars might join a society to investigate psychic phenomena, and the SPR was founded in 1882.

**Clodd, Edward,** (1840–1930). Banker, popular anthropologist, member of the Royal Astronomical Society and editor of the weekly scientific periodical *Knowledge.* He was also a leading folklorist of his generation.

A friend of Thomas Hardy, George Meredith and H G Wells, among others, he became famous for his condemnation of the superstitious roots of Spiritualism and Christian theology. He was chair of the Rationalist Press Association.

**Crawford, Dr William Jackson**, (1881-1920) born in New Zealand;

engineering professor at Queens University, Belfast. In 1914 he began investigating the physical phenomena of Kathleen Goligher and the group around her, known as the Goligher Circle. His investigation continued until his death in 1920.

**Crookes, Sir William F,** (1832–1919) was a chemist, science journalist and businessman. He developed early photographic processes and entered into business ventures such as commercial gold extraction, electric lighting and the creation of fertiliser from sewage. He was the first to isolate the new metallic element thallium, laid the groundwork for the discovery of X-rays; some of his experimental work was the foundation of nuclear physics and of electronic theory. 'Crookes's dark space' and the 'Crookes tube' have become part of the vocabulary of modern physics. In the 1870s and 1880s he investigated mediums and concluded that some mediums, including D D Home, had genuine psychic powers. More sensational was Crookes's support for the pretty young medium Florence Cook, who materialized a phantom called Katie King.

**Dallas, Helen Alexandrina,** (1856-1944) aka **Miss H A Dallas** was a member of the SPR, a writer on psychic matters and a frequent contributor to *Light*. She was encouraged in her early writing by the previous editor of *Light* Edmund Dawson Rogers. Over a long period she wrote and translated numerous books on Spiritualism, including *Gospel Records Interpreted By Human Experience* (1903), *Evidence For A Future Life* (translator, 1904), *Leaves From A Psychic Noter-Book* (1927) and *The Bridge of Death* (1936).

**Doyle, Sir Arthur Conan,** (1859-1930), as well as being the creator of Sherlock Holmes wrote horror, science fiction, historical romance, history, poetry and was a leading light in the Spiritualist movement. He was influential in setting up the Court of Appeal, was a pioneer of skiing as a leisure pursuit, was a volunteer doctor in the Boer War. He was married firstly to Louise Hawkins, who died in 1906, then to Jean Leckie in 1907.

**Doyle, Lady Jean Conan,** née Jean Leckie, (1874-1940) was Doyle's second wife. Born in London, the daughter of a silk and tea merchant, she trained as a singer, but met Doyle at the age of 23 and was invited to live with the Doyle family to help Doyle's sickly wife, Louise. Her relationship with Doyle has been characterised by biographers as both Platonic, and as a mistress. She married Doyle a year after the death of Louise and bore Arthur three children. Later in life, she became a medium, and was said to have great skill with automatic writing.

**Drayson, Major General Alfred Wilkes** (1827-1846) joined the Royal Artillery in 1846 and was posted to South Africa, where he was impressed by Zulu other native attitudes to nature, making him a proto-ecologist. Drayson converted to Spritualism in 1856. He served throughout the Empire, and was Professor of Surveying and Practical Astronomy at Woolwich. He also wrote for the *Boy's Own Paper* and was an expert at whist. Drayson ignored social distinctions and valued only friendship – and once turned down a knighthood. He retired in 1883 to Southsea, where he met Conan Doyle and influenced his early faith.

**Fielding-Ould, Rev F**, (unknown-1930), vicar of Christ Church, Regent's Park, London was a committed Spiritualist. Fielding-Ould wrote numerous books on religion and Spiritualism, including *Is Spiritualism of the Devil?*, *Wonders of the Saints* and *The Relation of Spiritualism to Christianity*, among others.

**Flammarion, Nicolas Camille**, (1842 – 1925), was a French astronomer and a prolific author of more than fifty titles, including popular science works about astronomy, several notable early science fiction novels, and works on psychical research and related topics. He also published the magazine *L'Astronomie*, starting in 1882. He maintained a private observatory at Juvisy-sur-Orge, France.

The **Fox Sisters** were three sisters: **Leah Fox**, (1814-1890), **Margaret Fox**, (1833-1893) and **Catherine Fox**, (1837-1892) who lived in Hydesville, New York. The two younger sisters were associated with apparently inexplicable "rappings" in their house, which attracted the interest of neighbours. Claimed to be messages from, variously, the spirit of a pedlar murdered in the basement and "Mr Splitfoot" (a nickname of the devil), the communications caused a sensation. "Kate" and Margaret Fox later emerged as mediums, were founders of the modern Spiritualist movement and travelled to Europe on missionary work. In later life they admitted their mediumship powers were fraudulent, though some argue that only one of the women did so, possibly as the result of a family feud and that they later retracted the admission. They died in poverty.

**Gow, David, (1866-1939 )**Born in Scotland in 1866, Gow was the editor of *Light* between 1914 and 1931. He was a small man, widely read and "never suffered fools gladly." Filled with nervous energy, he disdained public speaking, instead expressing himself through his pen. He was sensitive, artistic and quiet natured and found philosophical depth in mundane matters. A writer from early in his career, he emerged on the Spiritualist scene in 1899. He rose quickly through Spiritualist ranks, becoming a contributor and assistant editor to *Light*, taking over the editorship on E W Wallis's death in 1914. He guided *Light* through the economically difficult War years and beyond, taking on the editorship after the death of its previous editor. He retired due to ill health in 1931, and died in 1939 aged 73.

**Hageby, Lind Af,** (1878-1963) was from a wealthy, noble Swedish family. She was heavily involved in the early campaign against vivisection, founding the Animal Defence and Anti-Vivisection Society in 1906. A distinguished orator, she was also a strong advocate of feminism and was during World War I a member of the International Committee of Women for Permanent Peace. She saw spirituality as an integral part of her beliefs and was in later life closely associated with the London Spiritualist Alliance, becoming its first woman president between 1935 and 1943.

**Hodgson, Richard,** (1855-1905) was a psychical researcher, and member of the SPR. He investigated and declared fraudulent both Madame Blavatsky and Eusapia Palladino. However, he came to believe that another medium, Leonora Piper, had genuine powers.

**Home, D D,** (1833-1886) was considered the most gifted medium of his generation. Famous for his ability to cause a table to rock or rise into the air apparently of its own volition, he was said to be able to levitate in front of witnesses and produce many other impressive psychic phenomena.

**Lodge, Sir Oliver**, (1851-1940) Physicist, Fellow of the Royal Society and discoverer of radio waves. His experiments contributed to Einstein's conception of the special theory of relativity and he was a pioneer in wireless telegraphy and X-ray photography, among many other accolades. He was an ardent Spiritualist, and more so after the death of his son, Raymond Lodge, during the Great War.

**McCabe, Joseph**, (1867-1955), was a former Roman Catholic priest who later become a prominent writer on free thought. He wrote prolifically on many subjects, including history and religion. He was a founder member of the Rationalist Press Association and a tireless public speaker and writer, who claimed to have written more books and pamphlets than any living writer. He was a staunch critic of Spiritualism.

**Moses, William Stainton**, (1839–1892), spiritualist, was curate of Maughold in the Isle of Man from 1863 to 1868, and assistant chaplain of St George's, Douglas, from 1868 to 1871, when he became interested in Spiritualism and resigned his curacy to become English master at University College School, London. He was the most prominent of the various Church of England clergy who involved themselves in Spiritualism. He was a founder of the London Spiritualist Alliance, an active member and one of the vice-presidents of the Society for Psychical Research, and a frequent contributor and editor of *Light*. In 1882 he was a founder of the Ghost Club.

**Myers, F W**, (Frederic William Henry), (1843–1901), psychical researcher and essayist. He was one of the founders of the Society for Psychical Research (the SPR), and one of its most enthusiastic early supporters and organisers. He coined the term 'telepathy' and was the first to describe in English the early work of Pierre Janet and Freud.

**Oaten, Ernest**, (1875-1952) Editor of *The Two Worlds* and president of the SNU, in 1934 Oaten became the first person to broadcast on the topic of Spiritualism in the BBC programme *My Experience of Spiritualism*. Ernest led an SNU parliamentary campaign seeking legal recognition of Spiritualism as a religion.

**Owen, George Vale**, (1869-1931) was a Birmingham-born clergymen ordained in 1893 as curate first in the parish of Seaforth, Liverpool and at several other parishes thereafter. His psychic abilities awoke after his mother's death in 1909 and he began receiving psychic communication in 1913. He converted to Spiritualism and wrote numerous books on the subject, notably his five-volume set, *Life Beyond the Veil*, prefaced by Conan Doyle, who was a great supporter. He was forced out of his parish by the Church and became an active Spiritualist lecturer, touring the United States and the United Kingdom before becoming pastor of a Spiritualist congregation in London.

**Palladino, Eusapia**, (1854 – 1918) Italian Spiritualist and physical medium. She claimed to possess powers such as the ability to levitate tables and communicate with the dead through her spirit guide John King, and other related supernatural phenomena. She convinced many of her powers, but was at times also caught in deceptive trickery.

**Peters, Vout**, (1867-unknown), British clairvoyant and trance medium, first became aware of the presence of ghostly children when he was a child and claimed to have precognitive dreams, see visions and hear voices. He began his mediumship in 1895 and frequently came under control by a guide named "Moonstone." He was featured in Lodge's *Raymond* (1916), and also came under the control of a living person in 1899, at a séance in London. Peters was a talented psychometrist who was tested by psychic researcher and fraud-debunker Harry Price in 1927, for which Peters claimed success. Date of death unknown.

**Piper, Leonora**, (1857-1950), née Leonora Evelina Simonds. A famous New Hampshire trance medium, whose parents claimed she had psychic abilities from childhood. As an adult, after being treated by a psychic healer, she claimed to hear spirit voices and performed automatic writing. As her fame grew, she worked as a paid medium at a dollar a sitting, and was later investigated by William James and the SPR. Psychic debunker Richard Hodgson became convinced of her powers in the 1890s, though others, notably Joseph McCabe, criticised his credulousness.

**Powell, Ellis Thomas,** (1869-1922), British barrister, journalist, and Spiritualist. Powell was born in Ludlow, Shropshire, and educated at Ludlow Grammar School. After an apprenticeship to a draper he came to London and became a journalist and then editor of the *Financial News*. A polyglot, and polymath, he studied law and became a barrister and among other roles, lectured at the London School of Economics and Political Science (University of London).

Powell became a supporter of Spiritualism, delivering psychic lectures throughout Britain. He was a member of the British College of Psychic Science and a council member of the London Spiritualist Alliance. He frequently contributed to *Light*.

**Scatcherd, Felicia Rudolphina,** (1862–1927), journalist and spiritualist, was active in two principal fields: spiritualism and international politics. She became editor of the *Psychic Review* and wrote and lectured on the continent in support of mediums, and as an expert in spirit photography. She made Arthur Conan Doyle aware of the Cottingley fairy photographs. She was a keen advocate of animal welfare, a proponent of the Baha'i faith and lived for many years with Greek socialist politician Platon Soterios Drakoulès. and his wife. A committed Imperialist, between 1916 and 1919 she was also editor of the *Imperial and Asiatic Quarterly Review*

**Shaw, George Bernard,** (1856 – 1950), Nobel-Prize and Oscar-winning Irish playwright, critic and socialist whose influence on Western theatre, culture and politics stretched from the 1880s to his death in 1950.

**Sinnett, A P,** (1840–1921), a journalist and theosophist who worked for or was editor for publications including *The Globe, The Hong Kong Daily Press,* and *The Standard.* Appointed editor of *The Pioneer* in India in 1872, he came under the influence of Madame Blavatsky and published letters from her superhuman "Mahatmas" in *The Occult World* (1881) and *Esoteric Buddhism* (1883) to spread Blavatsky's word.

Returning to London in 1883 Sinnett became the foremost theosophist in Britain. On Blavatsky' later return, he criticised Blavatsky's denial of human spirit communication and set up a rival lodge. From 1904 to 1907 he published *Broad Views,* a monthly periodical to challenge "conventional habits of thought". He condemned Western materialism and published 20 books on spirit development.

**Tweedale, Rev Charles Lakeman**, (1866-1944)  was an Anglican minister, and leading Spiritualist. His vicarage at Weston in Yorkshire, was described as a "much-haunted house." He authored numerous books on Spiritualism, including *Man's Survival After Death* (1909) and *News from the Next World* (1940). He also defended spirit photography in his book *The Vindication of William Hope* (1933).

**Vaughan, Father Bernard**, (1847–1922), one of of thirteen children born to Colonel John Francis Vaughan, Bernard Vaughan was educated at Stonyhurst College nine years before Conan Doyle, becoming a Jesuit noviciate in 1866. As a priest, he became famous as a powerful preacher and public speaker, delivering an impassioned style of oratory.

**Wallace, Alfred Russel**, (1823-1913) was a British naturalist, explorer, geographer, anthropologist, and biologist. He is best known for independently conceiving the theory of evolution through natural selection and prompted Charles Darwin to publish *On the Origin of Species*. Wallace was strongly attracted to unconventional ideas (such as evolution) and Spiritualism.

**Wallace, Abraham**, (1849-1930) Like Conan Doyle, Dr Wallace was a medical doctor. He had a long-term association with the LSA and with Spiritualism. He investigated psychic phenomena with a specific interest in the nature of Christ. In a 1904 lecture to the LSA, printed in *Light*, he took a Unitarian view, describing Jesus as "a highly gifted psychic" who didn't claim divinity, but was "the most divine expression of humanity," and thus an exemplar for all humans. Conan Doyle encouraged the lecture to be reprinted by *The Two Worlds* in 1920, under the title *Jesus* *of Nazareth and Modern Scientific Investigation: From the Spiritualist Standpoint.*

**Whiting, Lilian,** (1859 – 1942), American journalist and author, was literary editor of the *Boston Traveler* from 1880 to 1890, editor of the *Boston Budget* in 1890-93, and afterward spent much of her time in Europe. Whiting's interest in things seen and unseen led her to explore many different philosophies and religions, including Bahai, New Thought, and Theosophy.

## Organisations

**The Ghost Club** is widely believed to be the oldest paranormal investigation organisation in the world. Formed in 1862 in London, it had Charles Dickens and numerous Cambridge academics and clergy as early members. The group undertook practical investigations of Spiritualist phenomena, was dissolved in the 1870s after Dickens's death, but was revived in 1882 by Alfred Alaric Watts and the Reverend William Stainton Moses. It was distinguished from the SPR in those early years in that its members were convinced of the fact of psychic phenomena.

The Ghost Club still exists, and now also investigates cryptozoology, dowsing and UFOs as well as more traditional psychic phenomena. Sir Arthur Conan Doyle was also a member.
*http://www.ghostclub.org.uk/*

**The London Spiritualist Alliance** (LSA) was founded in 1884 under the instigation of William Stainton Moses, its first president. The LSA obtained a wide membership, including notable figures such as Percy Wyndham and Alfred Russel Wallace, and was dedicated to furthering the understanding of Spiritualism. In 1955, it changed its name to The College of Psychic Science, and in 1970, to the College of Psychic Studies.

Stainton Moses also founded the magazine *Light* in 1881, dedicated to the study and understanding of Spiritualism, both as a science and a religion. College of Psychic Studies continues to publish *Light*.
*https://www.collegeofpsychicstudies.co.uk/*

**The Society for Psychical Research** (SPR) was founded by 1882 in London by a group of eminent thinkers, including Edmund Gurney, F W H Myers, William F Barrett and others. It was the first research organisation dedicated to researching psychic phenomena with "exact and unimpassioned enquiry" on a scientific basis.

It drew its initial members from believers and sceptics, and originally set up six committees to investigate different aspects of the paranormal. It continues to this day to investigate psychic phenomena, and has over the years unmasked numerous frauds, at some time gaining a reputation among believers for being overly sceptical.

*http://www.spr.ac.uk/*

**The Spiritualists' National Union** (SNU) is a Spiritualist organisation founded in the UK in 1901. It is one of the largest Spiritualist groups in the world with an active following and numerous Spiritualist temples affiliated to it. Its motto is *Light, Nature, Truth.*

*http://www.snu.org.uk/*

## Appendix C.

## A Glossary of Spiritualist Terms Used In This Book

**Angel** - benign spiritual being.

**Apparition** - supernatural appearance of a person or thing.

**Astral Body** - spiritual counterpart to a person's physical body, which is able to leave the body in astral projection and at death.

**Astral Projection** – the astral body's travels when separated from the physical body.

**Astrology** - belief that astronomical events affect or correlate to earthly events, and a method of applying this belief.

**Aura** - energy field surrounding living creatures, sometimes described as a halo.

**Automatic Writing** – messages written apparently without conscious control.

**Cabinet** - screened or curtained enclosure or box inside which a physical medium may be secured whilst producing psychic phenomena.

**Christian Science** – founded by Mary Baker Eddy, a set of beliefs and practices belonging to the metaphysical family of new religious movements.

**Circle** – séance group.

**Clairaudience** - ability to hear psychically generated sounds or voices.

**Clairvoyance** – ability to see psychically generated visual data. Can also apply to any form of information, not necessarily visual.

**Clairvoyant / Clairvoyant Medium** – one who obtains information psychically.

**Communication** - in Spiritualism, a spirit message.

**Communicator** – in Spiritualism, spirit that communicates with a medium.

**Conjuring** – use of trickery to create magical effects.

**Control** – spirit who controls a medium.

**Direct Voice** - spirit's voice which does not come from any physical person.

**Discarnate Entity / Spirit / Intelligence** - non-physical entity or spirit, often referring to one who has left their body, such as a dead person.

**Divination** – methods designed to forecast future events.

**Double** - spirit duplicate of a body, such as an astral or etheric body.

**Ectoplasm** - substance exuded by a physical medium which may manifest physical phenomena. Ectoplasm may be fluid, viscous or solid.

**Etheric Body** – astral body.

**Fairy** - small, often winged mythical being in human form.

**Fortune Telling** - see divination.

**Ghost** – dead person's spirit.

**Guardian Angel** – protective, benign spirit.

**Guide** - spirit believed to aid a person's spiritual journey or inquiry.

**Hallucination** - sensory experience that does not exist outside the mind or subjective perception.

**Haunting** – prolonged period of paranormal activity within a specific location.

**Healer** – person with the ability to heal.

**Hypnosis** – state of consciousness rendering a person open to suggestion.

**Immortality** – belief that some aspect of an individual does not die.

**Invocation** – invitation to benevolent spiritual beings through speech.

**Levitation** – ability of a person or object to defy gravity.

**Magic** - (a) influence of events or people through supernatural means. (b) conjuring.

**Magician** – one who practices magic.

**Materialisation** – visible and concrete object or human shape which manifests during a séance.

**Medium** – one through whom spirits communicate with the living.

**Mediumship** - medium's activities.

**Mesmerism** – early form of healing similar to hypnosis developed by F A Mesmer. Mesmerised patients sometimes displayed clairvoyant abilities.

**Mystic** – person who believes that the human mind or soul can encounter the divine directly.

**Necromancy** – form of black magic that involves speaking with dead spirits.

**Ouija Board** - numbered and lettered board used to spell out messages from spirits by the moving of a glass or planchette while the fingers of a group of sitters rest upon the glass or planchette.

**Paranormal** – events that cannot be explained by our normal conception of the world. Beyond normal.

**Pendulum** – object suspended by a thread and free to move. Movements of a pendulum can be interpreted to reveal particular answers to questions or the location of objects.

**Physical Medium** - medium able to produce physical phenomena, including sounds, lights, levitation and materialization.

**Planchette** - small platform on wheels often used with a ouija board. May have a pencil attached to produce automatic writing.

**Poltergeist** – "noisy or troublesome spirit". Poltergeists are often cited as the cause of inexplicable movements of objects, noises, pricks or scratches to a person's body and other physical phenomena.

**Possession** – taking over of a person by another entity.

**Prediction** – forecast of future events.

**Psychic** - one displaying paranormal ability. A description relating to paranormal abilities.

**Psychical Research** – study of paranormal activity.

**Psychic Photography** - photographic images with a paranormal element.

**Psychometry** – ability to psychically draw information or knowledge from a physical object.

**Raps** - unexplained knocking sounds related to physical mediumship and poltergeist activity.

**Sceptic** – one who does not believe in psychic and or paranormal activity, often with a rationalist bias.

**Séance** - session during which a medium attempts to communicate with spirits.

**Sitter** – one who attends a séance.

**Sitting** - séance.

**Soul** – person's spirit, often thought to be immortal.

**Spirit** - disembodied entity, or soul.

**Spirit Photography** – photography which shows the presence of deceased persons.

**Spiritualism (Spiritism)** – religious belief including the idea that it is possible with spirits through a medium.

**Survival** - belief in the continued existence of a spiritual aspect of a person after death.

**Synchronicity** – Jung's term to describe coincidental events connected not by cause but by meaningfulness.

**Table-Tilting, Table-Turning** – spirit communication through the movements of a table on which sitters place their hands.

**Telepathy** – ability to communicate subjective experience or thoughts.

**Theosophy** - religious and philosophy founded by Madame Blavatsky in 1875, particularly concerning the nature of divinity.

**Trance** – altered state of consciousness which tends to focus the attention on internal experience.

**Trance Medium** - medium who first enters a state of trance before performing mediumship.

**Trumpet** - conical tube through which direct voice communication occurs in séances. A trumpet is often luminous so it can be seen during darkened séance conditions.

**Vision** - religious manifestation or hallucination.

# Appendix D.

## Bibliography

I have included what I hope is a reasonably complete bibliography of the written works of Sir Arthur Conan Doyle, sorted by genre headings, though I have not included his plays or pamphlets. Many of these works, such as the *Holmes* and *Professor Challenger* stories are well known – others less so.

I have also included a short list of books related to Doyle's life and to Spiritualism in this era which you may find useful for background reading.

Finally, if you are looking for further reading on the state of Spiritualism in the years during and after the Great War, I have included a list of the main periodicals mentioned in this book. You will also find them, along with all the books and stories mentioned herein, listed in italics in the Index

### Bibliography of the Works of Sir Arthur Conan Doyle

**Spiritualist Works**
The New Revelation, 1918
The Vital Message, 1919
Verbatim Report of a Public Debate on 'The Truth of Spiritualism'
between Sir Arthur Conan Doyle and Joseph McCabe, 1920
The Wanderings of a Spiritualist, 1921
The Coming of the Fairies, 1922
The Case for Spirit Photography, 1922
Our American Adventure, 1924
The Spiritualist's Reader, 1924
The History of Spiritualism, 1926
Pheneas Speaks, 1927
Our African Winter, 1929
The Edge of the Unknown, 1930

**Sherlock Holmes**
A Study in Scarlet, 1887
The Sign of Four, 1890
The Adventures of Sherlock Holmes, 1892
The Memoirs of Sherlock Holmes, 1894
The Hound of the Baskervilles, 1902
The Return of Sherlock Holmes, 1905
The Valley of Fear, 1915
His Last Bow, 1917
The Case-book of Sherlock Holmes, 1927

**Horror / Adventure / Mystery**
The Mystery of Cloomber, 1889
Mysteries and Adventures, 1890
The Captain of the Pole-Star, 1890
The Doings of Raffles Haw, 1891
The Gully of Bluemansdyke 1893
Round the Red Lamp: Being Facts and Fancies of Medical Life,
1894
The Parasite, 1894
The Green Flag and Other Stories of War and Sport, 1900
Round the Fire Stories, 1908
The Last Galley, 1908
Danger! and Other Stories, 1918
Three of Them, 1923
The Maracot Deep, 1929

**Science Fiction**
The Lost World, 1912
The Poison Belt, 1913
The Land of Mist, 1926

**Historical Fiction**
Micah Clarke, 1889
The Firm of Girdlestone, 1890
The White Company, 1891
The Great Shadow, 1892

The Refugees, 1893
Rodney Stone, 1896
The Exploits of Brigadier Gerard, 1896
Uncle Bernac, 1897
The Tragedy of the Korosko, 1898
The Adventures of Gerard, 1903
Sir Nigel, 1906

**Other**
The Stark Munro Letters, 1895
A Duet, with an Occasional Chorus, 1899

**Non Fiction**
The Great Boer War, 1900
The War in South Africa – Its Cause and Conduct, 1902
Through the Magic Door, 1907
The Crime of the Congo, 1912
The German War: Some Sidelights and Reflections, 1914
A Visit to Three Fronts, 1916
The British Campaign in France and Flanders, 1916-20
Memories and Adventures (autobiographical work), 1924
Dangerous Work: Diary of an Arctic Adventure, 2012

**Poems**
Songs of Action, 1898
Songs of the Road, 1911
The Guards Came Through and Other Poems, 1919
The Poems of Arthur Conan Doyle: Collected Edition, 1922

**Some Biographical Works About Doyle:**
Conan Doyle and the Spirits: The Spiritualist Career of Sir Arthur
Conan Doyle – Kelvin I. Jones
Conan Doyle, Teller of Tales – Daniel Stashower
Conan Doyle, The Man Who Created Sherlock Holmes – Andrew
Lycett
A Study In Southsea – Geoffrey Stavert

## Books, stories and periodicals mentioned in this book

**Paranormal Periodicals:**
Light: A Journal of Psychical, Occult, and Mystical Research
The Two Worlds
The International Psychic Gazette
The Occult Review
Psychic Review
Truth

**Mainstream Periodicals:**

Boy's Own Paper
The Courier
The Daily Chronicle
The Daily Dispatch
The Daily Express
The Daily Graphic
The Daily Mail
The Daily Mirror
The Daily News
The Daily Record and Mail
The Daily Sketch
The Daily Star
The Daily Telegraph
The Empire News (Salvation
Army Periodical)
The Evening News
The Evening Standard
Hibbert Journal

John O' London's Weekly
The Literary Guide
The Medical Press
The Monist
The Morning Post
Nash's Magazine
The Pall Mall Gazette
Pearson's Magazine
The Strand Magazine
The Sunday Boston Herald
The Sunday Chronicle
The Sunday Express
The Sunday Times
The Times
Tit-Bits
T.P.'s Weekly
Weekly Dispatch
Worcester Advertiser

## Appendix E.

## Index of Letters and Articles written by Doyle or strongly featuring him

The following list contains two distinct entities. Those in CAPITALS are either letters or articles written by Doyle specifically for *Light*. Those in Title Case are articles about Doyle. These include interviews Doyle gave to other magazines quoted in *Light*, quotes from books, editorials which mention Doyle and longer articles written about him.

Of the articles and editorials about him, I have been judicious about what to include – some only mentioned Doyle in passing. While they do not form his writings, they certainly shed light on his thinking. Some long articles, though mentioning Doyle in the third person, are essentially his thinking in strong detail. This is true of the talk he gave at Suffolk Street reported in *Light* between November 11th and 24th, in which he gave the programme for his book *The New Revelation*.

A TEST MESSAGE; 2nd July 1887                                          26
MR. HODGSON; 27th August 1887                                         30
WHERE IS THE SOUL DURING UNCONSCIOUSNESS?; 11th March, 1916     38
WHERE IS THE SOUL DURING UNCONSCIOUSNESS? 13th May, 1916        41
A NEW REVELATION. SPIRITUALISM AND RELIGION; November 4th, 1916 44
SPIRITUALISM AND RELIGION; 2nd December, 1916                    54
FATHER VAUGHAN AND SPIRITUALISM; 23rd June 1917                 59
Introduction to "Is Spiritualism of the Devil?"; 4th August, 1917   61
Reason and Revelation; November 11th, 1917                       65
The New Revelation. Address by Sir Arthur Conan Doyle; 11th November, 1917 68
The New Revelation. Address by Sir Arthur Conan Doyle; November 17th, 1917 75
The New Revelation. Address by Sir Arthur Conan Doyle; November 24th, 1917 81
Light on Conan Doyle and Sherlock Holmes in The Strand; December 17th, 1917
                                                                     88
THE MAINTENANCE OF LIGHT; January 26th, 1918                    89
THE MILITARY VALUE OF SPIRITUALISM; May 11th, 1918             91

Conan Doyle's Address to the National Memorial Service for the Fallen, Albert Hall; May 3rd, 1919                                                                                      97
JESUS CHRIST AND SPIRITUALISM; August 9th, 1919                                      112
Is Spirit Communion A Sin? Criticisms On The Bishop Of London's Address, from The Evening News; 9th August 1919                                                      115
The New Testament and the New Revelation (extract from The Vital Message); September 27th, 1919                                                                              117
As It Was In The Beginning (extract from The Vital Message); October 4th, 1919
                                                                                                                   119
Sir A. Conan Doyle At Leicester. Reply To Church Criticisms; October 11th, 1919
                                                                                                                   122
Sir A Conan Doyle and the Rev. A. V. Magee; November 15th, 1919            125
Sir A. Conan Doyle and Rev. Magee (letter to Daily Mail); December 13th, 1919 126
Is "Spiritism" Anti-Christian? Views Of Bishop Welldon And Sir A. Conan Doyle; November 15th, 1919                                                                              127
Doyle quoted in the Evening Standard; April 1920                                         128
Sir Arthur Conan Doyle  (Doyle's address at the anniversary celebrations.); April 10th, 1920                                                                                          129
DOYLE'S PLEA TO THE BISHOPS; May 15th 1920                                           131
Sir Arthur Conan Doyle's Wimbledon Address; October 11th, 1919                137
SIR A. CONAN DOYLE EXPLAINS; October 18th, 1919                                   137
A WONDERFUL SEANCE. SIR A. CONAN DOYLE'S ACCOUNT; December 27th, 1919                                                                                                     138
Sir A Conan Doyle's Interview in the Worcester Advertiser on the truth of Spiritualism; January 10th, 1920                                                              142
Sir A Conan Doyle's Interview in the Worcester Advertiser - Unfair Press Tactics; January 10th, 1920                                                                              143
SIR A CONAN DOYLE AT HOVE; July 17th, 1920                                           144
Sir Arthur Conan Doyle in The Strand; September 11th 1920                         146
Is Sir Oliver Lodge Right?; July 7th, 1917                                                     151
Interviews with Sir Arthur Conan Doyle; March 1st 1919                              155
Doyle's Challenge to the Press; March 22nd, 1919                                        157
Doyle's Address at the Queen's Hall criticising the Press; July 5th, 1919        158
Daily Record and Mail interview; April 12th 1919                                         161
Conan Doyle on remote viewing reported in The Daily Express; 27th December 1919                                                                                                     169
Sir A. Conan Doyle's Answer [to Press criticism]; 10th January 1920            171
Arthur Conan Doyle's response to the Magic Circle; August 9th, 1919           178

Sir Arthur Conan Doyle and Crystal Gazing, Sunday Express; August 9th, 1920

179

Sir Arthur Conan Doyle and the Sideric Pendulum; 14th August 1919   180

Sir Arthur Conan Doyle on Invisible Air Records; May 8th, 1920   181

A Critic's "Logical Questions" answered; January 17th, 1920   187

THE NEED FOR ENERGY; January 11th, 1919   190

Sir Arthur Conan Doyle's Scottish Tour, The Meeting in Edinburgh; April 19th, 1919   192

Sir Arthur Conan Doyle's Scottish Tour, The Meeting In Glasgow; April 19th, 1919

193

ARTHUR CONAN DOYLE ON THE IMMEDIATE NEED; May 10th, 1919   195

Sir A Conan Doyle On Spiritualism As A Revolutionary Force; May 31st, 1919   196

Sir Arthur Conan Doyle In London.Address At The Queen's Hall; June 21st 1919

197

Sir Arthur Conan Doyle At Queen's Hall. Second Meeting. Lord Glenconner Presides.   199

Sir Arthur Conan Doyle Address At Queen's Hall. Finall Address: Viscount Molesworth Presides; July 5th, 1919   202

A CENTRAL INSTITUTE FOR SPIRITUALISM; 16th August 1919   205

The Challenge of Spiritualism, Daily Chronicle; August 23rd, 1919   206

A Proposal To Tour Australia And New Zealand; September 20th, 1919   206

Death And The Hereafter; September 20th, 1919   206

New Statesman Article; October 4th, 1919   207

Sir A Conan Doyle At Wimbledon; October 11th, 1919   207

Mr Bean's Address To The Institute Of Journalists; November 8th, 1919   209

Announcement of Doyle-McCabe Debate; December 6th, 1919   210

The Line Of Spiritual Advance; December 27th, 1919   211

A New Year Message For The Sunday Express; January 3rd, 1920   212

The Uncharted Coast, January 10th, 1920   212

Conan Doyle Engagements; February 14th, 1920   212

Lecture in London; March 4th, 1920   213

Conan Doyle At The Deanery Of Durham; March 4th, 1920   213

Sir A. Conan Doyle's Ghosts. Mr. McCabe's Pleasantries; February 14th, 1920   215

Anticipation of Doyle-McCabe Debate; 13th March, 1920   216

LETTER FROM SIR A. CONAN DOYLE; March 20th, 1920   223

Sir A. Conan Doyle And Mr McCabe; June 5th, 1920   227

Criticisms From Edward Clodd Answered; July 10th, 1920   228

Conan Doyle And His Spiritual Mission; May 1st, 1920   229

The Farewell Luncheon To Sir Arthur And Lady Conan Doyle; August 7th, 1920
232
The Farewell Luncheon To Sir Arthur Conan Doyle, Presentation Of The Illuminated Address; August 14th, 1920 240
THE NEEDS OF SPIRITUALISM IN THE METROPOLIS; August 7th, 1920 244
Death And The Hereafter Reported At Exeter; August 4th, 1920 246
Announcement of Departure; 21st August, 1920 246
A LETTER FROM SIR A. CONAN DOYLE, Religious Discussions On Shipboard; September 11th, 1920 246

# Index

A Brief History and Examination of Modern Spiritualism - Edward Clodd - 150

Abbey Grange - A C Doyle - 20

Aberdeen - 210

Adare, Lord - 224, 225

Adventures of Sherlock Holmes, The - A C Doyle - 20

Af-Hageby, Lind - 105

After Death - W T Stead - 151

Ames, Julia - 79

Armicis, Professor - 223

Art of Practical Whist, The - Alfred Wilkes Drayson - 24

Ashton, Harold - 151, 152, 153

Australia - 206, 213, 229, 231, 233, 236, 239, 244, 245, 248, 251

Balfour, Gerald - 78

Ball, Henry - 23, 24, 289

Ballantyne, Serjeant - 45

Banner, The - 145

Barnes, Canon - 131

Barrett, Sir William F - 45, 49, 50, 54, 62, 78, 80, 88, 90, 156, 157, 184, 223, 253, 270, 289

Bates, E. Katharine - 284

Bean, Mr - 209

Bean, Mr. - 209

Beard, Ernest - 207

Belfast - 176

Benson, E F - 202, 203, 204

Béraud, Marthe - 221, 222

Berry, George - 231

Berry, John (Communicating spirit) - 274

Bible, The Holy - 50, 51, 53, 57, 152

Bigot, The - A C Doyle - 142

Binito, Professor Sans - 223

Bishopsgate - 108

Black Hawk (Communicating spirit) - 139

Blake, Frank - 138

Blavatsky, Madame - 24, 30, 295

Boddington, H - 58

Boer War - 7

Book of Job - 164

Booth, General Bramwell - 106, 107

Bourne, Cardinal - 119

Bournemouth - 206

Bowmen, The - Arthur Machen - 158, 159, 163, 269

Boy's Own Paper, The - 24

Brittain, Annie (AKA Mrs B) - 136, 157, 158, 203

Brofferio, Professor - 223

Budge, Dr E Wallis - 284, 286

Burry, Henry B Pullen - 35

Bussler, M A - 267

Butler, Samuel - 166

C, Eva (medium) - 175

Cabell, Richard - 14
Caesar, Julius (Communicating spirit) - 110
Caesar, Tiberius - 129
Calderbank, Rev A - 265
Captain of the Polestar, The - A C Doyle - 19, 261
Cardiff - 153, 154
Carus, Paul - 57
Case for Spirit Photography, The - A C Doyle - 14, 249
Challis, Professor - 223, 227
Chambers, Rev Arthur - 78
Chambers, Robert - 198
Chaplin, Alderman - 122
Charmouth - 32, 33
Chiaia, Professor - 223
Chichester, Bishop of - 56
Christ, Jesus - 10, 52, 111, 112, 113, 120, 121, 133, 177, 282, 296
Church Congress - 124
Church Council - 108
Church of England - 111, 148
Claude's Second Book - L Kelway Bamber - 211
Clodd, Edward - 150, 151, 158, 164, 219, 228, 289
Cloister and the Hearth, The - Charles Reade - 36
Coates, James - 113
Cobb, Rev W F - 111, 116, 122, 179
Colley, Archdeacon - 122
Comic Dramatists of the Restoration - Leigh Hunt - 27, 40
Conan Doyle and the Spirits - Kelvin I Jones - 11, 15, 43
Conan Doyle, Teller of Tales - Daniel Stashower - 15, 43, 58, 93

Conan Doyle, The Man Who Created Sherlock Holmes - Andrew Lycett - 15, 34
Congreve, William - 27
Cook, E Wake - 104
Cook, Florence - 173, 174, 290
Cooper, Reverend G - 56, 57
Corson, Professor - 223
Cottingley - 250, 251
Cottingley Fairies - 11, 250, 259, 295
Coues, Elliott - 223
Crawford, Dr William J - 45, 78, 115, 158, 176, 177, 178, 187, 201, 221, 223, 228, 258, 289
Crawford, Lord - 225
Crespigny, Mrs Philip Champion de - 49, 216
Crookes, Sir William - 9, 21, 45, 54, 62, 70, 115, 149, 173, 174, 175, 187, 191, 198, 223, 233, 290
Cruikshank, George - 152
Cumberland, Stuart - 188, 189
Curie, Marie - 21, 149
Curie, Pierre - 149
Daily Chronicle, The - 101, 104, 157, 178, 206
Daily Dispatch, The - 106
Daily Express, The - 101, 137, 156, 157, 159, 167, 169
Daily Mail, The - 101, 126, 127, 155, 157, 168, 169, 210, 211, 287, 288
Daily Mirror, The - 101, 189
Daily News, The - 101
Daily Sketch, The - 101, 157
Daily Star, The - 101, 126
Daily Telegraph, The - 101
Dallas, H A - 113
Danger! - A C Doyle - 43

Darwin, Charles - 21, 70, 78, 104, 149, 296
Davis, Andrew Jackson - 130
Dawbarn, Charles - 206
de Morgan, Augustus - 223
de Morgan, Mrs Sophia - 79, 191, 211, 260
Decline and Fall of the Roman Empire - Edward Gibbon - 36
Denton, Professor - 223
Dickens, Charles - 152, 169
Dixon, John H - 164
Do Thoughts Perish? - Recorder (Nom de plume) - 92
Dodd (Communicating spirit) - 72
Doré, Gustave - 152
Doyle, Adrian Malcolm Conan - 38, 240
Doyle, Arthur Alleyne Kingsley Conan - 51, 93, 136, 140, 190
Doyle, Charles Altamont - 22, 34
Doyle, Denis Percy Stewart Conan - 38, 240
Doyle, John Frances Innes Hay (ACD's brother) - 136
Doyle, Lady Jean Conan - 43, 122, 153, 193, 200, 216, 231, 232, 233, 234, 240, 241, 243, 290
Doyle, Lena Jean Annette Conan - 240
Doyle, Louise Conan - 24, 36, 290
Drayson, Major-General Alfred Wilkes - 24, 26, 29, 41, 45, 71
Duguid, Mr (Communicating spirit) - 273, 275
Dumfries - 34
Dunraven, Lord - 198, 225, 226
Edalji, George - 7
Edmonds, Judge - 26, 45, 69, 187

Einstein, Albert - 178, 183, 293
Elmore, Colonel - 33
Empire News, The - 106
Engholm, Harry - 138, 139, 141, 216, 232, 233, 238, 239, 240, 241
Ermacora, Professor - 223
Esoteric Buddhism - A P Sinnett - 296
Evening News (Portsmouth) - 29
Evening News, The - 101, 115, 155, 157, 159, 269
Evening Standard, The - 101, 125, 128, 157, 184, 187
F L (Anonymous donor) - 102
Falcomer, Professor - 223
Felkin, Dr - 35
Festubert - 43
Fielding-Ould, Rev F - 10, 15, 57, 61, 62, 64, 78, 107, 108, 111, 113, 117, 122, 132, 291
Five Orange Pips, The - A C Doyle - 261
Flammarion, Nicolas Camille - 45, 70, 149, 266, 291
Foa, Professor Pio - 223
Foch, Marshal - 209
Foley, Ida (née Doyle - ACD's sister) - 51
Forbes, Alec - 136
Forro, Professor - 223
Fox (Sisters) - 120, 131, 291
Fox, Kate - 21, 174
Fox, Leah - 21
Frankenstein - Mary Shelley - 19
Freethinker, The - 210
Freud, Sigmund - 257, 280, 293
Frohman, Charles - 43
From Matter To Spirit - Sophia De Morgan - 191
Galilei, Galileo - 78
Galvani, Luigi - 78

Gardner, Edward - 251
Geeson (Nom de plume) - 134
Geley, Gustave - 175, 176, 187, 205
Gemmi Pass - 34
Gentle, Mildred - 208
Geresa, Professor - 223
Ghost Club, The - 50, 52, 293
Ghosts I Have Seen - Violet Tweedale - 127
Gigli, Professor - 223
Gillette, William - 43
Gladstone, W E - 127, 128
Glenconner, Lord - 199, 200
God The Invisible King - H G Wells - 164
Godfrey, Goff - 154
Golden Dawn, The Hermetic Order of the - 35
Goligher, Kathleen - 176, 228
Gollomb, Joseph - 165, 166, 167
Gordon, General Charles George - 50
Gordon, Mary - 102
Gordon, Rev Stanley - 192
Gow, David - 15, 154, 156, 159, 163, 165, 168, 216, 238, 253, 254, 292
Green, Richard Lancelyn - 7, 8
Griffiths, Frances - 251
Grimard, Professor - 223
Grobe-Wutischky, M - 267
Guards Came Through and Other Poems, The - A C Doyle - 141
Gurney, Edmund - 39, 62, 82
Hackney - 174
Hageby, Lind Af - 292
Haggard, Sir H Rider - 38
Haig, Marshal - 209
Halifax, Lord - 57
Hall, Sir Edward Marshall - 216

Hampshire Psychical Society - 29
Harding, Newman - 184, 185, 186, 187, 188
Hare, Professor - 223
Harmonial Philosophy - Andrew Jackson Davis - 130
Harward, Lieutenant-General Thomas - 24
Harward, Nancy - 24, 25
Hastie, Henry - 25
Hawkins, Louise - (see Doyle, Louise Conan) - 290
Hendry, W S - 276
Henslow, Professor - 223
Hill, J Arthur - 45, 60, 77, 79
History of Spiritualism, The - A C Doyle - 37, 173, 174, 176, 177
History of the Great War - A C Doyle - 104
Hodgson, Richard - 30, 31, 34, 39, 62, 233, 292, 295
Holmes, Oliver Wendell - 66
Holmes, Sherlock - 1, 7, 10, 13, 14, 19, 20, 23, 36, 43, 88, 89, 194, 209, 241, 252, 253, 261, 283, 290
Holy Bible, The - 78, 113, 127, 134, 236
Home, Daniel Dunglas - 73, 76, 173, 174, 191, 198, 218, 220, 221, 222, 224, 225, 290, 292
Hope, William - 249, 259
Hopkins, Matthew - 153
Hornung, Oscar - 43, 136
Horstead, Mr - 25
Houdini, Harry - 11, 188, 189, 248
Hound of the Baskervilles, The - A C Doyle - 14, 20
Human Personality and its Survival of Bodily Death - F W Myers - 36, 74

Hume, David - 123
Hunt, J Ernest - 257
Hunt, Leigh - 27, 28
Hunter, A - 228
Huxley, Thomas Henry - 41, 70
Hyde, Charles - 227
Hyde, Professor - 223
Hydesville - 21, 120, 291
Hyslop, Professor - 187, 188, 223, 233
Ilfracombe, W - 280
Imperator (Communicating spirit) - 52, 53, 113
In Quest of Truth - Hubert Stansbury - 148
Incidents In My Life - Daniel Dunglas Home - 191
Inge, Dr (Dean of St Paul's) - 123, 129
Institut Métapsychique - 176
International Psychic Gazette, The - 43, 60
Is Spiritualism Based On Fraud - Joseph McCabe - 228
Is Spiritualism Of The Devil? - Rev F Fielding-Ould - 61, 78, 291
Jack The Ripper - 121
Jacolliot, Louis - 73
James, William - 62, 223
Jerome, Jerome K - 164
John O' London's Weekly - 162
Johnson, E Roberts - 272, 275
Jones, Kelvin I - 11, 15
Jung, Carl - 179, 280
Kernahan, Coulson - 127
King, Katie - 174, 290
Kipling, Rudyard - 42
Kirk, Harriet - 214
Knapp, R - 268
Lambert, Rudolf - 175

Lambeth Conference - 131, 132, 133, 134, 135
Lankester, Sir Ray - 220
Lazarus - 121
Leaf, Horace - 210
Leckie, Jean - 36, 290
Leckie, Malcolm - 37, 43, 44, 136
Letters and Tracts on Spiritualism - Judge Edmonds - 69
Letters from the Other Side - H Thibault - 211
Lewis, John - 238
Life After Death - Prof James H Hyslop - 188
Lindsay, Lord - 198, 223, 224
Loder-Symonds, Lily - 37, 43, 44, 136, 139
Lodge, Raymond - 51, 52, 57, 62, 79, 83, 84, 180, 219, 293
Lodge, Sir Oliver - 10, 34, 45, 51, 52, 54, 56, 58, 59, 62, 68, 77, 85, 86, 89, 107, 114, 115, 144, 148, 149, 150, 151, 164, 165, 166, 170, 171, 180, 187, 188, 192, 218, 219, 223, 226, 227, 253, 293, 294
Lombroso, Cesare - 62, 187, 223
London Spiritualist Alliance - 9, 10, 11, 52, 204, 208, 244, 245, 293, 295, 296
Loraine, Robert - 168
Lost World, The - A C Doyle - 7, 13
Lot No 249 - A C Doyle - 20
Lusitania, RMS - 43
Lycett, Andrew - 15, 33, 34
M E (Nom de plume) - 272
MacFarlane, Mr and Mrs - 138
Machen, Arthur - 158, 159, 162, 163, 269, 270
Magee, Rev A V - 124, 125, 126, 131, 135
Malachi - 52

Malmesbury, Susan, Countess of - 177

Man's Survival After Death - Rev Charles L Tweedale - 131, 296

Manchester, Dean of - 118, 122

Mapes, Professor - 223

Marghieri, Professor - 223

Marie Curie: A Life - Susan Quinn - 150

Marriott-Watson, H B - 49, 54

Martext, Rev Boanerges (Nom de plume) - 257

Masked Medium, The (AKA "Miss Smith") - 159, 160, 161, 167, 168

Maskelyne, Nevil - 139, 154

Maugham, W Somerset - 134

Maupassant, Guy de - 34

Maxwell, Professor - 223

Mayo, Professor - 223

McCabe, Joseph - 15, 150, 189, 210, 213, 214, 215, 216, 217, 218, 219, 220, 221, 222, 223, 224, 225, 226, 227, 228, 229, 239, 293

McCabe, William Thomas - 214

McClure, Canon - 123

McKenzie, J Hewat - 248

Medical Press, The - 178

Memories and Adventures - A C Doyle - 24, 25

Mercier, Dr Charles A - 163

Meyer, Jean - 205

Micah Clarke - A C Doyle - 7

Minchin, Hamilton - 267

Molesworth, Lord - 202

Mons - 43, 269, 270

Mons, Angels of - 16, 163, 269, 270, 271, 276

Montrose Royal Mental Hospital - 22

Moore, Vice-Admiral Usborne - 45, 79, 139

Morambo (Communicating spirit) - 113

Morning Post, The - 101, 221

Morse, J J - 102

Morselli, Professor - 223

Moseley, Sydney - 167

Moses, W Stainton - 9, 52, 79, 87, 131, 293

Muir, Rev G Gilbert - 64

Murphy, Father - 22

Murray, Douglas - 285, 286, 287

Myers, F W - 34, 36, 39, 62, 74, 223, 233, 293, 298

Mystery of Cloomber, The - A C Doyle - 20, 24

Mystery of Edwin Drood, The - Charles Dickens - 169

Nash's Magazine - 104, 117

National Memorial Service for the Fallen - 104, 190

National Review, The - 45

National Spiritualists' Association (Washington, USA) - 205

New Revelation, The - A C Doyle - 14, 23, 29, 43, 65, 90, 91, 92, 104, 121, 128, 252

New York - 21

New Zealand - 206, 229, 231, 233, 236, 244, 248

News from the Next World - Rev Charles L Tweedale - 296

Nostradamus - 267

Oaten, Ernest - 10, 95, 122, 231, 238, 240, 241, 293

Occult Review, The - 13, 40

Occult World, The - A P Sinnett - 24, 239, 296

Ochorowicz, Professor - 223

Old, W Gorn - 267

Oldham, Major Leslie - 43
On The Origin Of Species - Charles Darwin - 149, 296
On The Threshold Of The Unseen - Sir William F Barrett - 78
Our Self After Death - Rev Arthur Chambers - 78
Owen, Dale - 212
Owen, George Vale - 294
Oxford Dictionary of National Biography, The - 149
Pall Mall Gazette, The - 59, 225
Palladino, Eusapia - 21, 75, 149, 218, 219, 292, 294
Parasite, The - A C Doyle - 261
Parr, Edward (Communicating spirit) - 110
Payn, James - 33, 34
Pearsons Magazine - 35
Pemberton, Max - 88
Peters, Vout - 44, 102, 294
Pictet, Professor - 223
Pilate, Pontius - 81
Piper, Leonora - 34, 294
Podmore, Frank - 32, 33, 34
Pole, W Tudor - 282
Portsmouth - 7, 206
Portsmouth Association Football Club - 7, 23
Portsmouth Central Library - 13
Portsmouth City Council - 7
Portsmouth Library Service - 7
Postlethwaite, Dorothy - 72
Powell, Ellis T - 96, 104, 177, 184, 216, 295
Powell, Evan - 138, 139, 220
Prel, Professor Carl du - 223
Press Association, The - 183

Price, Harry - 11
Psychical Investigations - J Arthur Hill - 77, 151
Psychical Research Committee of St. Ethelburga's Church, The - 108
Psychological Foundations of the Belief in Spirits, The - Carl G Jung - 179
Rasputin - 64
Raymond, Or Life And Death - Sir Oliver Lodge - 51, 52, 57, 72, 77, 92, 149, 150, 151, 192, 219, 226, 294
Red-Headed League, The - A C Doyle - 283
Reichel, Professor - 223
Reminiscences of Judge Edmonds - Judge Edmonds - 69
Report on an Address at Merthyr Tydfil; March 1st, 1919 - 148
Revue Spirite, La - 204
Richet, Charles - 62, 149, 187, 223
Ring Of Thoth, The - A C Doyle - 29, 283
Robinson, Fletcher - 14
Rochester - 22, 47
Rodney Stone - A C Doyle - 7
Rogers, Edmund Dawson - 13
Rogers, Ulyss - 157
Sass, General - 266
Scandal In Bohemia, A - A C Doyle - 283
Scatcherd, Felicia R - 11, 194, 216, 250, 295
Scheibner, Professor - 223
Schiaparelli, Professor - 223
Schriebner, Professor - 220
Scott, Robert Falcon - 7
Scott, Sydney - 32, 33
Seiling, Professor - 223

Selbit, P T - 167
Seneca - 129
Shackleton, Ernet - 7
Sharpe, James W - 42
Shaw, George Bernard - 165, 166, 295
Shelley, Mary - 19
Shirley, Ralph - 265
Sidgwick, Professor - 32
Sign of Four, The - A C Doyle - 20, 261
Silver Star (Communicating spirit) - 273, 274, 275
Simpson, James Young - 78
Singh, Guru Govind - 271, 272
Sinnett, A P - 24, 239, 295
Slade, Henry - 220
Slater, Oscar - 7
Smith, A C (A C Doyle's pseudonym) - 23
Smith, Miss (see "Masked Medium, The") - 159
Snelling, Harold - 251
Soal, S G - 183
Society for Psychical Research - 9, 10, 30, 32, 49, 52, 61, 74, 175, 179, 289, 293, 295
South Norwood - 32, 34
Southsea - 19, 23, 24, 28, 29, 32, 36, 54, 58, 71, 253, 277
Southsea (séance with Kingsley) - 138
Special and General Theory of Relativity - Albert Einstein - 183
Speckled Band, The - A C Doyle - 261
Spencer, Herbert - 70
Spirit Teachings - W Stainton Moses - 9, 79
Spiritualism, Volume I - Judge Edmonds - 69

Spiritualism, Volume II - Judge Edmonds - 69
Spiritualism: Its Present-Day Meaning - Huntly Carter (editor) - 58
Spiritualists National Union - 10, 94, 95, 122, 231, 293
Springett, Bernard H - 86, 87
Stansbury, Hubert - 148
Stark Munro Letters, The - A C Doyle - 23, 30
Stashower, Daniel - 15, 43
Stavert, Geoffrey - 15, 19
Stead, W T - 45, 62, 79, 151, 187, 233
Stephen, Father (Communicating spirit) - 110
Stonyhurst College - 22, 58, 296
Strand Magazine, The - 20, 43, 88, 145, 151, 165, 181, 192, 210, 212, 251
Street, Mona - 232
Street, Percy R - 102, 238
Study in Scarlet, A - 253
Study In Southsea, A - Geoffrey Stavert - 15, 19
Summerland - 52
Sunday Boston Herald, The - 30
Sunday Chronicle, The - 172
Sunday Express, The - 161, 163, 179, 212
Sunnyside - 22
Survival of Man - Sir Oliver Lodge - 51, 151
Swedenborg, Emanuel - 130
T.P.'s Weekly - 41
Tallmadge, Governor - 146
Tennant, David - 200
Tetrazzini, Luisa - 206
The Ear of Dionysius - Gerald Balfour - 78

The Principles of Nature - Andrew Jackson Davis - 130
The Question: "If A Man Die Shall He Live Again?" - Edward Clodd - 150
The Reality of Psychic Phenomena - Dr W J Crawford - 78
The Relation of Spiritualism to Christianity - Rev F Fieldling-Ould - 291
The Undying Fire - H G Wells - 164
The Unexplained - Peter Brookesmith, magazine - 13
The Voices - Vice Admiral W Usborne Moore - 79
The White Company - A C Doyle - 7
Theory of General and Special Relativity - Albert Einstein - 178
Theosophical Society - 149
Theosophist - 24
Thomas, Tom - 153, 156
Thomas, Will - 153
Three Character Sketches, Sir Arthur Conan Doyle, Light, June 19th, 1920 - 253
Times, The - 91, 101, 114, 122, 154, 169, 170
Tit-Bits - 151
Togo, Admiral - 98
Tompkins, Rev Charles Russell - 30
Tornebom, Professor - 223
Turner; Major-General Sir Alfred E - 45, 50
Tweedale, Rev Charles L - 106, 122, 126, 131, 134, 296
Tweedale, Violet - 127
Two Worlds, The - 10, 13, 122, 125, 138, 182, 296
Tyndall, John - 70

Uncertainty of Spiritual Intercourse - Judge Edmonds - 69
Vale Owen, George - 59, 106, 107, 116, 122, 131, 231, 232
Valley Of Fear, The - A C Doyle - 261
Vaughan, Father Bernard - 15, 58, 59, 60, 61, 106, 107, 122, 296
VCD (Nom de plume) - 60, 104
Verbatim Report of a Public Debate on 'The Truth of Spiritualism' between Sir Arthur Conan Doyle and Joseph McCabe - A C Doyle, Joseph McCabe - 226
Vesme, C de - 265, 266
Vindication of William Hope, The - Rev Charles L Tweedale - 296
Vital Message, The - A C Doyle - 14, 104, 117, 119, 121, 136, 182, 196
Voltaire (Nom de plume of François-Marie Arouet) - 123
Wade, A - 168
Wallace, Alfred Russel - 9, 21, 26, 45, 62, 70, 149, 166, 223, 233, 296
Wallace, Rev Abraham - 167, 168, 174, 175, 198, 231, 233, 296
Wallis, E W - 102
Weber, Professor - 220, 223
Weekly Dispatch, The - 225, 284
Welldon, Bishop - 127, 212, 213
Wells, H G - 150, 164, 165, 289
Wesley, John - 74
Western Mail, The - 155
Whiting, Lilian - 40, 41, 178, 297
Whitman, Walt - 62
Wilberforce, Archdeacon - 45, 78, 122
Williams, Charles T - 213
Williams, J Howard - 183
Wilson, Canon - 142, 143, 144

Wimbledon - 137, 207

Windlesham Manor - 37

Winington-Ingram, A F (Bishop of London) - 108, 114, 115, 116, 126

Winslow, Dr Forbes - 121, 123, 125, 126

Witchcraft and Vagrancy Acts - 58, 269

Wonders of the Saints - Rev F Fielding-Ould - 291

Wordsworth, William - 62

World War One - 7, 10, 16, 33, 37, 43, 44, 51, 88, 107, 121, 126, 132, 151, 153, 209, 229, 230, 234, 252, 269, 270, 273, 275, 276, 277, 283

Wreck On Loch McGarry, The - A C Doyle - 142

Wright, Elsie - 250

Wright, Orville - 257

Wright, Wilbur - 257

Wycherley, William - 27

Wynn, Rev Walter - 225, 240, 241, 287, 288

Wynne, Charlie - 225

Ypres - 43

Zollner, Professor - 220, 223